H
1
A4
v.461

17443

DATE DUE

[illegible]			
OCT 15 '84			
FEB 18 '86			
MAY 19 '86			
JUN 10 '86			
[illegible] 14 '92			
NOV 22 [illegible]			

North Hennepin
Community College Library
7411 85th Avenue North
Brooklyn Park, MN 55445

VOLUME 461 MAY 1982

THE ANNALS

of The American Academy *of* Political *and* Social Science

RICHARD D. LAMBERT, *Editor*
ALAN W. HESTON, *Associate Editor*

YOUNG CHILDREN AND SOCIAL POLICY

Special Editors of this Volume

WILLIAM M. BRIDGELAND
Associate Professor
Department of Social Science
Michigan State University
East Lansing, Michigan

EDWARD A. DUANE
Professor
Department of Social Science
Michigan State University
East Lansing, Michigan

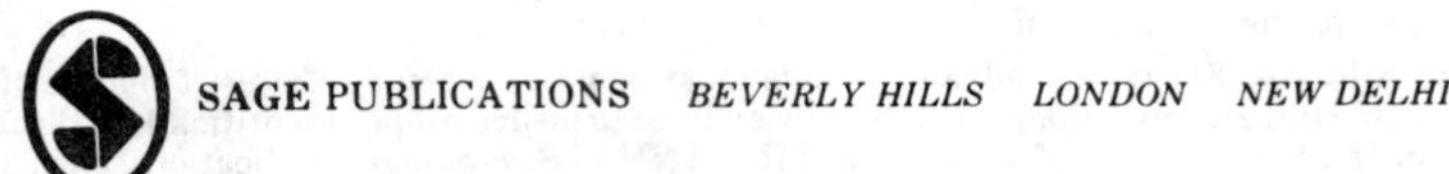
SAGE PUBLICATIONS *BEVERLY HILLS LONDON NEW DELHI*

H
/
A4
v. 461

THE ANNALS

© 1982 *by* The American Academy *of* Political *and* Social Science

PRISCILLA A. ESTES, *Assistant Editor*

All rights reserved. No part of this volume may be reproduced or utilized in any form or by any means, electronic or mechanical, including photocopying, recording, or by any information storage and retrieval system, without permission in writing from the publisher.

Editorial Office: 3937 Chestnut Street, Philadelphia, Pennsylvania 19104.

For information about membership (individuals only) and subscriptions (institutions), address:*

SAGE PUBLICATIONS, INC.
275 South Beverly Drive
Beverly Hills, Calif. 90212 USA

From India and South Asia, write to:
SAGE PUBLICATIONS INDIA Pvt. Ltd.
P.O. Box 3605
New Delhi 110 024
INDIA

From the UK, Europe, the Middle East and Africa, write to:
SAGE PUBLICATIONS LTD
28 Banner Street
London EC1Y 8QE
ENGLAND

**Please note that members of The Academy receive THE ANNALS with their membership.*

Library of Congress Catalog Card Number 82-80533
International Standard Serial Number ISSN 0002-7162
International Standard Book Number ISBN 0-8039-1832-1 (Vol. 461, 1982, paper)
International Standard Book Number ISBN 0-8039-1831-3 (Vol. 461, 1982, cloth)

Manufactured in the United States of America. First printing, May 1982.

The articles appearing in THE ANNALS are indexed in *Book Review Index; Public Affairs Information Service Bulletin; Social Sciences Index; Monthly Periodical Index; Current Contents: Behavioral, Social, Management Sciences;* and *Combined Retrospective Index Sets.* They are also abstracted and indexed in *ABC Pol Sci, Historical Abstracts, Human Resources Abstracts, Social Sciences Citation Index, United States Political Science Documents, Social Work Research & Abstracts, Peace Research Reviews, Sage Urban Studies Abstracts, International Political Science Abstracts,* and/or *America: History and Life.*

Information about membership rates, institutional subscriptions, and back issue prices may be found on the facing page.

Advertising. Current rates and specifications may be obtained by writing to THE ANNALS Advertising and Promotion Manager at the Beverly Hills office (address above).

Claims. Claims for undelivered copies must be made no later than three months following month of publication. The publisher will supply missing copies when losses have been sustained in transit and when the reserve stock will permit.

Change of Address. Six weeks' advance notice must be given when notifying of change of address. Please send old address label along with the new address to insure proper identification. Please specify name of journal. Send change of address to: THE ANNALS, c/o Sage Publications, Inc., 275 South Beverly Drive, Beverly Hills, CA 90212.

17443

The American Academy of Political and Social Science

3937 Chestnut Street Philadelphia, Pennsylvania 19104

Board of Directors

HOWARD C. PETERSEN
ELMER B. STAATS
MARVIN E. WOLFGANG
LEE BENSON
A. LEON HIGGINBOTHAM, Jr.
RICHARD D. LAMBERT
REBECCA JEAN BROWNLEE
COVEY T. OLIVER
THOMAS L. HUGHES
MATINA S. HORNER

Officers

President
MARVIN E. WOLFGANG

Vice-Presidents
RICHARD D. LAMBERT, *First Vice-President*
STEPHEN B. SWEENEY, *First Vice-President Emeritus*

Secretary
REBECCA JEAN BROWNLEE

Treasurer
HOWARD C. PETERSEN

Counsel
HENRY W. SAWYER, III

Editors, THE ANNALS

RICHARD D. LAMBERT, *Editor*
ALAN W. HESTON, *Associate Editor*
THORSTEN SELLIN, *Editor Emeritus*

Business Manager
INGEBORG HESSLER

Origin and Purpose. The Academy was organized December 14, 1889, to promote the progress of political and social science, especially through publications and meetings. The Academy does not take sides in controverted questions, but seeks to gather and present reliable information to assist the public in forming an intelligent and accurate judgment.

Meetings. The Academy holds an annual meeting in the spring extending over two days.

Publications. THE ANNALS is the bimonthly publication of The Academy. Each issue contains articles on some prominent social or political problem, written at the invitation of the editors. Also, monographs are published from time to time, numbers of which are distributed to pertinent professional organizations. These volumes constitute important reference works on the topics with which they deal, and they are extensively cited by authorities throughout the United States and abroad. The papers presented at the meetings of The Academy are included in THE ANNALS.

Membership. Each member of The Academy receives THE ANNALS and may attend the meetings of The Academy. Membership is open only to individuals. Annual dues: $24.00 for the regular paperbound edition (clothbound, $36.00). Add $6.00 per year for membership outside the U.S.A. Members may also purchase single issues of THE ANNALS for $5.00 each (clothbound, $7.00).

Subscriptions. THE ANNALS is published six times annually—in January, March, May, July, September, and November. Institutions may subscribe to THE ANNALS at the annual rate: $42.00 (clothbound, $54.00). Add $6.00 per year for subscriptions outside the U.S.A. Institutional rates for single issues: $7.00 each (clothbound, $9.00).

Second class postage paid at Beverly Hills, California.

Single issues of THE ANNALS may be obtained by individuals who are not members of The Academy for $6.00 each (clothbound, $7.50). Single issues of THE ANNALS have proven to be excellent supplementary texts for classroom use. Direct inquiries regarding adoptions to THE ANNALS c/o Sage Publications (address below).

All correspondence concerning membership in The Academy, dues renewals, inquiries about membership status, and/or purchase of single issues of THE ANNALS should be sent to THE ANNALS c/o Sage Publications, Inc., 275 South Beverly Drive, Beverly Hills, CA 90212. *Please note that orders under $20 must be prepaid.* Sage affiliates in London and India will assist institutional subscribers abroad with regard to orders, claims, and inquiries for both subscriptions and single issues.

THE ANNALS

of The American Academy *of* Political *and* Social Science

RICHARD D. LAMBERT, *Editor*
ALAN W. HESTON, *Associate Editor*

FORTHCOMING

THE AMERICAN JUDICIARY: Critical Issues

Special Editors: A. Leo Levin and
Russell R. Wheeler

Volume 462 July 1982

INTERNATIONAL TERRORISM

Special Editor: Marvin E. Wolfgang

Includes papers presented at the 1982 Annual Meeting of The Academy.

Volume 463 September 1982

MIDDLE AND LATE LIFE TRANSITIONS

Special Editor: Felix M. Berardo

Volume 464 November 1982

See page 3 for information on Academy membership and purchase of single volumes of **The Annals**.

CONTENTS

BOOK DEPARTMENT CONTENTS

INTERNATIONAL RELATIONS AND POLITICS

AFRICA, ASIA, AND LATIN AMERICA

EUROPE

UNITED STATES

SOCIOLOGY

ECONOMICS

PREFACE

There is some merit in the assertion that the twentieth century is "the century of the child."[1] In this regard, industrialization has represented both unprecedented opportunities and special problems. As a consequence, social policy for the young child, the newborn to 5- or 6-year-old, is fraught with paradoxes. The combination of declining birthrates and infant mortality rates is associated with increased parental concern about the health, nutrition, and development of their children. In contrast, the ascendance of out-of-home economic activity has altered traditional child care systems and weakened family support structures. Furthermore, the competition from mass media, schools, and peers has placed severe strains on the bonds between parent and child. One result has been an increasing social concern with supplementary services to families.

There are few areas of social policy that do not have at least some ramifications for young children, for example, housing, health, welfare, and education. The variety of relevant programs presents problems of policy coherence, gaps, and redundancies. Recently, child advocates have been trying to addess these and other related issues as part of the global agenda under the International Year of the Child in 1979. In the past, addressing such issues appears to have been an outgrowth of economic abundance in advanced industrial societies, but now these same societies are moving from accelerated growth to very slow or zero growth. This is not only leading to an abrupt retrenchment in public programs, but is also being reinforced, at least in the United States, by mass alienation from "big government" and the reemergence of a laissez faire or libertarian outlook.[2] Such a trend results in contradictory policies for the young child. For instance, more young mothers are working both out of economic necessity and self-fulfillment; the latter is a libertarian attitude. Yet this attitude, when translated into opposition to public supported facilities for child care, becomes an obstacle to pursuit of individual opportunity. In such an environment, proponents of early childhood programs, for example, Head Start, must provide either cogent cost-benefit analyses mixed with sophisticated advocacy, and/or be innovative in exploring alternative nonpublic arrangements to meet the varying needs of the young child.

American policy focused on early childhood has certain distinctive features. First, the rearing of children has been the historic monopoly of the family. Families have been regarded as the best means of realizing at least two fundamental societal functions, the inculcation of basic societal values in the young and the protection of dependent family members. It is not surprising that the care of young children is a core societal concern. But children have only recently become the focus of more explicit public enactments as well as a clear target population for public intervention, for example, the growth of interest in and thus laws on child abuse.

1. A. H. Halsey, *Change in British Society* (London: Oxford University Press, 1978), p. 106.
2. Joseph Veroff, Elizabeth Douvan, and Richard A. Kulka, *The Inner American: A Self Portrait from 1957 to 1976* (New York: Basic Books, 1981).

Second, many other policy domains have relatively coherent and focused objectives and programs, for example, transportation, labor, and even education. In other areas, public policy toward early childhood is diffused and even inchoate both where children are indirectly affected, for example, Aid to Families of Dependent Children, and where they are directly targeted, for example, immunization programs. At the very minimum, public policy for the young child cuts across health, welfare, and educational policy.

Third, these policy initiatives are incremental. In this regard, the consequences of public reticence to intrude into family jurisdiction have been abetted by the American tradition of abjuring comprehensive planning in favor of making specific moves on discrete problems.[3] As a result, early childhood policy is disjointed. It is a shibboleth, therefore, that the early childhood area, let alone national family policy, can be integrated into a unitary policy framework. This whole area is not one cause, but many causes with many followers.

A modification of our view of the policy arena is one way of achieving a focused perspective, and thereby better appreciating the scope of issues represented in the present volume.[4] Such a view includes at least three dimensions:

—a policy culture that includes the goals, methods, and processes in the general area of early childhood policymaking;

—a network of political organizations that includes the key governmental officials and agencies as well as special interest groups concerned with the young child; and

—a variety of social concerns that gives rise to a set of interrelated programs for the young child.

The preceding scheme helps to illuminate the overall thrust of the articles in this volume. To begin with, the articles in the first section are concerned with major value questions, including the political function of policy research. Those in the second section address the issue of policy actors and process. Finally, there are the particular areas of widespread concern relevant to the young child, which have elicited special programmatic responses. The article that focuses on health concerns is found in the third section, those that focus on education of the young child are in the fourth section, while those that focus on family concerns are in the last section.

In the following discussion, we have placed policy culture with social concerns and public programming. This brief discussion emphasizes unifying values that provide coherence, since the values that are important for children and family policy in general also permeate ongoing programs and set much of their direction.

A core value in early childhood policy is the commitment to privatism in child rearing. This has manifested itself in the historic resistance to public

3. Gilbert Steiner, *The Futility of Family Policy* (Washington, DC: Brookings Institution, 1981), p. 193.

4. William M. Bridgeland and Edward A. Duane, "Introduction: Early Childhood Education and Public Policy," *Education and Urban Society*, Feb. 1980, pp. 141-46.

intervention in family processes. Until recent decades, this value was translated into policy wherein public involvement was almost exclusively confined to so-called maintenance or reactive approach.[5] Specifically, governmental intervention was seen as legitimate only under conditions of social crisis, for example, economic depression and war, or in the case of children-in-crisis, for example, extreme neglect or abandonment. This minimalist tradition clearly underlies Doris Bergen Sponseller and Joel Fink's contention that among the basic sources of early childhood policy problems is the tendency to insist on parental rights over children's needs. It can be seen in their assertion that Americans tend to respond only to crises with action on children's problems especially vulnerable to this "crisis mentality."

With the recent economic affluence culminating in a spate of social legislation in the 1960s, children's programs expanded under an emergent, "reform-oriented" rationale.[6] While the family continued to be regarded as fundamental in child care, it was now assumed that government could share in family responsibilities and provide necessary support. Within this new perspective, one policy objective stood out: the prevention of developmental defects in poor children through ensuring adequate medical and nutritional care and compensatory preschool education.[7]

This reformist notion is clearly represented in Edward Zigler and Victoria Seitz's article on the emotional and intellectual benefits of Head Start, the premier child care program sponsored by the federal government. The reformist rationale also seems to guide the systematic research of David J. Irvine and his colleagues at the New York Department of Education. They trace longitudinally the positive effect of preschool programs for the disadvantaged. From this same perspective, both Irvine et al. and Douglas R. Powell identify important benefits for parental education that arise from publicly sponsored programs for children, and/or for parents and families. And in health care, Sara Sullivan Medley also reflects this reformism in her research on lead toxicity, a man-made disease that both professionals and the public have become aware of only recently. She suggests it be given a policy priority.

Following a decade of stagflation and mounting anti-big government reaction, children's programs are now under threat of curtailment or elimination. In order to meet this libertarian reaction in an atmosphere of increasingly scarce public dollars, child advocates are being pressured into assuming more sophisticated defensive postures to keep losses to a minimum. As reflected by many articles in this volume, this attempt is characterized by more empirically sound research and more effective policy recommendations.

In this regard, Linda Brookover Bourque suggests that superficial policy research has politically negative consequences. She found that evaluation research on children's programs has had little or no effect on governmental policy or programmatic decisions. Sandra McConnell Condry and Irving Lazar provide some useful guidelines for more effective policy research on

5. Kathleen H. Dunlop, "Child Care and Parent Education: Reformist Rationales for Government Intervention," *Education and Urban Society*, Feb. 1980, pp. 175-91.

6. Ibid.

7. Ibid., pp. 179-81.

children. They maintain that policy recommendations must include cost-benefit analyses, congruence with prevailing values, and readable results.

More child-oriented researchers are exploring voluntary and nongovernmental alternatives. Specifically, Elizabeth Jones and Elizabeth Prescott discuss a wide array of possible child care arrangements in the light of what children, families, and the economy need. Eunice L. Watson and Alice H. Collins explore "natural helping networks," an approach that parallels a new interest in the social sciences for mediating structures between individuals and government.[8]

Given the current social conservatism, it is quite natural for researchers to emphasize children's needs in a family context. This could give greater legitimacy to children's programs than they might have otherwise. Marsha Hurst and Ruth E. Zambrana investigate child care needs for the young, poor working mother in the city. They found that for Puerto Rican mothers, family continuity in child care is the most important factor in labor force participation. John C. Moore puts this in the larger context of parental preferences for child care, concluding that parents, not professionals, must have control over child care decisions. Complementary to this, Watson and Collins's networking and Powell's parent education provide insights into the ways that the family can be supported.

As conflicts in policy toward early childhood increase in response to the scarcity of public resources, more social scientists are beginning to explore directly the political processes and actors in the policy arena. At the overall process level, the findings of W. Norton Grubb and Julia Green Brody indicate that the impact of state governments as mediators between federal mandates and local funding allocations has been to perpetuate inequality in program expenditures among communities rather than to correct it. Focusing directly on policy actors, Mark E. Stern and we uncover a pattern where state agencies tend to dominate early childhood groups in policymaking. Furthermore, these agencies tend to exhibit "goal displacement" wherein agency self-perpetuation rivals public service as the prime goal. Complementary to this, Bourque reveals how government agencies, by manipulating research funds and deadlines, can change the results of program evaluation from a searching criticism of programmatic status quo into a pseudo-scientific defense for its perpetuation.

In conclusion, as Jones and Prescott note, well over 40 percent of all women with young children were in the labor force in 1979. The need, therefore, for early childhood programming is as great as ever. And yet this area faces a formidable set of obstacles, including economic contraction, public alienation, program fragmentation, and political inexperience of child advocates. However, as in many American crises, the challenge for policy for young children presents both real dangers and some opportunities to improve ongoing programs and to experiment with new options.

The articles in this volume represent a step in this direction. They outline the dimensions of some salient needs and concerns relative to the young child. They suggest guidelines for program evaluation and provide a wide array of empirically based programmatic recommendations. They also

8. Peter Berger and Richard Neuhaus, *To Empower People: The Role of Mediating Structures in Public Policy* (Washington, DC: American Enterprise Institute, 1977).

probe directly some political patterns to show what should be avoided as well as what should be pursued. It is, therefore, hoped that this volume will not only inform the interested public, but also act as a catalyst for more policy research centered on the young child.

WILLIAM M. BRIDGELAND
EDWARD A. DUANE

ANNALS, *AAPSS*, **461**, May 1982

Public Policy Toward Children: Identifying the Problems

By DORIS BERGEN SPONSELLER and JOEL S. FINK

ABSTRACT: This article identifies four problems with the way American society deals with children's needs: the discussion of children's problems seldom results in effective legislation or social action; child advocates are unable to achieve sufficient consensus on policy recommendations to provide direction to legislators; services needed by all children are provided only to special groups and even in these cases the help is not sustained; and much of the aid provided is directed toward adults and does not necessarily have the desired impact on children. Some possible explanations for these problems are offered: the cultural belief in parents' rights, the devaluing of children as recipients of economic investment, the cultural tendency to respond only to crises, and the political inexperience of child advocates are all identified as forces that contribute to the inadequacies in the way children's needs are met.

Doris Bergen Sponseller is dean of the Graduate School at Wheelock College. Her major fields of interest are early childhood education and educational psychology. She is particularly interested in social policy issues related to child advocacy.

Joel S. Fink is an associate professor at Oakland University, where he specializes in foundations of education and in social studies curriculum development and teacher training. He is interested in the formulation of public policy in the area of equal educational opportunity.

WHEN the International Year of the Child (IYC) drew to a close, persons who were especially concerned about the plight of children in contemporary society expressed doubts that the heightened focus on children's needs that IYC forums, conferences, and publications provided would bear fruit in legislative and social action. There is no question that IYC activities increased public awareness of children's needs and problems. What remained doubtful, however, was whether the plethora of information outlining these needs and the recommendations for action proposed in these forums would have any deep or lasting effect on budgetary decisions and legislative mandates. These doubts have subsequently been substantiated by current public policy stances advocating decreasing federal and state financial aid for children's programs.

It is the gap between identification of children's needs and societal action to meet these needs that is of interest to us in this article. Why is it that an area of expressed concern for so many people results in so little substantive improvement in the condition of children in our society? The purpose of this article is twofold. First, we will identify the problems with the way children's needs have been addressed by child advocates. Then we will hypothesize about the societal forces—psychological, economic, cultural, and political—that might be contributing to the existence of the identified problems.

PROBLEMS WITH CHILD ADVOCATES' METHODS AND ACTIONS

Even those persons most committed to promoting the care, education, and general welfare of young children have had difficulty transmitting their goals into effective policy. Four of the problems with child advocates' methods have been:

—substitution of talk for action;

—inability to form consensus goals;

—attention to needs of some children, but not others; and

—promotion of indirect, not direct, solutions.

Talk instead of action

A major way people concerned with child advocacy have dealt with children's needs has been to hold conferences or to convene meetings to talk about the problems. Typically these sessions are devoted to the documentation of the problems and to exhortations that something must be done. Statistics on nutritional deficits, infant mortality rates, child abuse, poor foster care, paucity of adequate child care, and changes in family structure affecting children—for example, divorce, teenage pregnancy, and working mothers—are repeated over and over. Discussions of solutions, however, are usually general and idealistic, resulting in lists of nonspecific recommendations. Seldom are concrete action policies agreed on or strategies planned for achieving political goals. Having engaged in general discussion about the problems, many people have either believed—or acted as if they believed—that they have made their contribution to the solution of the problems and have expended sufficient individual effort. Further, when no legislative or social action results, their reaction has frequently been disillusionment or cynicism, not increased devotion of energy to political action.

No consensus on action

When legislators or public officials have asked for policy direction, or when child advocates do agree that political action is necessary, ideological differences between groups make agreement on specific proposals for action difficult to achieve. Legislators and others in positions to affect policy thus may lack direction because they receive either vague suggestions or conflicting specific proposals from groups that they perceive as having similar interests. As one legislator put it, "If the corn farmers and the pig farmers can agree on legislative action why can't you child care people tell me what you want?" Unfortunately, various groups have wanted their solution to be adopted *in toto* and have resisted efforts at compromise. Unless a solution is suggested that allows a group's viewpoint to be incorporated without compromise, some of these groups prefer that no solution to the problem be proposed. When child advocates have taken specific policy stances, it is often to support programs whose legitimacy is no longer in question. For example, they agree to support Head Start or child health programs but not comprehensive child care.[1] Recent attempts to draw the child care community to a consensus position on day care, even on relatively noncontroversial stands, is proving to be a difficult and time-consuming process.[2]

Action limited in focus

Legislation that has been approved, policies that have been adopted, and actions that have been taken tend to be focused only on children identified as "needy," not on all children.[3] Although a case could be made that services should be provided for all children, only children who have been labeled "disadvantaged," "handicapped," "minority," "poor," "abused," or "delinquent" have been the focus of concern. There has been little commitment in action, and often not even in rhetoric, to the needs of all children.

In addition, those needy groups that are identified and assisted usually experience a cyclical type of assistance. Federal programs have often been started and then dropped, only to be replaced by others not necessarily better, but more in vogue. Because of problems in timing, promising programs have not been pursued because the target groups from one year have not necessarily been in vogue the next. Indeed, the good grant writer's task has often been to repackage the needy group in next year's label in order for a program to be refunded. Thus the sustained commitment that should be made to all children is not even evident for those groups of children who do have primary needs and major continuing problems.

The present federal and state moves to cut programs and to revise or to reduce sources of funding bear little relationship either to the quality of programs presently funded or to the level of need of the group being served. The lack of commitment to the needs of all children may have put in jeopardy service even to those children who are most in need.

1. M. W. Edelman, "Expanding Roots," *Childhood Education*, 55(1):14-21 (Oct. 1978).

2. "National Day Care Campaign Platform" (Draft statement, Kansas City, Kansas, Jan. 1980).

3. V. Kerr, "One Step Forward—Two Steps Back: Child Care's Long American History," in *Child Care: Who Cares?* ed. P. Roby New York: Basic Books, 1973), pp. 157-71.

Advocacy of indirect solutions

Much action that has been provided comes only indirectly to children. Its purpose has been to help adults, and as a by-product, children are supposed to be helped.[4] Child abuse prevention focusing on parents but providing no direct service to children is an example of this type of intervention. It is true, of course, that problems children face are complex, and total family intervention or larger society intervention may often be necessary if the child's welfare is to be served in a complete way. However, indirect solutions may not always be the best way to help children. Indeed, indirect solutions often give an illusion of doing something for children but may be diffuse and unpredictable in effect. For example, family financial or psychological assistance may or may not improve the condition of the children in that family. By the time assistance gets to the child's level, a distortion of the policy's intent may have occurred that actually may make it harmful to children. Or during a lengthy adult-oriented process, damage to children may occur that cannot be easily remediated. Programs that combine direct service to children with adult-oriented service have usually been among the most effective. They are usually more costly than an indirect approach.

POSSIBLE EXPLANATIONS

A number of possible hypotheses can be advanced to explain the occurrence of these problems with child advocates' methods and actions. Why is there such little translation of discussion into action? Why is there difficulty in reaching consensus? Why is action directed only to special needy groups rather than to all children? Why are the action strategies often indirect rather than targeted directly to children? Four hypotheses that may provide partial answers are:

—individualistic and family-oriented cultural values impinge on action possibilities;

—economic priorities influence action directions;

—crisis-oriented rather than planned-change-oriented action is the societal norm; and

—advocates are inexperienced in political action strategies.

Family-centered cultural values

There is a fundamental belief in American society that parents have the major responsibility and the right to make decisions concerning their children's welfare and future. This belief is complemented by a conviction that in a pluralistic society there are multiple correct ways to rear children. Therefore government intervention is considered legitimate and warranted only if there are deficiencies in parents' ability or will to provide adequate physical care or educational opportunities for their children. That is, a "deficit model" that "fills in the gaps" is preferred to a "full potential model" that commits the society to maximizing the development of all children. The weight of "societal" versus "familial" responsibility for children has been on the

4. Marilyn M. Smith, "How Could Early Childhood Education Affect Families?" *Young Children*, 33(6):6-14 (Sept. 1978).

familial side throughout our history.[5]

A fear that social action might disrupt the parent-child bond or might infringe on family rights has been found even among professional early childhood educators and may contribute to their propensity to talk and exhort parents to act rather than to advocate specific societal policies that might conflict with parents' practices and value systems.[6] Even when advocates are aware of research supporting the conclusion that fear of child care disrupting the family is unwarranted, they may persist in basing action recommendations on other studies that support the cultural norms. For example, they may discount studies indicating that children's attachment to parents is not harmed by out-of-home care, while citing authors who point out dangers in this care arrangement.[7]

The belief that the family must remain inviolate might also explain why only those groups with deficits, that is, families in which norms are already violated, are appropriate targets for public policy. Similarly, action strategies often are not focused directly on children but rather on parent education or therapy or on general family assistance. The belief that cultural diversity is to be valued may also contribute to the difficulty advocates have in reaching consensus and to their inability to compromise. Even when there is recognition of the need for some services that are supplementary to those provided by the family, individualistic socioeconomic attitudes support private enterprise solutions rather than publicly sponsored programs. For example, although the families' need for child care is acknowledged, proprietory and industrial day care are being advocated in place of a strong publicly supported and monitored system.

Children's low economic priority

The lack of implementation, the limitation of attention to circumscribed groups, and the choice of indirect rather than direct interventions are often related to concern with excessive cost. These economic considerations are often stated as a major roadblock to legislation for children and to expansion of children's programs. For example, even at a time when federal regulation and assistance for child care was being considered as a policy option, prohibitive child care costs were cited as the reason why no comprehensive assistance could be provided. Proposed federal interagency guidelines did not require adequately trained child care givers even though data indicate training makes a difference in the quality of adult/child interactions in programs.[8] Prohibitive costs of societally supported child care have been

5. B. Greenblatt, *Responsibility for Child Care* (San Francisco: Jossey-Bass, 1977), pp. 2-10.

6. D. B. Sponseller and J. S. Fink, "Early Childhood Education: A National Profile of Early Childhood Educators' Views," *Education and Urban Society*, 12(2):163-73 (Feb. 1980).

7. B. Caldwell, "Child Development and Social Policy," in *Current Issues in Child Development*, eds. Scott and Grimmett (Washington, DC: National Association for Education of Young Children, 1977), pp. 61-88.

8. R. Ruopp et al., *Children at the Center: Summary Findings and Their Implications*, vol. 1, *Final Report of the National Day Care Study* (Mar. 1979), pp. 54-56, 160-1.

cited in the majority of research reviews on child care policy.[9]

It should be recognized, however, that implicit in this economic cost argument is the belief that the welfare of adults is preferred to that of children in our society. Rhetoric to the contrary, children are neither inherently valued nor treated as valuable resources in which investment will bring later return. Indeed, the pattern of indirect assistance to children may be explained by the rationale that the primary societal concern is with solving adults' problems. Thus policies that provide jobs for welfare mothers, parent education and therapy, and subsidies for child care have not been motivated by concern for children, but have been offered as direct solutions for adults' problems. Historically, children's assistance has been a byproduct of concern for adults' economic well being. In a discussion of rationales that have influenced child care, Dunlop cites five that are adult or societal-oriented and only one that is child-oriented.[10]

This conclusion is further supported by the fact that the evidence being amassed indicating that direct, sustained investment in the early education of children can be cost-effective in terms of later societal benefits has not been translated into strong public support for these programs.[11] Long-term cost effectiveness has not usually been the basis on which policy decisions related to children have been made in this country.

"Crisis-mentality" public policymaking

The shifting focus on various special groups and the lack of commitment to children who are not identified as special may result from the "crisis mentality" with which this society approaches the formulation of public policy. Problems do not receive attention and are often not even recognized as problems unless there is a major disruption in the functioning of the social order or until a particularly vocal group convinces decision makers that a crisis will occur. Also, once a problem situation has been identified and some action taken, there is a tendency to prematurely redirect social resources to new problems or to old problems with new labels.

Research on children's issues has often been funded with this same mentality. Implicit in acceptance of a grant has been the researcher's promise that the study not only will solve a complex question with a simple answer but will also require only a modest and short-term expenditure of funds. Public decision makers exhibit an impatience with sustained efforts directed to a particular problem, preferring immediate and visible payoff. The present tenor of public policy even implies that these problems will go away if they are ignored by the federal government. Since the problems of children rarely can be resolved with short-term effort and effective

9. M. A. Larson, "Federal Policy for Preschool Services: Assumptions and Evidence" (S.R.I. Project 2158, Report EPRCO2158-24, Stanford Research Institute, Educational Policy Research Center, Menlo Park, CA, May 1975).

10. K. H. Dunlop, "Child Care and Parent Education: Reformist Rationales for Government Intervention," *Education and Urban Society*, 12(2):175-91 (Feb. 1980).

11. I. Lazar, "Social Research and Social Policy—Reflections on Relationships," in *Care and Education of Young Children in America*, eds. R. Haskins and J. Gallagher (Norwood, NJ: Ablex, 1980), pp. 59-71.

action strategies rarely generate immediate results, social action related to children's problems is especially vulnerable to the crisis mentality. The budgetary cuts of 1981 have emphasized this instability in long-term societal commitment to children.

Advocates' political inexperience

Even when it is clear to advocates that an intervention is needed and a policy is agreed upon that protects cultural values, is economically viable, and meets immediate needs, this policy may be difficult to implement because of the political naiveté of the proponents. Many of them have come only recently to a position of commitment to action. They are inexperienced in understanding the political process and in using political strategy. They often believe that simply identifying a problem and giving reasons why certain steps should be taken will result in implementation of their proposals. They are unaware of political strategies that could advance their cause in the face of competing programs.[12] This results in the phenomenon identified earlier of problem identification being viewed as sufficient to ensure problem solution.

Moreover, many potential advocates for children seem to believe that attention to the political realities contaminates children's causes. They exhibit an unwillingness to engage in the political skills of compromise, alternative strategy planning, and consensus group mobilization to achieve desired ends. The Children's Defense Fund recognized this issue as a problem when they proposed a national network of political organizers for children's causes. As Edelman has put it, "We can no longer delude ourselves that children are above politics. Their lives are deeply affected by political decisions, and we must become as effective as others who wield political clout."[13] Child advocates are only now beginning to take these words to heart.

CONCLUSION

There are problems with the way children's needs have been addressed by child advocates. We have identified some of these problems and have hypothesized about the forces that might be contributing to their existence. It is necessary that advocates of societal sharing of family responsibility to provide for the needs of children be clear about both these problems and the society's underlying values if they wish to act effectively to influence public policy. Once this clarification and analysis has been done, child advocates must then be prepared to take the further step of constructing methods of action that can effectively counter these forces in order to improve the conditions of all children in our society. This effort requires not only the understanding of the forces involved but also a long-term, sustained effort in the public policy arena.

12. J. S. Fink and D. B. Sponseller, "Practicing for Child Advocacy," *Young Children*, Mar. 1977, pp. 49-54.

13. M. W. Edelman, "Develop a National Agenda for Children" (Position paper commissioned by the Association for Childhood Education International, the National Association for the Education of Young Children, and the U.S. National Committee for Early Childhood Education, for International Year of the Child, 1979. Reprinted from *Young Children*, 34:2-3 [Nov. 1978]).

ANNALS, *AAPSS*, **461**, May 1982

American Values and Social Policy for Children

By SANDRA McCONNELL CONDRY and IRVING LAZAR

ABSTRACT: Social science research that has affected social policy is discussed, focusing on the follow-up studies of the Consortium for Longitudinal Studies. It is argued that a study is likely to influence social policy if (1) it uses direct outcome measures so that the results are comprehensible to nonscientists, (2) it addresses the economic implications of the policy recommendations and so is congruent with contemporary political values, and (3) it is communicated directly to political professionals.

Sandra McConnell Condry is a research associate with the Foundation for Human Service Studies, working with the Consortium for Longitudinal Studies. She earned her Master's degree from UCLA and her Ph.D. from Cornell University. During her graduate career she was a lecturer of developmental psychology at several colleges. She has been an active experimental researcher and has published studies of the development of reading skills and the development of sex differences. Since receiving her Ph.D., she has performed several types of preschool education evaluation research.

Irving Lazar is a professor and member of the graduate fields of human service studies, psychology, and public policy at Cornell University. He has worked as a teacher, as a clinician, as an administrator, and as an evaluator of social programs for federal and state agencies and private foundations. He served as associate director of the Appalachian Regional Commission, as a Congressional Fellow, and as a member of the board of several national voluntary organizations. He organized and is executive officer of the Consortium for Longitudinal Studies.

IN the United States social research has only rarely influenced the few federal policies that specifically address the needs of children. Although children have been the beneficiaries of a number of policies, rarely are these specifically for children or for all children. The few exceptions stand out. The Childen's Bureau, which had significant effects on the lives of children by way of educating parents, bringing about reform in society's treatment of neglected and dependent children, and developing child labor and delinquency laws, was established in 1912. The other exceptions are policies directed toward children with special needs, such as handicapped or economically deprived children. Other American policies that have benefited children have done so indirectly, for instance, Aid for Families with Dependent Children (AFDC) and Maternal Health Care (MHC).

NATIONAL DAY CARE POLICIES IN THE UNITED STATES AND IN EUROPE

As an example of the differences between the United States and other western countries, let us look at day care provisions. U.S. federally supported day care has been provided only during wars and depressions. During the depression of the 1930s, day care centers were set up under the federal government's Works Progress Administration, primarily to provide employment for teachers and domestic workers. During World War II, the Lanham Act provided funds for day care and extended school services to free women for work in war-related industries. At the end of World War II, the Lanham Child Care Centers were closed; however, state and local funds continued them in California, Philadelphia, and New York City.

In contrast, for 50 years France, Italy, and Germany have provided day care for 2-month- to 3-year-old children of working mothers. While parents meet part of the costs on a sliding scale of fees, government allowances for working mothers offset this expense.[1] In 1918, Great Britain established nursery schools as part of the national school, and today, Health Department centers are open for 10 hours per day. In Belgium nearly all 3- to 6-year-olds attend early childhood education centers that are integrated with the compulsory school system.[2] Denmark has a day care system for children up to 18 years old, supported by the federal and local governments and by parents.

Day care programs are provided in many East European countries also. Czechoslovakia provides universal day care programs financed completely by the national government. The Soviet Union, the German Democratic Republic, and Hungary also provide day care programs.[3]

1. F. Davidson, *Day Care Centers in Paris and its Suburbs*, World Health Organization Working Paper no. 13 (Geneva: Joint UN/WHO Committee on the Care of Well Children in Day Care Centers and Institutions, 1962).

2. International Year of the Child, *Discussion Paper on Early Childhood Education*, pt. 1 (New York: International Year of the Child Secretariat, 1979), p. 13.

3. D. R. Meers, "International Day Care: A Selective Review and Psychoanalytic Critique," in *Day Care: Decisions for Resources*, Office of Planning, Research, and Evaluation PRE/R, 4-27, Office of Economic Opportunity Pamphlet 6106-1, ed. E. H. Grotberg (Washington, DC: Office of Economic Opportunity, Office of Planning, Research, and Evaluation), pp. 4-27; M. G. Wagner and M. M. Wagner, "Day Care Programs in Denmark and Czechoslovakia," in Grotberg, *Day Care: Decisions for Resources*, pp. 28-49.

In contrast, the United States supports day care programs only for the children of AFDC mothers enrolled in work training, and few states or cities provide day care for children of working mothers. There have been unsuccessful attempts to institute more universal federally supported day care programs. In 1971, Congress authorized a major new program for day care and other child development programs, which was vetoed by President Nixon. Subsequent efforts at legislation were discouraged by the Carter administration.

THE ROLE OF AMERICAN VALUES IN SOCIAL POLICY FOR CHILDREN

In his classic study of American values, Jones[4] demonstrated that the relative rank and importance of three core values—life, liberty, and property—was highly predictive of the social, political, and economic attitudes held by various groups of Americans. In general, property rights have been ascendent among our legislators; individual liberty has ranked second, and values related to the quality or preservation of life have held lowest rank. The polarization of property rights versus values related to life has become more pronounced than ever; property rights are clearly held in greater value than the others by the present administration. It is no surprise that when policy decisions raise a conflict between property and the lives of children, property has usually won. For example, in the mid-1970s there was political and social pressure to develop and enforce strict federal day care standards in response to the documented horrors of some day care facilities. However, strict standards would also have increased the costs to private day care providers; the proposed standards were gutted. In American society, children are considered to be the property of their parents and there is strong resistance to actions that would deprive parents of their rights to do with their children as they see fit.

However, there is a ray of light here. Because children are considered to be property and because private property is of primary importance in American society, policies that enhance the economic value of children might be acceptable. Evidence that a social policy can increase the value of children or decrease the cost of children should be looked upon favorably. Unfortunately, such evidence is difficult to accumulate because it is the nature of children that their positive economic value is usually not apparent until they near adulthood. We will return to this point.

SOCIAL RESEARCH THAT HAS AFFECTED SOCIAL POLICY

Social scientists have played a role in the few policies for children our government has advanced. Generally, that role has not been central, but there are striking instances where research has been influential. Some of these instances may provide insights into promising relationships between the social science researcher and social policy; these may be able to increase those relationships.

In the 1940s and 1950s, several studies elucidated the effects of

4. A. W. Jones, *Life, Liberty, & Property* (Philadelphia: J. B. Lippincott, 1941).

institutionalization on infants, and these reinforced the trend away from institutionalization and toward foster family care and adoption. Spitz[5] compared the development of two groups of institutionalized infants. One group consisted of infants who were abruptly separated from their mothers at 3 months of age to be reared in a foundling home in an unstimulating environment. The other group lived in a nursery connected to a penal institution; this arrangement allowed the imprisoned mothers to interact with their children each day. Spitz found that the mothered infants developed normally for the first two years while the unmothered infants showed dramatically delayed behavioral and cognitive development. In addition, 37 percent of the foundling home infants died during the first two years, while the mothered infants remained healthy.

A second set of studies, performed by Goldfarb,[6] compared the later development of children who had spent their first three years in institutions before being placed in foster homes with similar children who had been reared in foster homes from infancy. This series of investigations found that the institution-reared children developed a greater frequency of problem behavior—such as aggressiveness, hyperactivity, and social immaturity—lower IQ scores, and greater school difficulties even after four or more years of foster home care. As a result, these institution-reared children required several foster home replacements during their childhoods. Goldfarb concluded that institutional rearing tended to produce damaged personalities.

These studies had direct effects on child welfare policies. In 1955, the executive director of the Child Welfare League of America, J. H. Reid, stated, "We have more than ample scientific proof that . . . it is criminal for institutions to provide care for normal pre-school children."[7] This view was widely accepted by social service professionals, as evidenced by dramatic decreases in the number of children residing in voluntary institutions. National statistics on the placement of neglected and dependent children show that in 1933, 144,000 children lived in institutions, while in 1969, only 74,000 children lived in such institutions. Over that same period, the number of children under foster care increased from 105,000 to 249,000.[8] In New York State, the percentage of neglected and dependent children who resided in voluntary institutions declined from 43 percent in 1940 to 24 percent in 1968.[9] In California, from 1928 to

5. R. A. Spitz, "The Role of Ecological Factors in Emotional Development in Infancy," *Child Development*, 20(3):145-55 (1949).

6. W. Goldfarb, "Infant Rearing and Problem Behavior," *American Journal of Orthopsychiatry*, 13:249-66 (1943); idem, "Effects of Early Institutional Care on Adolescent Personality: Rorschach Data," ibid., 14:441-7 (1944); idem, "Psychological Privation in Infancy and Subsequent Adjustment," ibid., 15:247-55 (1945).

7. J. H. Reid, *Child Welfare Perspectives; Selected Papers of Joseph H. Reid*, ed. A. W. Shyne (New York: Child Welfare League of America, 1979), p. 101.

8. White House Conference on Children, Youth, and Families, *Profiles of Children* (Washington, DC: Government Printing Office, 1970), p. 147.

9. New York State Office of Social Research and Program Information, Bureau of Program Information and Analysis, "Major Trends in Foster Care of Children, New York State, 1965-1968," New York State Department of Social Services Public Notice no. 1108 (Albany, 1970), p. 11.

1964, the capacity of voluntary institutions for neglected children dropped 40 percent, while California's child population increased by 300 percent.[10]

A second striking example of social science research influencing social policy is the Clark and Clark study[11] on racial identification and preference in Negro children. In this study, individual black children, aged three to seven, were questioned about four dolls, which were identical except for skin and hair color: two were white with yellow hair, and two were brown with black hair. The children had no difficulty identifying a white doll or a black doll—94 percent and 93 percent correct. When asked preference questions—for instance, "Which doll is a nice doll?" or "Which doll looks bad?"—about 60 percent of the children attributed the positive characteristics to the white doll and the negative characteristics to the black doll. The evaluative rejection of the black doll was most pronounced among 5-year-olds. In response to a self-identification question—which doll "looks like you?"—only 66 percent of the children selected a black doll. With age there was an increase in correct racial identification; however, even among 7-year-olds, 13 percent of the children still said they "looked like" a white doll. This research figured prominently in the 1954 Supreme Court decision on *Brown* v. *Topeka (Kansas) Board of Education,* which banned segregated schooling.

CONSORTIUM FOR LONGITUDINAL STUDIES

A more recent example of social science research having an effect on social policy will be discussed in greater detail. In 1965, as part of President Johnson's war on poverty, summer Head Start programs were funded by the newly created Office of Economic Opportunity. Before the summer was over, it was decided that Head Start should be run as full-year programs, as it continues to be today.

Social science research was one impetus for Head Start; the social and political milieu were equally important. By the early 1960s, many social scientists were rejecting the view that intelligence was determined solely by heredity. The conclusion drawn from several lines of research was that the environment, and particularly the child's early environment, could drastically affect the final level of intellectual ability; this heredity/environment argument is still raging, two decades later.[12] Social activism during the late 1950s increased public sensitivity to poverty and racial discrimination in America. President Kennedy's plan to alleviate poverty was continued by President Johnson. Reports of the Deutsch's preschool program in Harlem[13]

10. National Study Service, "Planning for Care and Protection of Neglected Children in California" (Report of a Study by National Study Services for the Joint Study Committee on Children's Services," Anselmo, CA, 1965), p. 74.

11. K. Clark and M. P. Clark, "Emotional Factors in Racial Identification and Preference in Negro Children," *Journal of Negro Education,* 29:341-50 (1950).

12. C. M. Jencks, H. Smith, M. B. Ackland, M. Bane, D. Cohen, H. Gintis, B. Heyns, and S. Michelson, *Inequality: A Reassessment of the Effect of Family and Schooling in America* (New York: Basic Books, 1972); N. J. Block and Gerald Dworkin, eds., *The IQ Controversy: Critical Readings* (New York: Pantheon, 1976).

13. M. Deutsch, E. Taleporos, and J. Victor, "A Brief Synopsis of an Initial Enrich-

convinced him that the war on poverty should include, in addition to the Job Corps, a "kiddie corps." Amid a whirlwind of activity, Head Start was planned and implemented during the first half of 1965.[14]

For political reasons the program was instituted on a national full-scale level rather than as a carefully conducted pilot program. As a result, Head Start was not amenable to careful evaluation that, at a minimum, requires random assignment of children from the same population to treatment and control status. Because Head Start was open to all children of poverty, random denial of services was out of the question from a political standpoint. Nevertheless, evaluations of Head Start programs were undertaken. The most prominent was the Westinghouse Study[15] in which a large sample of children who had attended summer or full-year programs in 1966-67 was compared with a sample of their grade school peers who had not attended Head Start. Tests revealed disappointingly few advantages of Head Start children over the non-Head Start children.

Criticisms of the study were quick to surface. It was argued that the evaluation was premature and that the children should have been followed further in their school careers. The inadequacy of the research design received strong criticism—particularly the noncomparability of the control group. The choice of measurement instruments was also criticized.

An influential assessment of seven Head Start-like programs was performed by Bronfenbrenner.[16] Bronfenbrenner agreed with Moynihan that the immediate gains in IQ due to program participation "washed out" within a few years. The programs included in his summary evaluation were less subject to the criticisms regarding the control groups, but the measurement instruments were the same and many of the children were only two years beyond the programs when they were assessed.

These and other negative critiques of Head Start and related programs fed into political attempts to disband the war on poverty. In 1971, President Nixon vetoed the Equal Opportunities Amendments. In 1975, President Ford planned to phase out all support for Head Start.

In this political environment, Irving Lazar of Cornell University and Edith Grotberg of the Administration for Children, Youth, and Families (ACYF) agreed that it was essential to gather the data appropriate to the central evaluative question of Head Start: does preschool education help children avoid failure in their school careers? It was impractical to set up the appropriate prospective evaluation study by randomly assigning children to Head Start or control groups and then following and testing them throughout their school careers. The

ment Program in Early Childhood," in *A Report on Longitudinal Evaluations*, vol. 1, ed. S. Ryan (Washington, DC: Office of Child Development, Department of Health, Education, and Welfare Publication no. [OHD] 74-24, 1974), pp. 49-60.

14. Edward Zigler and Jeannette Valentine, *Project Head Start: A Legacy of the War on Poverty* (New York: Free Press, 1979).

15. Westinghouse Learning Corporation, *The Impact of Head Start on Children's Cognitive and Affective Development, Executive Summary, Ohio Report to the Office of Economic Opportunity*, ED036321 (Washington, DC: Clearinghouse for Federal Scientific and Technical Information, Jun. 1969).

16. Urie Bronfenbrenner, "Is Early Intervention Effective?" in Ryan, *A Report on Longitudinal Programs*, vol. 2.

ongoing follow-up studies of early Head Start participants could not address this question because of the absence of random controls and baseline measures.

Fortunately, in the 1960s several early childhood researchers and practitioners had independently designed and run experimental or demonstration education programs for children of low-income families. Most had collected background data, developed control groups, and followed the children for several years beyond program completion. These children, in 1975, ranged in age from 8 to 18, and thus they had accumulated enough school experiences to provide the data necessary for determining academic success and failure. These research projects appeared appropriate for providing the necessary information if funding could be found, if the researchers would participate, if the children could be located, and if the families would cooperate.

ACYF provided funding, and Irving Lazar, with the help of Kuno Beller and Edward Zigler, approached many of the researchers. In 1975 the Consortium for Longitudinal Studies—originally known as the Consortium for Developmental Continuity—was formed as a voluntary association of independent investigators. The consortium members agreed (1) to develop a common protocol for follow-up testing of their original experimental and control groups, (2) to locate and test as many of these children as possible, and (3) to send both their original raw data and the follow-up data to an independent group in Ithaca for analysis. The consortium has been operating for five years, and the positive impact of this collaboration has proved greater than had been anticipated.

It will be recalled that in the previously mentioned evaluations of preschool education, a central measure of effectiveness was IQ differences. While useful for other purposes, IQ is not a direct measure of success in school. The consortium analyses did not need to depend on this substitute measure; because the school records of the children were available for up to a 12-year period, it was possible to focus on demonstrated school success and failure.

Three measures of school performance were selected as the most appropriate indicators of academic outcomes of preschool education: assignment to special education classes, retention in grade, and high school completion. The results of the consortium analyses showed that low-income children who had attended some type of preschool education program differed from similar children who had not attended preschool in that they (1) were less likely to be placed in a special education program at some time in their school careers (14 percent versus 29 percent); (2) were less likely to be retained in grade (25 percent versus 31 percent); and (3) were somewhat more likely to complete high school (69 percent versus 58 percent).[17]

17. Consortium on Developmental Continuity, *The Persistence of Preschool Effects*, Final report, grant no. 18-76-07843 from the Administration for Children, Youth, and Families, Office of Human Development Services (Washington, DC: U.S. Department of Health, Education, and Welfare, Oct. 1977), pp. 74-81; idem, *Lasting Effects After Preschool*, Final report, grant no. 90C-1311 from the Administration for Children, Youth, and Families (Office of Human Development Services (Washington, DC: U.S. Department of Health, Education, and Welfare, Oct. 1978), pp. 53-74; C. D. Chang, "Evaluating the Long-Term Effects of Preschool Program on the Educational Attainment of Children from Low Income Families" (Ph.D. dissertation, Cornell University, 1981).

These results have had significant social policy effects. Since 1977, Head Start funding has been dramatically increased by Congress, and in 1981, in the midst of federal budget-slashing, the Reagan administration announced that Head Start would be expanded.

REASONS UNDERLYING SOCIAL POLICY EFFECTIVENESS OF RESEARCH

Three useful lessons derive from this discussion of the consortium. The first is the importance of focusing on direct outcome measures whose importance and validity are easily understood. The consortium measures have face validity; it is obvious that a child who is assigned to special education class is not coping well with school. Retention in grade is another clear sign of a child's failure to meet minimum school standards. High school completion is a good predictor of later labor market outcomes and is a benchmark of competence in our society.

It should be noted that these three measures were particularly appropriate for this population—grade failure, special education assignment, and failure to complete high school are unwelcome but all too probable school outcomes for children of poverty. Notice also that these measures of school failure are interpretable only in comparison with a control group from the same population. Individual schools vary in their school policies on assignment to special education and retention; at a minimum, schools tend to favor one over the other. Because of this, the actual percentage of program children retained in grade is only informative in comparison with the percentage of similar nonprogram children, attending the same school, who were retained.

A second lesson from the consortium experience is that economic analyses are particularly forceful. Economists performed cost-benefit analyses of the Ypsilanti Perry Preschool Project, one of the consortium member studies.[18] For two years of preschool education, the undiscounted benefits[19] were about $15,000 per child in 1979 dollars against a cost of $6000 per child—a 248 percent return on the original investment. In our cost-conscious society, dollar analyses are central to political decision-making processes. In discussions of the consortium findings, legislators have focused on the cost-benefit findings. Here again, the advantage of working with direct outcome measures is clear. Placement in special education is an expensive decision for a school to make and the difference in costs between special education and regular class placement is easily computed. By contrast, a cost-benefit analysis of the effectiveness of preschool education based on IQ scores would require correlational inferences that are easily questioned.

A third lesson from the consortium experience is that rapid and

18. C. U. Weber, P. W. Foster, and D. P. Weikart, "An Economic Analysis of the Ypsilanti Perry Preschool Project," Monographs of the High/Scope Educational Research Foundation, no. 5 (1978); L. J. Schweinhart and D. P. Weikart, "Young Children Grow Up: The Effects of the Perry Preschool Program on Youths through Age 15," Monographs of the High/Scope Educational Research Foundation, no. 7 (1980).

19. The benefits included in this computation were the value of the mother's released time during the preschool years, the reduced cost of public education (due to lower rates of special education assignment and grade retention), and the increase in projected lifetime earnings of the child.

broad dissemination of the findings is critical for affecting social policy. A sizable proportion of the consortium budget was earmarked for dissemination activities. The target of these activities was not the academic world but rather the political one: congressional staffs, state legislators, governor's staffs, and chief state school officers.

The three lessons, then, of the consortium are (1) that ecologically valid, easily understood outcome measures are essential; (2) that an analysis of the research outcomes in economic cost-benefit terms is of particular interest to policy decision makers; and (3) that rapid and broad dissemination of this information greatly increases the likelihood of social scientific work affecting social policy.

As was discussed previously, the Spitz, Goldfarb, and Clark and Clark studies were critical elements in earlier social policy decisions. A brief consideration of apparent reasons for their effectiveness will broaden and reinforce the present argument. The Spitz and Goldfarb studies were evaluations of the widely practiced and well-accepted policy of institutional rearing of homeless infants. The studies provided pictures of children irreparably harmed by established social policy. The researchers developed some superb measures. A search for ecologically valid, easily understood outcome measures can find few that outrank the death of the subject. Spitz's finding on the high death rate of institutionalized babies demanded public attention and a policy response. A different direct-outcome measure was developed by Goldfarb in his finding that an institution-reared child, more than a foster family child, was likely to require several foster home placements because of unacceptable behavior. The Clark and Clark study of young black children painted a heart-rending picture of black children denying their racial identity.

A study that uses ecologically valid measures is relatively easy to interpret; an easily interpreted study is more easily disseminated. A widely known study can affect attitudes of policymakers and the public. The policy and economic implications of a study are more easily grasped when the measures are direct.

A second generalization is that economic issues play a central role in social policy formation: it is pertinent that institutionalization of homeless infants and children is more costly than foster family care; resettling a child in a new foster home is an additional expense; segregated schooling is more expensive than integrated schooling; and a preschool education is less expensive than later special treatment in public schools. All these social policy decisions promised tax savings. At a more general level, we argue that to affect social policy, social scientists should clarify the link between research implications and the values of policymakers and society by describing findings in practical and economic terms.

PRACTICAL ADVICE FOR RESEARCHERS

Research that hopes to affect social policy must, of course, have a good experimental design. Every social policy decision has its foes, and any weakness is fair game for the critics. A good comparison group is often missing because program developers feel they cannot deny services to people—even if they cannot serve them. One solution to this problem is for researchers from different areas to collaborate in the development of treatment and control groups. If the expected effects of the two programs are different, for instance, an early education experiment and a study of early physical development, then participants who are assigned to treatment status in one program can serve as control subjects for the other.

We have argued strongly that cost-benefit analyses are essential. It is an unfortunate truism that while the costs for children's programs are immediate, the benefits are not, particularly the economic benefits to society. This means that evaluations of child programs should be designed to allow later follow-up even during lean funding years. Weikart,[20] for instance, staggered his follow-up data collection throughout the year rather than scheduling a single concentrated period each year since the latter procedure would require a larger staff.

Another major problem with longitudinal or follow-up studies is attrition. Levenstein, for her Mother-Child Home Program,[21] keeps track of her treatment and control groups by sending out birthday cards each year, with an enclosure for updating a family's address. Another strategy for counteracting the effects of attrition is for individual researchers to collaborate on follow-ups so that several studies can pool their findings. This tactic requires some planning and organization regarding data collection, such as a standardized format for demographic information and agreement on some basic common outcome measures. Parental consent forms should authorize collection of future data, such as school records.

Although scientists working in child development rarely do so, effective dissemination of their findings to policymakers and public administrators is at least as important as the design of the research itself. Most investigators are concerned with publication in scholarly journals, a form of dissemination that principally benefits the author. Many academics still consider direct efforts to influence the people who make public policy as less than respectable.

Perhaps the most difficult barrier to effective dissemination stems from the socialization of social scientists themselves. Believing that very little is really surely known about anything—or indeed that it can ever be known—many social scientists are unwilling to make a clear statement about the practical and policy implications of the current state of the art in child development. We hedge our statements so carefully that we wind up straddling issues in ways that eliminate any influence our knowledge might have on political decisions. Vice President Mondale once expressed his wish to find a one-armed social scientist—one who would not, in the midst of answering a simple question, say "on the other hand."

20. D. P. Weikart, J. T. Bond, and J. T. McNeil, "The Ypsilanti Perry Preschool Project: Preschool Years and Longitudinal Results," Monographs of the High/Scope Educational Research Foundation, no. 3 (1978).

21. P. Levenstein, "Cognitive Development Through Verbalized Play: The Mother-Child Home Program," in *Play*, eds. J. S. Bruner, A. Jolly, and K. Sylva (New York: Basic Books, 1976), pp. 286-300.

SUMMARY

Social research can influence social policy under certain circumstances. A study must be well designed and must be comprehensible to a nonscientist. It must have recommendations that do not fly in the face of contemporary political values. It must be communicated directly to political professionals. Social scientists will not influence policy by limiting their reports to their colleagues, by ignoring the role of values in policy formation, or by waiting to be asked.

ANNALS, *AAPSS*, **461**, May 1982

Applied Research in the 1970s: Can Anything Be Learned about Children?

By LINDA BROOKOVER BOURQUE

ABSTRACT: This article presents the findings from a careful examination of evaluation studies funded by the U.S. Department of Health, Education, and Welfare in 1974 and 1975. Particular attention is paid to their methodological adequacy and potential applicability to the development of child-relevant policies and practice procedures. The conclusion is that persons interested in developing a cohesive, national policy for children's welfare or for research on children will find little useful information in evaluation studies of the seventies.

Linda Brookover Bourque, Ph.D., is an associate professor in the Divisions of Epidemiology, and Population, Family, and International Health, School of Public Health, University of California. She received her Ph.D. in sociology from Duke University in 1968. Before joining the UCLA faculty, she held a postdoctoral fellowship in mental health and gerontology at Duke University and was assistant professor of sociology at California State University, Los Angeles. Author or coauthor of 18 articles, her areas of research interest include survey design methodology, social psychology, epidemiology, and application of research to policy issues. Her current research focuses on instrument design and analysis of psychosocial data in various medical studies.

NOTE: This is a revised version of a presentation made at the Annual Meeting of the Pacific Sociological Association, San Francisco, April 1980. Research was supported by a grant from the Foundation for Child Development entitled "Monitoring Evaluation Research On and About Children," Howard E. Freeman and Linda B. Bourque, codirectors; by BRSG S07 RR5442, awarded by the Biomedical Research Support Grant (BRSG) Program, Division of Research Resources, National Institutes of Health; by grants 3004 and 3552 from the University of California, Los Angeles, Committee on Research of the Academic Senate; and by PKI053, 1977-80, Intramural Funds, Office of Academic Computing, University of California, Los Angeles.

PERSONS interested in developing a cohesive, national policy for children's welfare or for research on children will find little useful information in evaluation studies done in the past decade. This conclusion is supported by careful examination of studies conducted during the 1970s, with particular attention to their methodological adequacy and potential applicability to the development of child-relevant policies and practice procedures. Some relevant findings from such a set of evaluation studies for child advocates are presented in the following pages.

CONTEXT OF THE EVALUATION STUDIES

During the International Year of the Child and the White House Conference on the Family, child development specialists, social program practitioners, policymakers, the media, and representatives of practically every identifiable institution in American society expressed concern about the future of our children in the 1980s.

Data used by groups interested in child advocacy usually were of necessity by-products of formal research projects or the administrative functions of agencies and governments. In many instances, the original objective for data collection did not resemble the desires or needs of groups who wanted to influence policy formulation.[1] A type of data thought to be closer to the needs of policymakers and practitioners was collected under the auspices of evaluation research.[2]

Evaluation research investigates the extent to which social programs are delivered according to specification and the extent to which they affect their targets according to stated intent. Since many programs are developed and financed by the public sector, we assume that their evaluation will influence the formulation of public policy and will enable practitioners and sponsoring agencies to make administrative decisions on the future status of programs. Consistent with this assumption, support for the need to evaluate the impact of federal programs in health, education, and welfare has increased during the last decade.[3] Evaluation research has emerged as a method by which federal programs might be monitored, implemented, expanded, or terminated. To the extent that evaluation research has been assumed to be a viable administrative tool within the federal government, groups outside government made similar assumptions. Thus people interested in developing a cohesive national policy regarding children believed that information and data available in evaluation studies might provide valuable assistance in attaining their goal.

WHAT DO CHILD ADVOCATES EXPECT FROM EVALUATION RESEARCH?

Research and advocacy have coexisted uneasily for generations.

1. L. B. Schorr, "Issues in the Formulation of a National Child Health Policy" (Paper presented at a special session on "Assuring Basic Health Care for Children and Families in the United States," Annual Meeting of the American Public Health Association, New York, Nov. 1979).

2. P. H. Rossi, H. E. Freeman, S. R. Wright, *Evaluation: A Systematic Approach* (Beverly Hills: Sage, 1979).

3. J. G. Abert, *Program Evaluation at HEW: Research versus Reality*, pt. 1: Health; pt. 2: Education; pt. 3: Welfare (New York: Marcel Dekker, 1979).

Research findings have been made to serve the needs of advocates and have led to the development or demise of social movements. As a result, some children's advocates fear that findings from evaluation studies can be used to terminate programs with humanitarian value that are judged to be administratively ineffective or inefficient. Other advocates believe that evaluation research represents a largely untapped source of information that can help them present their case. These advocates see evaluation research as a possible source of information usable in expanding policy and in maximizing the development of efficient, effective children's programs. Assuming the second perspective, a series of questions can be generated representing what advocates might want to know about or from evaluation studies.

First, how many evaluation studies investigated programs that were directly or indirectly targeted on children? What kinds of programs were they? Who funded them? How much did they cost and so on.

Second, when child-targeted programs were evaluated, what were the characteristics of the evaluation? Who funded such evaluations? Who conducted them? What did they cost? What was the objective of the evaluation? What kinds of evaluations—impact, process, comprehensive—were conducted? How good were the evaluations methodologically?

Third, what conclusions did evaluation studies reach about child-targeted programs? What were the implications of the conclusions for policymakers and practitioners? Was Clark Abt[4] correct when he observed that evaluation studies emphasize analytical procedures to the exclusion of design and data collection procedures and that evaluations reporting sophisticated analyses tended to show the least program efficacy? If through sophisticated analysis programs were shown to be ineffective, did evaluators conclude that such programs were bad and thus should be terminated?

Fourth, what were practitioners doing with the results of evaluations? Did they terminate or change programs in accordance with the findings?

The brief answer to all four questions is that evaluation studies frequently targeted on programs for children. But the nature of the programs studied and the inadequacies of the studies themselves provide few definitive conclusions for practitioners or policymakers. The nonutility of evaluation studies suggests that there is little to gain or to fear from the act of evaluation; decisions to terminate, to change, or to expand programs are probably independent of the data provided by such studies.

DESIGN OF THE EVALUATION STUDIES[5]

In this study, 243 final reports of evaluation studies funded by the Department of Health, Education, and Welfare (DHEW) were analyzed. To be included, a study had to meet three criteria: (1) the study had to be completed and a report filed

4. C. Abt, "Current and Future Prospects for Interdisciplinary Social Policy Research" (Institute for Social Science Research Seminar, University of California, Los Angeles, 1979).

5. L. B. Bourque, "The Role of Evaluation Research in the Federal Government" (Unpublished manuscript, Institute for Social Science Research, University of California, Los Angeles, 1980).

during 1974 or 1975, (2) an identifiable human service program or social intervention had to be assessed, and (3) assessment had to focus on the effectiveness or efficacy of the intervention or on ways the program was being delivered. To obtain reports, inquiries were made about 1700 grants and contracts. Studies were reviewed whether or not they were designated by DHEW as evaluations. Since their definitions on the scope of evaluation research change frequently, all 243 reports coded were studies of action programs. State-of-the-art papers, conferences, reports on planning, and efforts to develop methodological procedures were not included.

Studies were identified as impact evaluations, process evaluations, or comprehensive evaluations. Impact evaluations assess the extent to which a social program or intervention directly or indirectly affects targets of the program. Process evaluations investigate the extent to which a program is delivered or organized as specified. Comprehensive studies include both an impact and a process component.

Data were taken from reports using an auditing form designed to collect information about the contractual characteristics of the intervention being evaluated, the characteristics of the evaluative research, and the study's relevance for children and families.

Data on children and families are the focus of this article. Major variables are the extent to which (1) the evaluated social programs were relevant to children and/or families, (2) the evaluations themselves were relevant to children and/or families, and (3) the implications of the stated conclusions were relevant for child-oriented policy or practice formulation. Frequency distributions were examined, and a single composite variable was constructed. Forty-eight percent of the programs were directly or indirectly targeted on children; in 71 of these 116 evaluations children were also research subjects. Reports are thus divided into three groups: those in which children were both targets of the program and subjects of the evaluation (29.9 percent); those in which children were targets but not subjects (18.5 percent); and those in which children were neither targets nor subjects (52.3 percent).

In answering the questions just raised, the association between this composite variable and various characteristics of the social programs evaluated, the research conducted, and the circumstances under which it was conducted will be examined.

RESULTS OF THE EVALUATION STUDIES

While the majority of these evaluation studies are found in the health area, most of the studies in which children were both program targets and research subjects were educational studies with a "fine-tuning" objective. They were conducted under grants in universities (Table 1). During data collection, we categorized interventions with respect to sector and objective. Briefly, sector refers to the human-resource system or set of institutional arrangements that provide a context for the program. Objective, on the other hand, refers to the stated purpose of the evaluation. Policy-oriented evaluations may result in major changes in the delivery system, in the targets served, or in expanding or terminating a program. Fine-tuning evaluations focused on increasing efficiency by

TABLE 1
CHARACTERISTICS OF EVALUATION STUDIES (in percentages)

CATEGORY	CHILDREN ARE: TARGETS AND SUBJECTS	TARGETS ONLY	NEITHER
Program sector distribution*			
Health	23.9	46.7	52.8
Education	49.3	28.9	18.9
Human service	12.7	15.6	10.2
Other†	21.1	17.8	25.2
Objective of evaluation‡			
Policy	11.3	24.4	26.0
Administration or monitoring	2.8	6.7	26.0
Fine-tuning	85.9	68.9	48.0
Type of evaluation			
Impact studies	62.0	31.1	33.1
Process studies	21.1	60.0	47.2
Comprehensive	16.9	8.9	19.7
Total number (not in percentages)	71	45	127

*Studies are identified as having multiple sector affiliations.

†Includes programs identified as being in the psychological, social, economic, political, legal, and communications areas.

‡$\chi^2 = 34.0$, $p < 0.0001$.

modifying elements within a program. Administrative or monitoring evaluations were done to assure conformity between program designs and procedures.

The majority of all evaluations completed in 1974 and 1975 had a fine-tuning objective and were in the health or education area. Educational evaluations generally were funded by grants, were conducted by universities, and the programs usually had more targets and program elements. While not common in evaluations, theories were cited more often in educational studies. When children were targets but not subjects, studies were health-related, conducted by a variety of organizations, and policy-oriented.

Information on funding devoted to programs, the evaluations themselves, and the duration of the evaluation often were not available. Program funding information was available for 60 percent, and information on evaluation funding was available for 59 percent of the studies. Information on study duration was available for 67 percent. The average cost of a study was $163,000 while the average duration was 17.9 months. Those studies targeted on children and in which children were subjects averaged $145,000 and lasted an average of 19 months. Those in which children were only targets had similar average costs but lasted a significantly shorter period of time (13.7 months). Studies in which children were neither targets nor subjects were both more expensive ($185,924) and lasted a longer time (18.7 months).

Characteristics of the studies

Most evaluation studies in which children were both targets and subjects were impact or comprehensive evaluations (Table 1). Those in which children were targets but not subjects were usually process studies. Educational evaluations were usually impact studies, while health studies were more often process studies. Adopting traditional definitions of research quality, the studies in which children were research subjects were among the better studies in our sample.[6]

Study results can confirm, partially confirm, or fail to confirm initial hypotheses. Impact studies less often reported confirmed hypotheses and were more cautious in drawing definitive conclusions from their findings. Since studies with children as targets and subjects were usually educational impact evaluations, the same conclusions can be made about these studies (Table 2).

Most evaluation reports recommend that the programs evaluated should be developed, modified, or expanded. Rarely did an evaluator recommend program termination nor were study results thought to be useful for the development of either knowledge or policies. Although program maintenance was recommended, practitioners were perceived as the greatest single barrier to implementing change. And the dissemination of results to practitioners appeared to be remarkably sparse (Table 2). Although reports rarely gave information about dissemination, we can infer certain things. For example, since studies in which children were both targets and subjects were so heavily dominated by educational studies, we know that many of these studies were available to a national audience through the Educational Resources Information Center (ERIC). We do not know, however, whether practitioners made any effort to obtain copies from ERIC.

6. Designs of impact studies were categorized as to whether they were experiments, quasi-experiments, or something else; process studies were categorized as to whether they were qualitative, quantitative, or mixed in research approach. Of all impact studies, 18 percent were true experiments and 57 percent were quasi-experiments; these categories were combined and equated with "better quality." Of the process studies, 54 percent used exclusively qualitative approaches; 36 percent used quantitative approaches; and 6 percent used a combination. For process studies, the latter two categories were equated with "better quality."

DISCUSSION OF THE EVALUATION STUDIES

Persons seeking to develop a cohesive national policy for the welfare of children or for research focused on children will find little in completed evaluation studies. Evaluation research is not in the vanguard of policy formulation, but at most, is a reactive enterprise in relation to policy. The programs studied decisions of policy and practice from documents made in the 1960s, rather than previewing policy directions for the 1980s. For example, while a plurality of the studies in our sample dealt with issues in the health area, the majority of the questions asked focused on adults, national health insurance, or other issues not particularly pertinent for children. Few studies focused on children or on how children's health status might be affected by the programs under investigation. An exception is a series of 11 evaluations sponsored by the Office of

TABLE 2
CHARACTERISTICS OF FINDINGS, CONCLUSIONS, AND THEIR IMPLICATIONS (in percentages)

	CHILDREN ARE:		
FINDINGS AND CONCLUSIONS	TARGETS AND SUBJECTS	TARGETS ONLY	NEITHER
Comparisons possible with related studies*	63.4	46.7	34.6
Impact studies			
Hypotheses confirmed	29.5	14.3	66.7
Characteristics of conclusions			
Useful for:			
Theory	4.5	0.0	0.0
Practice principles	61.4	64.3	45.2
Policy	6.8	7.1	19.0
All others, plus combinations	25.0	21.3	16.7
No references	2.3	7.1	19.0
Qualifications are attached:			
Yes	61.4	42.8	45.1
No	25.0	28.6	19.0
No information	13.6	28.6	35.7
Utility:			
Develop, continue, modify, or expand program	86.4	49.9	54.5
Curtail/terminate program	4.5	21.4	0.0
All others†	2.3	7.1	4.8
No information	6.8	21.4	40.5
Process studies			
Hypotheses confirmed	46.7	74.1	70.0
Characteristics of conclusions			
Useful for:			
Practice principles	73.3	59.3	55.0
Policy	6.7	3.7	13.3
All others, plus combinations	20.0	14.8	26.7
No reference	0.0	22.2	5.0
Qualifications are attached:			
Yes	59.3	55.5	43.3
No	26.7	7.4	26.7
No information	13.3	44.4	30.0
Utility:			
Develop, continue, modify, or expand program	60.0	51.8	70.1
All others†	26.7	7.4	15.0
No information	13.3	40.7	15.0

*In recording information about findings, the coder specified whether—according to the report or in the coder's own judgment—the findings could be compared with those of other studies in the same substantive area. In many instances, regardless of what the report implied, the coder indicated that such judgments could not be made. Frequently, this reflects inadequacies in the study design, data collection, or analyses. Percentages in this line of the table represent the proportion of studies for which, in our judgment, sufficient information existed to make comparisons.

†Primarily meeting legislative/contractual requirements.

Child Development. In this series a manual by which maternal health centers could evaluate their services was tested.

Children in the studies

In contrast to the initial assumptions, a substantial proportion (47.7 percent, N = 116) of the programs evaluated were targeted on children. Of that group, 61 percent—71 studies—collected data on or about children as part of the evaluation study. These studies were heavily dominated by educational programs in which the objective was to modify or fine tune an existing program. Grants were the funding mechanism, with universities conducting the evaluation. Where children were the central focus, studies were superior methodologically, and the evaluator was cautious in drawing conclusions.

Of greater interest are two other types of studies: (1) those evaluation programs that clearly targeted on children, but in which children were not research subjects and in which the evaluator failed to examine the implications for children; and (2) those programs that did not target on children, but where the program and findings from the evaluation had relevance for children and families. When children were targets but not subjects, the study was frequently a process evaluation in which the objective was to examine whether services were delivered as specified. Failure to collect data directly from children is not unusual.

This failure characterizes many studies where children are research subjects as well as those where they are not. Recording children as subjects simply means that some kinds of data were collected about or on children; it does not mean that children were directly interviewed. Many researchers when studying children depend on parents, usually the mother, teachers, trained observers, or existing records for their data. Children are rarely formally interviewed, and on the few occasions when they have been, their opinions frequently contradicted those given by parents and teachers on their behalf.[7] Reluctance to interview children or otherwise obtain data directly from them may indicate that researchers do not consider children capable of acting as research subjects. In addition, restrictions imposed by human subjects legislation and the necessity of obtaining permission from parents or guardians to study minors probably discourages investigators from using children as research subjects.[8] The fact that children, particularly older children, are avoided as research subjects may introduce an unknown but systematic bias into all studies about children or of potential relevance to children.

When children were neither subjects nor targets, the evaluated programs often were targeted on large, categorically defined groups, such as Aid to Families with Dependent Children (AFDC) recipients, or on other adults, such as teachers or parents who interacted with children. These programs involved such

7. N. Zill, "Reports on American Family Life from a National Sample of Children and Parents" (Paper presented at the 1977 Biennial Meeting of the Society for Research in Child Development, New Orleans, Mar. 1977).

8. Department of Health, Education, and Welfare, "Report and Recommendations of the National Commission for the Protection of Human Subjects of Biomedical and Behavioral Research, P.L. (93-348), Regulations on Research Involving Children, pt. 3," *Federal Register*, 43: 2084 (13 Jan. 1978).

things as delivery of health care and financial aid, programs for alcoholics and Indians, or community health centers. All these programs, whether or not targeted on children, could quite possibly affect children if adults with whom they were involved were also affected.

Thus, in addition to the evaluation reports in which children were targets, subjects, or both, there were a substantial number of additional programs that could affect children. At the same time, the importance of these studies for children's advocates was probably limited. Although the ideal evaluation study was assumed to contribute to policy-relevant decision making and to affect the development of innovative social programs, these data suggest that studies rarely had a policy objective, were rarely perceived as adding to knowledge, and rarely involved innovative programs.

Using evaluations to formulate policy or to modify programs

The research component of these evaluation studies was not particularly sophisticated. The more sophisticated studies usually involved analytical procedures rather than design and data collection. There is no evidence in this data set that evaluators use study findings to recommend that social programs be curtailed or terminated. The more sophisticated the study, in fact, the more cautious the evaluator was in making definitive statements as to what should happen to the program under study. The strongest statements on the future and/or adequacy of programs were made in reports where the information provided about both the program and the evaluation was minimal or where the evaluation component was weak or inadequate, using traditional research standards. In such reports, findings were generally reported as conclusive, and therefore they supported the expansion or maintenance of the evaluated program.

Whereas evaluators rarely recommended major modification or termination of a program, conclusions were often perceived to be relevant for practice principles. Practitioners were perceived to be the single greatest barrier to implementing changes or modifications that might—on the basis of the evaluation—be considered meritorious. Only five reports recommended program termination. In three of the five, the evaluated program was highly controversial, and strong lobbying efforts were directed against the program prior to full implementation or adequate testing.

These data provide overwhelming evidence that evaluation research was not directed at questions of policy formulation or program development. Moreover, this pattern was so strong in the early 1970s that it is doubtful it has changed in the post-1975 evaluations.

Consistent with Gallagher's observation that "certain research problems can not be addressed by the individual investigator,"[9] most evaluation studies concentrate on minor questions, not necessarily because the investigators are incompetent, but because evaluation funds do not provide sufficient time and resources to address major questions. Nor is the timing of evaluation

9. J. J. Gallagher, "Research Centers and Social Policy," *American Psychologist*, 34:997 (1979).

studies such that they have a major effect on the development of policies and programs. Most evaluations focus on existent programs, and the resultant findings, if used at all, are used to modify or refine components of the program.

Rather than using completed evaluations as a source of information about programs and policies currently being formulated, it may be possible to use them to describe the extent to which policies established during a prior period of time did in fact result in actual programs. Children's advocates should be cautious in using them even for this purpose, however, for there are wide variations in the quality of the reports, the quality of the research conducted, and the care with which the programs evaluated were described. Certainly, the universe of evaluation research studies can give a group such as the Select Panel for the Promotion of Child Health only suggestive information.[10] Such studies do provide a data base, but it is a selective data base—selective in the programs studied, in the questions addressed, and in the dependability of the findings reported and the conclusions reached. Used with caution and with knowledge of their inadequacies, these studies can provide insight into programmatic questions, particularly in the educational area.

While these studies were by definition applied, and made little pretense of contributing to knowledge or of testing questions of theoretical interest, it is doubtful that methodological quality differs significantly from more traditional, academic research. Unlike research conducted in academic settings where there is at least some pressure to publish in academic journals, undoubtedly most evaluation studies—and particularly those not conducted in universities—were seen only by the evaluator, persons involved in the specific program evaluated, and the sponsoring agency.[11] Since educational studies were frequently conducted by universities and were the ones most frequently specifying children as targets of the program and subjects of the research, these studies seem more likely to have been disseminated and read by constituent groups for whom they should have relevance. In contrast, health studies not conducted in universities and in which the evaluator frequently failed to recognize any relevance for children probably were never disseminated to people interested in children's health. Consequently, children's advocates with a specific interest in health might want to obtain evaluation studies in the health area. These studies will not necessarily provide information about children, but they will suggest some of the health issues preceived as major during the 1970s, the kinds of programs that existed, and may even give some insight into the federal government's future programmatic plans.

Finally, despite the fact that studies were usually reported as relevant for practitioners rather than for academics or policymakers, and that only rarely was it suggested that programs be terminated, practitioners were seen as the major barrier to implementing suggested

10. Schorr, "Issues in the Formulation of A National Child Health Policy."

11. M. Useem and P. DiMaggio, "An Example of Evaluation Research as a Cottage Industry: The Technical Quality and Impact of Arts Audience Studies," *Sociological Methods & Research*, 7:55 (1978).

programmatic changes. This suggests that practitioners—and possibly advocates—have a fear of or resistance to evaluation research and that this fear or resistance was readily perceived by evaluation researchers and possibly by sponsoring agencies. Whether or not this fear inhibits the actions of practitioners, evaluators, and sponsors cannot be answered from these data. Others have suggested, however, that the politics of evaluation research creates a pull on all the interested parties—practitioners, researchers, and sponsors—and as a result distorts the findings. Persons more familiar with the day-to-day activities of social programs—social providers and constituency-specific advocates—may be able to assess accurately the existence or extent of possible bias.

CONCLUSION

Evaluation researchers have undertaken assessment of many programs targeting children, while a significant number of evaluations collected data on or about children. Additional studies have relevance for children that was not recognized by the evaluators. Few studies assessed innovative or policy-relevant programs; many were useless for interested people because they were poorly done or inadequately reported.

Programs studied in the best evaluations were those of least relevance to persons with broadly defined interests in innovative program and policy development. Such studies were in the educational area and had as their objective the minor modification or fine tuning of well-established programs. Those evaluations specifying a policy objective characterized the health area; they were potentially of greatest interest. Because of methodological weakness, lack of recognition of relevance to children, and sparse dissemination, however, they were least likely to be incorporated into the deliberations of policymakers.

If findings from health studies are being used to formulate intragovernmental policy regarding children, there is good reason for advocates outside government to be concerned. The data in this study suggested that many policy-oriented evaluations focused on innocuous programs or on programs that were already well established and thus were unlikely to be modified in response to an evaluation. Few were suitably timed for decision making to affect the program. Assuming that some studies do evaluate programs with broad or controversial policy relevance, few of these studies collected data on or about children or even considered their potential relevance to children. Evaluations that were policy-oriented and failed to study children using sophisticated methodology were among the weakest. Thus if intragovernmental policy and programmatic decisions are being based—even partially—on the results of such evaluations, they are being made in the absence of information about children and in the absence of high-quality information about all aspects of the programs and their recipients.

ANNALS, *AAPSS*, **461**, May 1982

Relationships Between Early Childhood Groups in Three States

By EDWARD A. DUANE, WILLIAM M. BRIDGELAND, and MARK E. STERN

ABSTRACT: The state-level services arena for the young child has been subjected to little systematic study, especially that focused on early childhood policy people themselves. Using analysis from state kindergarten through twelfth grade educational policymaking, the present effort focuses on the interaction patterns among key policy groups in three states: Michigan, California, and New York. Respondents include people within state agencies, nonagency governmental people, and early childhood specialists. The findings suggest that agency and interest groups are cooptative and that proprietary child care providers are the most active participants in policymaking.

Edward A. Duane is a professor in the Department of Social Science and the Department of Educational Administration, Michigan State University, East Lansing. His Ph.D. is from the University of Pennsylvania, Philadelphia, in political science. He has contributed to numerous professional journals in the area of educational policymaking and the theory of political power.

William M. Bridgeland is an associate professor in the Department of Social Science, Michigan State University, East Lansing. He holds a Ph.D. in sociology from the University of Illinois, Urbana, has done postdoctoral work in social policy at the University of Michigan, Ann Arbor, and has contributed to a variety of professional journals in such areas as educational policymaking, environmental movements, and community poverty programs.

Mark E. Stern is director of Stern and Associates-Education Consultants, Rochester, Michigan. His Ph.D. is in education from Michigan State University.

NOTE: An earlier draft of this article was presented at the Annual Meeting of the American Educational Research Association, Special Interest Group: Politics of Education, Toronto, Ontario, Canada, March 1978. The analysis for this article was completed while William M. Bridgeland was a visiting scholar at the University of Michigan Center for Research on Social Organizations.

THE policy process in early childhood services can be usefully conceived of as an "arena," that is, as a network of policy values—or a "culture"—public programs, and related actors, both individuals and organizations. While analysis of early childhood policy is a relatively new area of inquiry, some work has been done on the first two of the three foci: policy rationales[1] and especially public programming.[2] And yet apart from Steiner's[3] historical overview of Washington lobbying, there has been almost no systematic analysis of early childhood policy people themselves, the decision makers and advocate groups, especially, as well as their interactions. This is a real research void. Central to all policy analysis is the question, Who does what to whom with what effect? More specifically, for analysis of policy for early childhood some of the key questions are as follows:

—Who are the major participants in early childhood policymaking?

—What policy resources do they have?

—How do these actors seek to influence the policy process?

—What are the significant relationships—conflict and collaboration—in the policy process?

TERRAIN FOR THE PRESENT RESEARCH ON POLICY

Elsewhere, we have attempted to identify the key policy actors, their political styles, and their relative effects.[4] In contrast, the overriding concern in this inquiry is with exploring the political interaction patterns among the agencies and interest groups. The research findings should therefore help illuminate the basic theoretical question about the types of power structures that exist in early childhood policymaking.

The state level is chosen as the unit of analysis because state government is a mediator between federal mandates and local allocation. It is the fulcrum in early childhood policymaking. While much of public funding comes from the federal government, state agencies write crucial rules, oversee programs, and allocate resources. California, Michigan, and New York are the focus of this research because they clearly lead their respective regions in the range of early childhood programming and the amount of funding.

To direct this inquiry, the salient features of policymaking for state early childhood services are con-

1. Kathleen Dunlop, "Reformist Rationales for Governmental Intervention Into Child Care," *Education and Urban Society*, 2:175-210; Leon Keyserling, "Making Politics Work for Children," *Child Welfare*, 53:483-92 (Oct. 1974).

2. Dennis Young and Richard Nelson, *Public Policy for Day Care of Young Children* (Lexington, MA: D. C. Heath, 1973); Sheila Kamerman and Alfred Kahn, "The Day-Care Debate: A Wider View," *Public Interest*, 54:79-93 (Winter 1979).

3. Gilbert Steiner, *The Children's Cause* (Washington, DC: Brookings Institution, 1976).

4. William Bridgeland and Edward Duane, "The Politics of Pre-Kindergarten Education: An Inquiry in Three States," *Education and Urban Society*, 12:211-26 (Feb. 1980); idem, "Pre-Kindergarten Educational Politics as a Policy Arena in the 1980s," *Child Care Quarterly*, 9:149-57 (Fall 1980); idem, "Policymaking Styles in State Early Childhood Education" (unpublished, 1979).

trasted with those of policymaking for state kindergarten through twelfth grade (K-12).[5] First, in the K-12 policy arena, political demands are transmitted through formalized channels by complex bureaucratic organizations, that is, associational interest groups. In the early childhood policy area, by contrast, more informal and intermittent political communications come from small-scale and often temporary interest groups, that is, nonassociational and even anomic groups.[6] Second, although state K-12 politics largely concerns the legislative process—policy formulation—state early childhood politics more usually involves state agencies—policy implementation. Third, the basic power configuration among state K-12 policy groups has shifted from a monolithic mode involving a close concert of most interested parties to achieve common objectives to a fragmented pattern wherein educational power groups pursue sharply competitive interests.[7] In contrast, the programmatically more incoherent preschool area appears much more as a mix of disparate and syndical power patterns.

Typically, some local child care practitioners will temporarily coalesce around a single issue of importance in the policy process—a nonassociational interest group exhibiting a disparate pattern. Moreover, the relevant state agencies who are institutional interest groups seem to be politically linked to practitioner organizations and client groups—a syndical relationship with agency ascendance but sometimes dependence. Fourth, while people from the K-12 world focus on the more limited schooling process, prekindergarten programs involve the more embracing process of social, psychological, and physical development and care of the young child. And this situation has resulted in a host of governmental programs dispersed across many public agencies, especially social services, education, public health, and mental health. As a result, interagency competition or so-called turfsmanship pervades preschool politics.

What are the basic findings anticipated from such an exploration of the political interaction patterns among state groups concerned with early childhood? First, given overlapping program responsibilities, it is reasonable to expect that there will be much jurisdictional infighting among early childhood agencies, for example, social service versus education departments over programming control. Second, in the relationship beween the several agencies—bureaucratic power centers—and their informal and politically unsophisticated groups of practitioners and clients, it is assumed that the respondents would emphasize domination and cooptation of practitioners and clients by agencies. Third, as a consequence of the low level of political mobilization among practitioners, it would be anticipated that there would be a paucity of perceptions concerned with the political exchanges between these largely nonassociational interest groups themselves.

5. See Duane and Bridgeland, "Pre-Kindergarten Educational Politics as a Policy Arena in the 1980s."

6. Gabriel Almond and James Coleman, *The Politics of Developing Areas* (Princeton, NJ: Princeton University Press, 1960), pp. 33-8.

7. Laurence Iannaccone, "State Politics of Education," in *The Politics of Education at the Local, State and Federal Levels*, ed. Michael Kirst (Berkeley, CA: McCutchon, 1969), pp. 284-99.

People from California, Michigan, and New York who are knowledgeable about the early childhood arena were the respondents to this survey on the perceptions of power. Each person was asked to describe the relationships between state agencies—for example, education and public health—and interest groups—for example, the state branch of the National Association for the Education of Young Children or various feminist groups. The types of behavior that seem to fit these potential relations best are open conflict, quiet competition, cooptation, partnership-coalition, and indifference. A structured questionnaire with some complementary semistructured items was mailed to the respondents in 1978.

Respondent panels within each of the respective states were developed from three general categories of people: those within the various state departments or agencies, governmental people outside of agencies, and early childhood specialists outside the government. A total of 84 respondents completed and returned the questionnaire: 35 for Michigan, 27 for California, and 22 for New York.[8] Those findings that focus on the power patterns between the various groups are reported next.

POLITICAL INTERACTIONS AMONG GROUPS AFFECTING POLICY

Two sets of relationships were especially identified and characterized by some of the respondents. These included interactions between child-affecting state agencies and relationships between these agencies and interest groups.

Interagency relationships

The relationships that elicited the greatest number of responses from the policy panel were those involving agencies responsible for programs for the young child (Table 1). As several respondents in each state pointed out, the agencies administer policy but do not establish it. The governor and legislature do that. The questionnaire did not really get at this fact. The thrust was rather on the relationship between agencies and interest groups over policy issues and not how such policy was formulated in nonagency spheres of state government. Surveying the latter would have taken much more time and money than was available to this modest study.

This point relates, of course, to the first hypothesis. The scattering of preschool programs across various "soft," or social, public policy-making units leads to intense territorial struggles. But where there are clear agency distinctions, as between the State Department of Education (SDE) and the others, there is a distinctly significant pattern of variation between the three states (Table 1). Specifically, the National Consortium report (1980) notes that in Michigan there is

> an interesting picture of program fragmentation and overlapping agency function with potential inter-agency conflict. The most dramatic example is that of Medicaid administration located in the State Department of Social Services (SDSS) rather than the State Department of Public Health (SDPH). Also, food distribution is a function of two large programs: the Women, Infant and Children Program (WIC) in the SDPH,

8. See Bridgeland and Duane, "The Politics of Pre-Kindergarten Education" and "Pre-Kindergarten Educational Politics" for a more extensive discussion.

TABLE 1
RELATIONSHIPS BETWEEN CHILD-AFFECTING STATE AGENCIES
(in percentages)*

	CONFLICT	COMPETITION	COOPTATION	COALITION	INDIFFERENCE	NO OPINION
SDE and SDSS†						
Michigan	05.7	51.4	05.7	28.5	00.0	08.5
California	44.4	14.8	07.4	11.1	00.0	22.2
New York	09.1	27.3	22.7	13.6	09.1	19.2
Total	19.0	33.3	10.7	19.0	02.4	15.5
Total χ^2 0.01 (10) = 34.58						
SDE and SDPH†						
Michigan	00.0	05.7	08.5	34.2	25.7	25.9
California	25.9	22.2	18.5	14.8	03.7	14.9
New York	04.5	13.6	22.7	09.1	13.6	36.5
Total	09.5	13.1	15.5	21.4	15.5	25.0
Total χ^2 0.01 (10) = 28.61						
SDSS and SDPH						
Michigan	00.0	14.2	08.5	42.9	14.2	20.0
California	NA	NA	NA	NA	NA	NA
New York	00.0	13.6	13.6	27.3	18.2	27.3
Total	03.6	15.5	08.3	31.0	16.7	25.0

*N = 84; degrees of freedom = 10.

†SDE = State Department of Education; SDSS = State Department of Social Services; and SDPH = State Department of Public Health.

and the assistance payment administration of SDSS. Furthermore, SDSS has control over the administration and licensing of day care facilities (public, private-voluntary and proprietary, nursery schools, and Head Start). Vocal elements have been arguing recently that this entire area properly lies within the purview of the State Department of Education (SDE) under an office of preprimary or early childhood education. Several respondents spoke to us of (and lamented) these interdepartmental overlaps. However, pooling interdepartmental resources and efforts may arise but probably not on any systematic basis.[9]

9. Edward Duane and William Bridgeland, "Report to the National Consortium for Families and Children on Federally Funded Child Programs in Michigan" (unpublished); ERIC-ED 171 414, 1980, p. 8.

If the meaning of turfsmanship is confined to open and intense struggle between state agencies, then the data do not support the preceding hypothesis. However, if it includes, as we believe it should, both subtler conflicts and/or collaboration, then interagency transactions are clearly an important political reality.

The notable exception is the relationship of the SDSSs and the SDEs to the SDPHs. This interaction with the SDPHs elicits little behavioral reaction from the respondents in any of the three states: 40 percent of the entire panel either characterized the relationship as one of indifference or expressed no opinion about it at all (Table 1).

According to the current respondents, the relationship that

best seems to describe the SDE and the SDSS in Michigan is not conflict, but instead, competition (51.4 percent) or coalition (28.5 percent). On the other hand, open conflict seems to be the primary relationship in California (44.4 percent). This is interesting in light of the fact that there is but one umbrella agency, called the Department of Health, that includes both social services and public health; in addition, note that they perceive a 25.9 percent conflict between SDE and SDPH. These perceptions make apt Kirst's description:

> Issues in state governance that impact upon delivery of child care revolve primarily around the infighting between SDE and SDPH. The SDPH has been assigned single state agency responsibility for Title XX child care by HEW, and SDE assumed administrative responsibility by means of a state level interagency agreement. HEW, however, has filed an audit exception against the state charging that the SDPH is not fulfilling its obligations. SDPH claims that SDE does not allow sufficient monitoring of the child care by SDPH, and that SDE considers child care an educational service rather than a social service which it was intended to be under Title XX.[10]

The New York respondents saw relatively little conflict, though there is some competition perceived between agencies—27.3 percent between SDE and SDSS. The full spectrum of political behaviors was perceived as more or less present, with no particular type seen generally as dominant, although 6 of the 22 (27.3 percent) did cite a coalition between the SDSS and SDPH as important. On the other hand, Garms points out that all the state agencies in the child service area have been involved in some interagency squabbling.

> [Because] of Section 853 (The Education for All Handicapped Act), the state and the school districts are responsible for educating all students. They can even provide them with room and board and other expenses. As a result, sometimes when (the Department of) Mental Hygiene wants to discharge a patient there is a tug-of-war between the SDE and SDSS as to who will place the student and provide for him.[11]

How does one interpret this emphasis on muted conflict and even limited coalition? In the first place, there would appear to be little necessity for a zero-sum type of conflict. Traditionally comfortable funding levels for early childhood programs in states with high levels of social services should work to promote an environment conducive to a degree of accommodation. Beyond this, in an era of increasingly close legislative scrutiny, excessive public wrangling could affect the agencies adversely. There seems to be a real incentive here, at least, to keep damage from interagency disputes within acceptable limits.

Agency and interest group interactions

The reactions to the network of complex governmental organizations are in contrast to the perceptions of these agencies as they relate to organizations of pertinent practitioner and client surrogates. These organizations act as nonassociational interest groups informally

10. Michael Kirst, "Children's Services in California: A First Look" (unpublished, 1977), p. 21.

11. Walter Garms, "New York State Programs for Children" (unpublished, 1977), p. 4.

TABLE 2
RELATIONSHIPS BETWEEN CHILD-AFFECTING STATE AGENCIES AND INTEREST GROUPS (in percentages)

	CONFLICT	COMPE-TITION	COOPTA-TION	COALI-TION	INDIFFER-ENCE	NO OPINION
State agencies and NAEYC*						
Michigan	14.2	14.2	08.5	08.5	20.0	34.2
California	00.0	11.1	29.6	29.6	03.7	25.9
New York	04.5	04.5	13.6	13.6	18.2	45.5
Total	07.1	10.7	16.7	16.7	14.3	34.5
Total χ^2 nonsignificant = 16.13						
State agencies and school administrators and teachers associations						
Michigan	05.7	28.5	14.2	02.8	02.8	45.7
California	03.7	18.5	11.1	29.6	00.0	37.0
New York	00.0	00.0	22.7	27.3	00.0	50.0
Total	03.6	17.9	15.5	17.9	01.2	44.0
Total χ^2 nonsignificant = 18.03						
State agencies and private child care groups						
Michigan	45.7	22.8	11.4	02.8	02.8	14.2
California	00.0	33.3	18.5	22.2	03.7	22.2
New York	13.6	18.2	31.8	00.0	09.1	27.3
Total	22.6	25.0	19.0	08.3	04.8	20.2
Total χ^2 0.01 (10) = 31.06						

NOTE: Degrees of freedom = 10.
*NAEYC = National Association for the Education of Young Children.

forwarding intermittent demands. If the frequency of response is a crude index of perceived power, then it is not completely surprising to find that groups oriented to early childhood were given less attention than agencies (Table 2).

For instance, two organizations highly visible in the media—the National Organization for Women (NOW) and the American Federation of Teachers (AFT)—are largely ignored as forces in the policy arena of early childhood. (They are therefore excluded from Table 2.) The reason NOW is ignored might be that child care has been only one of the items on its agenda, and it has had a low priority. As for the AFT, it has had only one major intervention into the prekindergarten arena in the form of a nationally publicized pronouncement on policy.[12] However, this initiative has yet to be followed up by a sustained political presence in the domain of preschool policy.

Therefore a set pattern between school people and state agencies may not have emerged to date over early childhood; note the rather large percentage of "no opinions"—44 percent in the total study—in Table 2. Nonetheless, the respondents did identify competition in Michigan (28.5 percent) and coalition in California (29.6 percent). Only half the New York respondents

12. American Federation of Teachers (AFT) Task Force on Educational Issues, "Putting Early Childhood and Day Care Services into the Public Schools," Winter 1976.

actually characterized the relationships in any way whatsoever, with coalition being the dominant response (27.3 percent).

Two large aggregates of deliverers of early child care, the voluntary and the public Head Start people, also appear to be of little importance among this panel of policy observers. What might account for this situation? Head Start units are concentrated in inner cities, are fewer in number than other child care arrangements, and have a comparatively secure base of federal funding. They are, therefore, less likely to be the source of important policy initiatives. While numerically larger, the "voluntary" organizations are individually small in size, geographically dispersed, and programmatically influenced by heterogeneous and often conflicting philosophies—Piaget, Montessori, Reich, Dreikers, and so forth. Or they may provide merely "custodial" service with little apparent philosophy, although the results of the custodial care centers may be little different from those more concerned with development.[13] In any event, this environment of organizational fragmentation is unlikely to produce effective coalitions.

The National Association for the Education of Young Children (NAEYC) represents an organizational analog to the National Educational Association (NEA) before the latter became a union in the mid-1960s. NAEYC is basically a professional association of researchers, practitioners, and client-surrogates, and it has not been geared up as a vehicle for political influence over policymaking.[14] It is quite expected, then, that the reaction to the NAEYC would be low-keyed and mixed. At most, indifference seems to mark the relationship between the state agencies and NAEYC in Michigan (20.0 percent) and New York (18.2 percent), while cooptation and coalition mark this relationship in California (29.6 percent).

But one of these relationships between the agencies and the interest groups is important. In sharp contrast to other groups that affect children, it is the relationship between state agencies and proprietary child care groups that appears to be most easily isolated and labeled. This is understandable when one recalls that the profit-oriented organizations are likely to be impelled to scramble for financial resources and, in particular, to attempt to put themselves in a better position to obtain public subsidies. Whatever their commitment to professionalism and/or idealism, these profit-making groups clearly have tangible, material stakes in the policymaking process. In addition, some research into early childhood programs describes profit-making day care centers as providing programs of lower quality than those of the nonprofit.[15] In order to defend themselves from criticisms of their

13. Meredith Larson, "Federal Policy for Pre-School Services: Assumptions and Evidence," Research Memorandum ERPC 2158-24, *SRI International*, Jun. 1979, p. 11.

14. At the national level, the NAEYC has begun attempting to mobilize its members through its *Policy Alert* news sheet.

15. Richard Ruopp et al., *Children at the Center* (Cambridge, MA: Abt Associates, 1979), pp. xxxvi-vii, 122-5. See also AFT Task Force on Educational Issues, 1976, pp. 5-6; Advisory Committee on Child Development Assembly of Behavioral and Social Sciences National Research Council, *Toward a National Policy for Children and Families* (Washington, DC: National Academy of Sciences, 1976), p. 68.

programs that could eventually curtail their public support, they would be expected to be more politically organized and active than other provider groups.

There is, however, little agreement among states here, as the patterns in the three states significantly diverge (Table 2). Michigan appears to have a mixed relationship of conflict (45.7 percent) and competition (22.8 percent) between state agencies and proprietary child care groups. The respondents were asked to elaborate on their choices. It was on this latter relationship that they commented generally. For example, one Michigan prekindergarten specialist noted that the "private child care administrators are very critical of the SDSS on day-care licensing regulations." Another prekindergarten specialist said, "All organizations are in open conflict with the SDE about performance objectives." In California, this relationship was seen by part of the panel as competitive (33.3 percent), by part as a coalition (22.2 percent), and by a small part as cooptation (18.5 percent). In fact, several of the respondents really wanted to choose both characteristics. This was well articulated by one agency policy person who said, "California subsidizes many private agencies, which leads to both conflict and cooperation."

Of those on the New York panel who chose to characterize this relationship, 50 percent depicted the relationship between the agencies and private child care groups as one of cooptation. The reasons this group gave have to do with the ability of some of the private day care operations to escape day care SDSS licensure.

What might account for the diversity of these reactions? In the past, proprietary child care groups were small-scale, shoestring outfits with inherent limitations in playing political roles at the state and national levels. However, in recent years, there has been a notable increase in the well-capitalized franchises—Kindercare, Young World, and the like. These "chain" operations have emerged to meet the demands of the new cohort of middle-class working mothers for better child care outside the family. People who control such businesses are most likely to be the ones who know just how to approach pertinent agency operatives. Given the coexistence of the traditional and the streamlined proprietary organizations, viewpoints about the political efficacy of proprietary groups are bound to vary considerably.

CONCLUSION AND PROJECTIONS

All three hypotheses are basically, although qualifiedly, confirmed. Program fragmentation and overlapping does seem to be related to extensive political exchanges between agency people. Agencies seem to be able to limit tendencies toward the escalation of conflict and even to engage in some collaboration or "collusion." With control over child care as a major motive, it appears that what conflict exists revolves around the SDEs and SDSSs and, to a much lesser extent, other program areas such as mental and public health.

The relationship between agencies and interest groups was generally tilted toward agency cooptation and control. And yet cooptation potentially goes both ways. The controlling party, an agency, can absorb its potential opponents, the practitioners, only to discover that the absorbed parties can now "bore from within" and eventually alter the cooptor itself. There is some evidence here that something like this is occurring in California, where with public support for day care dating from World War II, practitioner organizations might have acquired more political experience.

The respondents were generally unimpressed by most potential—K-12 and feminist groups—and actual—NAEYC, voluntary, and public child care deliverers—early childhood interest groups. Both the public schools and the feminist groups appear to be perceived as unimportant "in this arena," at least at this moment. But it seems that actual child-oriented interest groups were similarly perceived. Perhaps they are in a political version of "culture lag" whereby the rising demand for early childhood programs, especially child care, has not yet been matched by an upgrading of political organization among people interested in the young child. There is, however, the notable exception of proprietary day care organizations, whose activism tends to confirm this interpretation. Having something significant to gain or lose in the public arena, the profit-oriented providers would be expected to be more consistent policy participants.

What are the likely trends in the interaction patterns among the agencies and interest groups? First, the spread of tax limitations legislation inspired by California's Proposition 13 could be expected to intensify competition among early childhood agency people over the diminished public funds. And yet, both as a matter of public relations in an era of governmental accountability and as an attempt to "minimize the maximum damage" from such infighting, there are likely to be stepped-up efforts at program coordination between agencies, ranging all the way from informal "treaties" through interdepartmental coordinating committees (Michigan) to institutionalized child-advocacy commissions, offices, and even supra-agencies (California). The emergence of such machinery is, of course, no guarantee of its achieving its manifest objective.

Second, how are the early childhood interest groups likely to respond to the combined pressures for more and better child care programs and to threats of sharply reduced public money? An increasing political consciousness will probably be translated into more efforts at sophisticated lobbying. And yet the small size of these groups will hamper their ability to allocate scarce resources for these activities. In trying to overcome such constraints, they might engage in organizational mergers. Any integration, however, will require protracted and complex negotiations to achieve a common policy strategy because these groups lack prior political experience and often have conflicting programs. Even when they do achieve a united front, they face the real challenge of trying to gain greater influence over public agencies without themselves becoming even more controlled by agency operatives.[16]

In conclusion, the present effort delineates the relationships among policy actors in state early childhood services. As such, it appears to advance the goal of developing a profile of power patterns and organizational effectiveness in this dynamic and largely unexplored arena.

16. See Duane and Bridgeland, "Report to the National Consortium" for additional discussion.

ANNALS, *AAPSS*, **461**, May 1982

Spending Inequalities for Children's Programs in Texas

By W. NORTON GRUBB and JULIA GREEN BRODY

ABSTRACT: Although researchers and reformers have attacked inequalities in school expenditures throughout this century, funding patterns in noneducational programs for children and youth have been generally ignored. This article presents measures of expenditure inequalities among the 254 counties in Texas for a variety of income support, nutrition, child care, and juvenile justice programs and for several social and psychological services. In every case nonschool spending differences are greater than variations in school spending. The intrastate variations result from a variety of mechanisms, some of which are difficult to ascertain and others difficult to correct, but the magnitude of the inequalities suggests that the problem is too serious to ignore.

W. Norton Grubb received his B.A. and Ph.D. in economics at Harvard. He currently teaches at the Lyndon Baines Johnson School of Public Affairs, the University of Texas at Austin. He and Marvin Lazerson have completed a book on the principles that have guided and limited public programs for children, to be published in the spring of 1982 by Basic Books, entitled Broken Promises: The State, Children, and Families in America.

Julia Green Brody received her B.A. from Harvard. She is currently a doctoral candidate in psychology at the University of Texas at Austin.

NOTE: Research for this article has been supported by grants from the Hogg Foundation and the Ford Foundation and is part of a larger project examining programs for children and youth, both within Texas and in other states.

THROUGHOUT this century, educational reformers have attacked differences in expenditures among school districts, charging that inequalities lead to varying educational opportunities and chances for adult success. Most recently, pressure toward reform increased during the 1970s through a series of court cases beginning with *Serrano* v. *Priest* in California. As a consequence of these cases and the resulting attention to spending patterns, many states increased their school aid and revised their distribution formulas to reduce expenditure differences. The effects of these changes are still small,[1] however, so school spending differences remain on the agenda of educational reformers.

In contrast to the attention school finance has received, the funding patterns of other programs for children have been almost totally ignored. In part, the indifference to nonschool spending may reflect conceptions of its importance: funds for education are by far the majority of public spending, about 77 percent of all public spending for children in Texas; and these expenditures reach almost all children, while other programs serve relatively few. In addition, education is widely interpreted as critical to adult success. The comparative novelty of noneducational programs for children—most of them creations of the 1960s—and the greater difficulty of studying them may also explain the lack of attention. Data available about these programs are much cruder than information about schools, and conceptual problems for studying them are more complicated, as we will discuss later.

Nonetheless, a smattering of evidence suggests that differences in spending levels within states on nonschool programs are large, perhaps larger than differences in school spending. Kirst, Garms, and Opperman found differences between a high-wealth and a low-wealth county in California of 82 to 1 in spending for child protective services, 29 to 1 for day care, and 75 to 1 for health services; they found differences of 25 to 1 between two New York counties for five social services.[2]

Anecdotal evidence about programs in Texas is consistent with these findings. The conventional wisdom holds that children in rural areas of the state have fewer services available to them than urban children, and differences in the availability of Title XX child care have been serious enough to generate a project of collecting funds from the private sector to remedy inequalities. Federal officials within the Aid to Families with Dependent Children (AFDC) program complain that it is harder for eligible individuals to receive welfare in west Texas and south Texas because of a greater hostility toward welfare recipients and a lack of bilingual caseworkers. Less than a third of the counties in Texas have a Women, Infants, and Children (WIC) program of nutritional supplements for pregnant women and infants, and the funds available are allocated through a bizarre procedure in which need levels are evaluated and then ignored. There is

1. See, for example, Stephen Carroll with Millicent Cox and William Lisowski, *The Search for Equity in School Finance: Results from Five States*, Rand Report R-2348-NIE, Mar. 1979. For a brief history of school finance reform, see W. Norton Grubb and Stephen Michelson, *States and Schools: The Political Economy of Public School Finance* (Lexington, MA: Lexington Books, 1974). ch. 2.

2. Michael Kirst, Walter Garms, and Theo Opperman, "State Services for Children: An Exploration of Who Benefits, Who Governs," *Public Policy*, 28:185-206 (Spring 1980).

every reason to believe, then, that intrastate differences in nonschool spending for children are at least as large as school spending differences.

Furthermore, nonschool services may be in some ways more critical to a child's development than is education, and they may influence the success of the educational system. The negative income tax experiments demonstrated that greater access to income support programs increases birth weight and improves school performance and retention.[3] For children in poverty, barriers to receiving AFDC, Medicaid, or food subsidies may lead to malnutrition, poor health, and other serious consequences. Children may also be threatened by less obvious dangers. A lack of subsidized child care may force parents to leave youngsters in inappropriate care or without care, as so-called latch-key children, for example; and an absence of children's programs in health, criminal justice, and social welfare means a lost potential for preventing serious harms in later life. The consequences of failing to receive public nonschool services have not been thoroughly documented; but most of these services go to children and youth in poverty or with some specific need, so there is every reason to believe that inequalities in the availability of these programs are grave, even life-threatening.

In this article we present some measures of spending inequalities among the 254 counties in Texas for a wide variety of programs serving children and youth. Although the results apply, strictly speaking, to Texas only, Texas is typical of many other states in several ways: it relies heavily on federal funding for most noneducational programs, state-level responsibilities for social programs have developed only in the last decade or two, and state funding remains low. As a growing sunbelt state, Texas will be influencing an ever-growing portion of the population, and may be representative of trends in the newly developing areas of the nation.

The results in this article are preliminary, since they may overstate the extent of inequity by failing to consider variations among counties in the need for different programs. Nonetheless, they confirm that serious inequalities exist in a wide variety of programs and that these inequalities are larger than differences in school spending. The preliminary results suggest some of the possible causes of inequalities, leading to a set of reform issues that are very different from those in school finance cases.

DATA AND PRELIMINARY RESULTS

In Texas, the number of counties—254—is large enough for statistical analysis without being overwhelming, and relatively accurate data comparable across counties are available. Other researchers have complained about the lack of information on nonschool programs, but data on a variety of Texas programs are published by several state agencies. In addition, some federal programs can be examined with the statistics collected by the Community Services Administration, though these figures must be used with care.[4] Unfortunately,

3. See the results from the Gary income maintenance experiments published in the *Journal of Human Resources*, 14 (Fall 1979).

4. Community Services Administration, *Geographic Distribution of Federal Funds in Texas, 1978* (Washington, DC: U.S. Government Printing Office, 1979). Some of the figures are prorated across counties by population or some other proxy, and so give no real information on county spending patterns.

there is currently no independent check on the accuracy of either state or federal figures

In considering intercounty variations in services, we can decompose funding per capita for a specific program into three components. For example, in the case of AFDC funding,

$$\frac{\text{AFDC funds}}{\text{population}} = \frac{\text{AFDC funds}}{\text{AFDC recipients}} \cdot \frac{\text{AFDC recipients}}{\text{AFDC eligibles}} \cdot \frac{\text{AFDC eligibles}}{\text{population}} \quad (1)$$

The relative number of AFDC eligibles in every county indicates county poverty levels, but variation in this component does not reflect inequities in the AFDC system itself. Therefore we are concerned with funds per eligible person:

$$\frac{\text{AFDC funds}}{\text{AFDC eligibles}} = \frac{\text{AFDC funds}}{\text{AFDC recipients}} \cdot \frac{\text{AFDC recipients}}{\text{AFDC eligibles}} \quad (2)$$

This variable is composed of a benefit rate, measuring benefits per recipient; and a participation rate, measuring the proportion of those eligible who actually receive AFDC. Each of these components may vary; and they may vary independently if, for example, some counties try to keep the numbers on welfare low but are relatively generous to those who are granted benefits.[5] We are concerned with both elements of funding patterns, since low participation rates mean that eligible families are being denied assistance, and low benefits indicate that some counties deny recipients all they are entitled. For many programs, however, data limitations allow us to examine only one or the other of these two components. Data on the numbers eligible for specific programs are rarely available, so proxies are necessary. For programs designed primarily to benefit low-income groups, we have used the population below 60 percent of state median income as estimated for 1978 by the Texas Department of Human Resources.

Table 1 presents the coefficients of variation for a variety of programs grouped into education, income support, nutrition, health, child care, juvenile justice, and social and psychological services. The coefficient of variation, or the standard deviation divided by the mean, is one of the best simple measures of variation.[6] It describes variation among counties, where the smallest and the largest counties have equal weight. An alternative measure is the coefficient of variation weighted by county size, which considers large counties more important than small counties and more accurately reflects the variation among individuals.[7] Adjustment by county size

5. In general, the variance of AFDC funds per eligible person will be a function of both the variances of the two components and their covariances. If we represent equation 2 as $f = b \cdot p$, or a funding rate as the product of a benefit rate and a participation rate, then an approximation is

$$\text{var } f = \bar{b} \text{ var } p + \bar{p} \text{ var } b + 2\, \bar{b}\, \bar{p} \text{ cov }(b,p)$$

Leo Goodman, "On the Exact Variance of Products," *Journal of the American Statistical Association*, 55:708-13 (Dec. 1960). In the Texas sample, benefit rates and participation rates tend to be positively correlated: the population-weighted correlation coefficients are .249 for AFDC individuals, .379 for AFDC families, and .131 for food stamp recipients.

6. For tests of different measures of variation, see Robert Berne, "Alternative Equity and Equality Measures: Does the Measure Make a Difference?" in *Selected Papers in School Finance, 1978* (Washington, DC: U.S. Office of Education, 1978), pp. 1-56.

7. The weight used is the number of children under 20. Since all measures of population size are so highly correlated across counties, it makes no real difference to the results whether the weight is the number of children or the population.

TABLE 1
MEASURES OF VARIATION AMONG TEXAS COUNTIES IN PROGRAMS FOR CHILDREN AND YOUTH

	UNWEIGHTED COEFFICIENT OF VARIATION	WEIGHTED COEFFICIENT OF VARIATION	WEIGHTED PERCENTILES	
			10th	90th
Education				
(1) Total expenditure* / Average daily attendance	1.268	.242	$1461	$1921
(2) Assessed valuation* / Average daily attendance	.965	.471	$24,496	$65,180
Income support				
(3) AFDC payments+ / Poor population	.653	.391	$14.18	$47.61
(4) AFDC payments+ / AFDC families	.102	.054	$1171	$1371
(5) AFDC families+ / Poor female-head families	.786	.493	9.5%	37.2%
(6) AFDC payments+ / AFDC individuals	.099	.038	$356.85	$384.02
(7) AFDC individuals+ / Poor individuals	.642	.378	3.88%	13.03%
(8) Low-income housing expenditures‡ / Poor population	2.00	1.100	0	$.0199
Nutrition				
(9) Food stamp bonus value* / Poor population	.766	.500	$30.32	$122.86
(10) Food stamp bonus value* / Food stamp recipients	.101	.021	$299.02	$376.62
(11) Food stamp recipients* / Poor population	.705	.500	8.95%	34.97%
(12) WIC children§ / Poor children under 6	1.848	1.030	0	–
(13) WIC mothers§ / Poor population	1.821	.754	0	–
Health				
(14) EPSDT medical patients‖ / Poor children 0-19	.690	.389	3.78%	13.04%
(15) Children served by maternal and child health‖ / Poor children 0-19	8.25	1.197	0	12.77%
(16) Children immunized for DPT‖ / Children 0-19	.678	.519	5.44%	11.02%

(continued)

TABLE 1 Continued

	UNWEIGHTED COEFFICIENT OF VARIATION	WEIGHTED COEFFICIENT OF VARIATION	WEIGHTED PERCENTILES 10th	WEIGHTED PERCENTILES 90th
(17) Children immunized for polio‖ / Children 0-19	.711	.535	4.46%	10.56%
(18) Children immunized for measles‖ / Children 0-19	.667	.643	1.55%	4.46%
Child care				
(19) Head Start funds‡ / Poor children under 6	3.416	1.586	0	$59.76
(20) Head Start children‖ / Poor children under 6	1.95	1.233	0	6.38%
(21) Children in public child care+ / Poor children under 6	3.778	5.055	0	5.6%
(22) Licensed child care capacity‖ / Children under 6	.986	.421	10.05%	25.02%
Juvenile justice				
(23) County spending for probation# / Children 10-17	1.209	.590	$3.73	$25.90
Social and psychological services				
(24) Community mental health patients 0-12** / Children 0-12	1.490	.708	.011%	.041%
(25) Community mental health patients 13-17** / Youth 13-17	1.296	.559	.073%	.197%
(26) Children under 6 in state schools for the mentally retarded‖ / Children under 6	3.368	2.073	0	.154%
(27) Number receiving services for abused and neglected children‖ / Children 0-5	2.668	4.529	.031%	9.24%
(28) County expenditures for child welfare# / Children 0-5	2.046	.807	$.269	$9.59
(29) Federal family planning funds‡ / Population	6.738	2.618	0	$1.21
(30) Handicapped early childhood education funds‡ / Children 0-5	14.150	7.671	0	$.963

TABLE 1 Continued

	UNWEIGHTED COEFFICIENT OF VARIATION	WEIGHTED COEFFICIENT OF VARIATION	WEIGHTED PERCENTILES	
			10th	90th
(31) Number served by crippled children's services‖ / Children 0-19	.636	.676	.095%	.647%
(32) Children under 6 in special education‖ / Children under 6	1.27	.833	.907%	3.48%

NOTES: AFDC = Aid to Families with Dependent Children; WIC = Women, Infants, and Children; EPSDT = Early and Periodic Screening, Diagnosis, and Treatment. Data on population by age and population below 60 percent of median income are taken from Texas Department of Human Resources, "Title XX Eligibles at 60 percent of Median Income for Texas, Texas Counties, and DPW Regions," November 1978.

*Computer print-outs for school year 1977-78 made available by the Texas Education Agency.

+Texas Department of Human Resources, *Annual Report, 1978*.

‡Community Services Administration, *Distribution of Federal Funds in Texas, 1978*.

§Mimeographed data provided by the Texas Department of Health showing enrollments in the WIC program, fiscal year 1979. The scale of these data is unclear, and so the 90th percentile has not been shown.

‖Texas Department of Community Affairs, *Family and Child Statistics Information System* (FACS), data for 1977 made available on computer tapes.

#Data collected by Beck Runte, Special Committee on the Delivery of Human Services, from county budgets for fiscal year 1978.

**Texas Department of Mental Health-Mental Retardation, *Data Book 1978*, vols. A and B.

is important because of the great variation in population among Texas counties—the largest county has 2,076,271 people, while the smallest has 140. The general finding that weighted variation is smaller than unweighted variation means that for most programs there are many small counties with extreme—high or low—values and that in general the variation in children's programs is greater among small rural counties than among the large urban counties where most of the population lives.

Since the coefficient of variation is not an intuitively meaningful number, we have also included the tenth and ninetieth percentiles as alternative indicators. These statistics are also weighted by the number of children; thus the results indicate, for example, that 10 percent of children live in counties where the AFDC payments per poor person are $14.18 or less, 10 percent live in counties where the spending level is $47.61 or more, and 80 percent live in counties where AFDC spending is between these two extremes. These percentiles give a sense of how meagre or generous programs for children generally are.

SOME INTERPRETATIONS

The most obvious finding of this examination is that intercounty variation for children's programs is substantial. We can use variation in total school spending as a comparison, since school spending differences have caused so much concern over the past decade. If we examine population-weighted results, the benefits of every program are distributed less equally than are school resources. These findings confirm the allegations of substantial spending differences.

The major welfare program for poor children—AFDC—suffers 50

percent more variation than school spending (.391 versus .242), and the major nutrition program—food stamps—has twice the variation (.5 versus .242). Given the inequalities in AFDC, inequalities in food stamp allocations are not surprising: nationally low participation levels in the food stamp program indicate that information about the program is limited and that access to AFDC is one of the important mechanisms by which eligible families find out about food stamps. The supposition that variations in AFDC spending then cause differences in food stamp spending is loosely confirmed in the Texas data, since the weighted correlation coefficient between food stamp bonus values per poor person and AFDC payments per poor person is .774. Variation in spending for these two programs comes largely from variation among counties in participation rates, while variation in benefits per recipient is relatively small (Table 1, lines 4, 6, and 10). This in turn suggests that the most serious problem is that those eligible for welfare programs are not uniformly certified for benefits.

Variations in the WIC program are even more substantial than for AFDC and food stamps; and these differences are especially disheartening, since the goal of this program is to provide supplemental nutrition to pregnant women, to lactating mothers, and to infants who are in great danger of malnutrition. The allocation process that produces these results is strange. The federal government requires each state to select counties in greatest need, based on factors like poverty, infant death rates, and other relevant indicators; however, federal officials do not examine the states' methods, and the procedure in Texas inadvertantly gives great weight to county population. Moreover, these ranking are then ignored and WIC funds are allocated in some other way, allegedly because more needy counties have no local agencies willing to administer the program.[8] As a result, only 82 counties have WIC programs.

Intercounty variation in publicly funded child care is also substantial, and certainly greater than the variation in the supply of licensed child care places (Table 1, line 22). The state requires Title XX child care programs to contribute 30 percent of total funds, and this may prevent poor communities from participating. A similar requirement for Head Start programs to provide 20 percent of their total costs—in cash or in kind—allegedly has the same effect. While these claims need further investigation, they are consistent with findings in other programs that matching requirements may exacerbate regional inequalities.

Of the other programs, health screening and immunizations are relatively more evenly distributed across Texas than most other services, though they are still more unequally distributed than AFDC benefits. Benefits under the Maternal and Child Health (MCH) program are more uneven than are other health benefits, probably because the Texas Department of Health has established MCH centers in 140 counties, and access to these centers by children in other counties may be difficult. Problems of access to a few centralized locations probably explains the variation in many other social and psychological services as well, especially use of the state's 28 community mental health/mental retardation centers, 14 state schools for the mentally retarded, and 10 state mental hospitals.

For a number of programs, the variations among counties are truly enormous by any standard. Many of

8. See the Texas State Plans for the WIC program, 1978, 1979, and 1980.

these services are funded directly by the federal government to local organizations. Funding is distributed by project applications rather than through formula grants or other mechanisms designed to ensure regional equity. Examples include federal family planning funds under Title X (Table 1, line 29), handicapped early childhood education funds (Table 1, line 30), and Head Start funds (Table 1, line 19). The issue in these cases is a difficult and common one: although there are good reasons for funding programs through project grants—especially in cases of experimental programs or programs that are supposed to reach special populations—allocations of funds through project application tends to reward grantsmanship and to favor established programs and fails to guarantee regional equity. The problem is sometimes compounded when the federal government requires local matching funds. Texas Head Start directors claim that the required match has prevented many poor communities from applying for funds, for example.

In contrast, child welfare spending and juvenile probation funds (Table 1, lines 23 and 28) are generated by rather different mechanisms than are most other programs. These funds are appropriated by elected county commissioners out of county revenues collected largely from property taxes. Like the inequalities in school spending, then, inequalities in county funding are probably functions of differences in property valuation and perhaps of other measures of ability to pay, like income. Variables measuring county "preferences"—perhaps measures of socioeconomic status and political views—may also explain these variations.

Even at this preliminary stage of analysis it is clear that the intrastate variations in nonschool programs for children and youth result from a variety of mechanisms, including some that are very different from the school finance case. Some inequalities, like those in child welfare and juvenile justice, arise from mechanisms similar to the processes of local choice under conditions of resource inequality that generate school spending differences. Other inequalities, like those of AFDC and the food stamp program, result from the inability or unwillingness of state officials to impose uniformity in administration and perhaps from hostility toward outreach programs that increase participation rates. Some inequalities, like those in the WIC program, originate in muddled allocation decisions of state officials; others, like those in Title XX day care, are caused in part by state requirements of a local match. Still others are probably due to problems of access to facilities that are necessarily centralized, and some are due to the decisions of federal officials who allocate project grants. Thus reducing intrastate inequalities in many children's programs will require administrative and policy changes, at both state and federal levels, that are substantially different from the familiar revision of state grants dominanting school finance remedies.

STILL TO COME

The results in Table 1 are very simple descriptions of intrastate variation. They indicate nothing about which kinds of counties provide high and low levels of services and they do not investigate hypotheses that might explain why variation among counties exists. In particular, the issue of variation in need is more important in nonschool programs for children than it is in the education case, where most researchers have been content to assume that variations in educational "need" are small. For example, the large variations in handicapped early childhood education funds (Table 1, line 30) might simply indicate that there are many counties with few handicapped children; the variation in use of community mental health facilities in some counties may reflect the lack of stress and mental health problems in some counties. The next task is therefore to examine how much of the intercounty variation displayed in Table 1 can be accounted for by different indicators of need. Once need-related variation has been considered, the remaining variation is a better measure of inequity.[9]

Once these variations in need have been considered and the remaining inequity has been calculated, the reason(s) why services to children and youth are unequally distributed remains to be explained. Investigating this issue requires analyses of individual programs, since allocation processes vary so much among different services described in Table 1. In some cases the causal mechanisms underlying inequalities are obvious; in other cases, formulation and testing of hypotheses about causal mechanisms that cannot be readily observed is required before remedies can be suggested. For example, we hypothesize that AFDC participation rates are affected by attitudes of citizens and caseworkers toward the poor and that therefore AFDC spending per poor person is higher in counties that are more liberal or more urban, that have a better-educated population and a lower concentration of poor, and that have a predominantly white rather than Black or Chicano population. In addition, demand for low-wage labor and characteristics of local welfare offices may affect intercounty variation.

It is hard to imagine, however, that subsequent analysis will overturn our basic, robust findings: the intrastate inequalities in nonschool programs for children and youth are substantial. Given the complexity and variety of the mechanisms that cause these inequalities, remedies may prove difficult to develop. They will necessarily take advocates, lawyers, and administrators into the difficult areas of intergovernmental relations, the structure of federal grants, and program administration.

Advocates for children will probably have their hands full in the coming decade with the general retrenchment in social programs, so it may seem a poor time to add another isue to the reform agenda. More optimistically, the upheavals that will be caused by President Reagan's proposed block grants for social services may provide a new opportunity to revise old and inequitable spending patterns. In any event, the underlying problem is critical and merits political attention. Differences in service levels violate a basic criterion of equity. Furthermore, current proposals to fund more programs through block grants to states will give state governments even more discretion over funding patterns, and information on current funding patterns could anticipate and help correct misallocations within states. Regional inequalities mean that, however meagre programs for children are, some children—in all likelihood, the worst off and most desperate children—have no access to even those programs that should be available to them.

9. That is, we plan to use the residuals, from regressions of service measures on indicators of need, as measures of inequity. Some indicators of need will also include composite variables from a factor analysis of a variety of social indicators. This method has been suggested in Leonard Kogan and Shirley Jenkins, *Indicators of Child Health and Welfare: Development of the DIPOV Index* (New York: Center for Social Research, CUNY, 1974).

ANNALS, *AAPSS*, **461**, May 1982

Childhood Lead Toxicity: A Paradox of Modern Technology

By SARA SULLIVAN MEDLEY

ABSTRACT: Lead toxicity, a man-made disease of young children, has only recently come to the focus of professional and public awareness. Lead has become increasingly bioavailable to humans as a direct result of industrial processing and manufacturing. While lead-based paint in older dwellings is the primary cause of lead toxicity among young children, airborne lead from gasoline fumes and factory emissions, plus dirt and dust into which high concentrations of lead have settled, are also significant sources of undue exposure. A variety of consumer products, including kitchen utensils, newsprint, and cosmetics are likewise potentially hazardous because of their high lead content. Exposure to excessive amounts of lead is especially harmful for young children: they are biologically and developmentally more vulnerable to its toxic effects. Even at levels of absorption that produce no medical symptoms, lead may impede children's overall developmental progress by interfering with their performance in several crucial areas. Although the United States has been reluctant to assume an aggressive regulatory position toward lead, the federal government currently supports comprehensive lead poisoning control programs in 60 American cities. The future of these programs is jeopardized by the shift from categorical to block grants. Unless continued funding is made available for lead management programs and a strong regulatory stance is assumed toward lead, young children will continue to become afflicted with this debilitating, yet preventable, illness.

Sara Sullivan Medley is a graduate research assistant in the Department of Psychology at the University of Louisville. Since joining the staff of the Child Development Lab in 1979, she has been involved in a study of the long-term effects of Head Start, conducted by Louise B. Miller, Ph.D. She has taught developmental psychology and currently serves on the board of directors of Community Coordinated Child Care of Louisville. Previously she studied political science and American history at Marquette University.

Lead poisoning is a serious disease developing from entirely man-made hazards which should be controlled by appropriate legislation.[1]

Lead toxicity is unique among childhood diseases. Unlike polio, whooping cough, or phenylketonuria (PKU), this crippling—often fatal—disease is man-made. Lead is a naturally occurring substance that becomes bioavailable to humans as a direct result of industrial processing and manufacturing. Children develop lead toxicity because their environment has become contaminated with this useful, but toxic, metal. In spite of remarkable advances toward the elimination of other pediatric disorders, such as vaccines for infectious diseases and dietary treatment of inborn errors of metabolism, childhood lead poisoning has been virtually neglected. Although it has been recognized since the turn of the century that lead poisoning could be eliminated by adequately controlling environmental sources of lead, few preventive efforts were undertaken until the early 1970s. Lead poisoning is indeed a paradox in modern industrial societies.[2]

Jane S. Lin-Fu, child welfare advocate and prominent authority on childhood lead poisoning, suggests several reasons why lead poisoning has been neglected among both the medical professionals and the general public. Primarily, the symptoms of lead poisoning have been frequently misinterpreted by parents and physicians alike. Abdominal pain, vomiting, constipation, anemia, irritability, apathy, sleep disturbances, and developmental delays can easily be misdiagnosed as manifestations of other childhood disorders. Even when lead poisoning has been properly diagnosed, it was generally regarded as an illness restricted to the children of the socioeconomically deprived. When health workers did try to deal with the problems of lead poisoning, their efforts had little real impact. Since few cities had adequate housing codes or financial resources to protect children from exposure to lead paint in their homes, repeated episodes of lead poisoning were inevitable. Finally, after titanium oxide began to replace lead in paint, many considered lead poisoning a problem of the past because they failed to recognize the hazards of lead paint in old dwellings.[3]

The general realization that lead poisoning was still common in the United States came in the wake of the civil rights movement and social awakening of the 1960s. During this time, several public agencies and private institutions launched extensive educational campaigns and widespread screening programs. The findings of this massive screening were totally unexpected. Thousands of youngsters with no clinical symptoms of lead poisoning were found to have blood lead levels that

1. R. K. Byers and E. E. Lord, "Late Effects of Lead Poisoning on Mental Development," *American Journal of Diseases of Children*, 66(5):484 (Nov. 1943).

2. J. S. Lin-Fu, "Lead Poisoning and Undue Lead Exposure in Children: History and Current Status," in *Low Level Lead Exposure: The Clinical Implications of Current Research*, ed. H. L. Needleman (New York: Raven Press, 1980), pp. 5-16.

3. J. S. Lin-Fu, *What Price Shall We Pay for Lead Poisoning in Children?* U.S. Department of Health, Education and Welfare (DHEW), Public Health Service/Health Services Administration/Bureau of Community Health Services, Pub. no. (HSA) 79-5144 (Washington, DC: Government Printing Office), p. 3.

exceeded normal limits. Moreover, children with elevated blood lead levels were not restricted to urban slums, but were also found in smaller cities and rural areas across the nation. With these discoveries, the very diagnosis of lead poisoning became somewhat controversial: did these asymptomatic youngsters with high blood lead levels have lead poisoning or not?[4] In light of this controversy, overt lead poisoning has been distinguished from undue lead absorption. Lead poisoning is reserved for those cases in which clinical symptoms are present, while undue or excessive lead absorption is used to describe cases in which the body lead burden is considered above normal but no clinical symptoms are manifest.

ENVIRONMENTAL SOURCES OF LEAD EXPOSURE

As Figure 1 illustrates, lead has infiltrated every phase of the ecosystem. Not only has lead become ubiquitous in the biosphere but lead concentrations are steadily increasing. In the chronological snow layers of Greenland's remote polar ice caps, the 1965 snow layer contained lead concentrations 400 times greater than the natural level present in the 800 B.C. layer.[5]

In addition to this overall increase in environmental lead, numerous sources are particularly hazardous to young children. Lead-based paint in old, ill-kept housing is the major source of exposure for youngsters. Children in urban slums have been identified as a population at risk for lead poisoning.[6] According to Dr. Vernon Houk, director of the Center for Environmental Health, "After nutrition, lead poisoning is the second most important public health problem facing older, urban neighborhoods."[7] Even children in well-maintained older houses are at risk. Removal of lead-based paint can produce potentially hazardous lead dust if appropriate measures are not taken to protect both workers and inhabitants.[8] As more homes in older, urban areas are being renovated and restored, there is increased risk to youngsters in these renewal neighborhoods.[9]

While lead paint is the major cause of lead poisoning among young children, airborne lead from gasoline fumes, factory emissions, and the clothing and shoes of lead workers, plus dirt and dust into which high concentrations of lead have settled, are also significant sources of exposure. Youngsters who live near major urban roadways,[10] ore smelters,[11] and lead bat-

4. Ibid, p. 5.

5. National Research Council, *Lead: Airborne Lead in Perspective* (Washington, DC: National Academy of Sciences, 1972).

6. R. A. Goyer and J. J. Chisolm, "Lead," in *Metallic Contaminants and Human Health*, ed. D.H.K. Lee (New York: Academic Press, 1972), pp. 57-95.

7. V. N. Houk, quoted in Jim Detjen, "Lead Poisoning Isn't a Problem of the Past or of the Poor," *Courier-Journal and The Louisville Times*, 251(25):1 (2 Nov. 1980).

8. Lin-Fu, *What Price Shall We Pay?*, p. 4.

9. Dwyla Griffin, Director, Louisville-Jefferson County Childhood Lead Poisoning Control Program, personal interview, 9 Jun. 1981.

10. R. J. Caprio, H. L. Margulis, and M. M. Joselow, "Lead Absorption in Children and Its Relation to Urban Traffic Density," *Archives of Environmental Health*, 28:195-97 (Apr. 1974).

11. P. J. Landrigan et al., "Neuropsychological Dysfunction in Children with Chronic Low Level Lead Absorption," *Lancet*, 1:708-12 (29 Mar. 1975).

FIGURE 1
SOURCES OF HUMAN LEAD CONSUMPTION

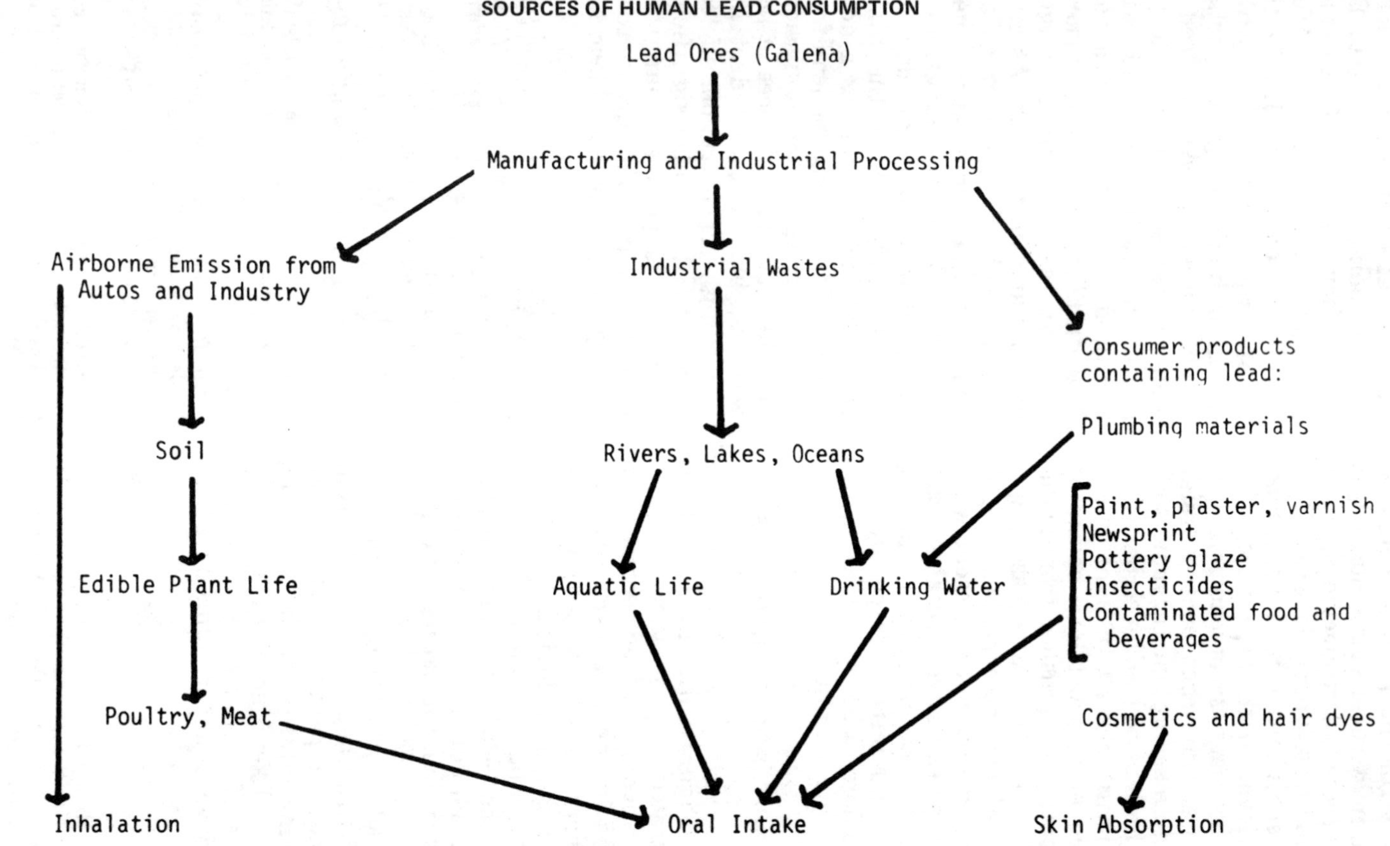

SOURCE: R. A. Goyer and J. Julian Chisolm, "Lead," in *Metallic Contaminants and Human Health,* ed. D.H.K. Lee (New York: Academic Press, 1972), p. 59.

tery factories[12] or whose parents work in lead-processing industries[13] are exposed to excessive levels of environmental lead. Elevated blood lead levels have in fact been found in many of these children.

Because of their high lead content, a variety of consumer products are likewise regarded as potentially hazardous sources of lead. Newsprint, lead curtain weights, silverplated holloware, lead-soldered electric water kettles, colored ink, cosmetics, food and beverages contaminated during processing—either at home or commercially—or packaged in lead-soldered cans, and some toothpastes have all been cited as sources of exposure in cases of lead poisoning.[14]

VULNERABILITY OF YOUNG CHILDREN

Whatever the source, young children exposed to lead are at a greater risk than adults exposed to the same levels. Youngsters apparently absorb and retain more ingested lead than older persons.[15] Because of their higher rate of metabolism and greater physical activity, children also inhale more lead per unit of body weight than adults.[16] Young children do not have the same degree of internal protection against absorbed lead afforded adults. Once lead has been deposited in mature skeletal tissue, it remains firmly bound. In children, on the other hand, the lead present in bone can readily reenter the circulatory system where it becomes available to more vulnerable soft tissue.[17] Finally, the brain and central nervous system of young children seem to be specific target organs for lead.[18] While adults often manifest peripheral nervous system involvement, children generally show central nervous system impairment in cases of lead toxicity.[19]

Not only are young children biologically more vulnerable to lead than adults, but they are also developmentally more likely to inhale or ingest more lead than adults do in similar situations. The lead concentration in ambient air is greater at the level at which young children breathe.[20] Other lead sources, such as paint chips, newsprint, dirt, and

12. J. M. Ratcliffe, "Developmental and Behavioral Functions in Young Children with Elevated Blood Lead Levels," *British Journal of Preventive & Social Medicine*, 31:258-64 (Dec. 1977).

13. R. A. Lansdown et al., "Blood-lead Levels, Behavior and Intelligence: A Population Study," *Lancet*, 1:538-41 (30 Mar. 1974).

14. J. S. Lin-Fu, "Undue Lead Absorption and Lead Poisoning in Children—An Overview" (Paper presented at the International Conference on Heavy Metals in the Environment, Toronto, Ontario, Canada, 27-31 Oct. 1975), pp. 29-52; P.S.I. Barry, "A Comparison of Concentrations of Lead in Human Tissues," *British Journal of Industrial Medicine*, 32:119-39 (May 1975); K. R. Mahaffey, "Environmental Exposure to Lead," in *The Biogeochemistry of Lead in the Environment*, pt. B, ed. J. O. Nriagu, (New York: Elsevier/North-Holland Biomedical Press, 1978), pp. 1-36.

15. E. E. Ziegler et al., "Absorption and Retention of Lead by Infants," *Pediatric Research*, 12(3):29-34 (Jan. 1978).

16. National Research Council, *Lead*.

17. P.S.I. Barry, "Distribution and Storage of Lead in Human Tissues," in *The Biogeochemistry of Lead*, ed. J. O. Nriagu (New York: Elsevier/North-Holland Biomedical Press, 1978), pp. 97-142.

18. H. S. Posner, T. D'Amstra, and J. O. Nriagu, "Health Effects of Lead," in Nriagu, *The Biogeochemistry of Lead*, pp. 173-224.

19. R. G. Feldman et al., "Lead Neuropathy in Adults and Children," *Archives of Neurology*, 34:481-8 (Aug. 1977).

20. D. K. Darrow, "Childhood Exposure to Environmental Lead," *Advances of Experimental Medicine and Biology*, 48:425-445 (1974).

dust present a hazard to young children because of their normal hand-to-mouth activities or because of pica (eating substances not generally considered edible), yet pose no health threat to adults.[21]

LONG-TERM CONSEQUENCES OF LEAD TOXICITY

Forty years ago, lead poisoning was a fatal disease of childhood.[22] Even though the incidence of mortality has been greatly reduced as a result of early detection and medical advances, those children who become afflicted with lead poisoning suffer long-term, pernicious consequences.

Among the children who survive acute lead encephalopathy (swelling of the brain and degeneration of nerve cells), permanent neurological complications, including palsy, treatment-resistant seizures, blindness, and mental retardation are frequently present.[23] It is estimated that in 3.4 percent of the cases of lead poisoning, youngsters sustain permanent mental retardation and an additional 12.5 percent require extensive medical treatment.[24] There is, furthermore, evidence that asymptomatic youngsters with only moderately excessive lead absorption also suffer long-term negative consequences. Low-level lead absorption is especially damaging when it persists over long durations. In some cases, "acute severe exposure was less damaging than prolonged exposure."[25]

During the last decade, research endeavors have made progress in understanding the relation between chronically elevated levels of lead absorption and intellectual/behavioral development. The primary focus of these investigations is to determine whether "the adverse effects of lead on behavior and cognition also appear at levels hitherto regarded as safe or acceptable."[26] A recent study conducted by Herbert L. Needleman and his colleagues[27] of numerous developmental measures relative to dentine lead levels among Boston school children is representative of the current wave of lead toxicity research. In this study, children with high levels of lead in their teeth performed significantly poorer than their low-lead counterparts on the Wechsler Intelligence Scale for Children (Revised) on three measures of auditory and speech processing and on a measure of attention. In addition, the incidence of nonadaptive classroom behavior, such as distractibility, hyperactivity, and inability to follow simple directions, as measured by teachers' behavior ratings, increased in a dose-related fashion. Interference with a child's performance in these areas obviously impedes overall developmental progress. These findings are particularly alarming in light of the large number of youngsters who

21. Lin-Fu, "Undue Lead Absorption and Lead Poisoning in Children," p. 40.

22. S. S. Blackman, "The Lesions of Lead Encephalitis in Children," *Bulletin of Johns Hopkins*, 61(1):1-62 (1937).

23. M. A. Perlstein and R. Attala, "Neurological Sequelae of Plumbism in Children," *Clinical Pediatrics*, 5(5):292-8 (May 1966).

24. Jim Detjen, "Lead Poisoning," p. 1.

25. R. K. Byers, "Introduction," in Needleman, *Low Level Lead Exposure*, pp. 1-3.

26. M. Rutter, "Raised Lead Levels and Impaired Cognitive/Behavioral Functioning: A Review of the Evidence," *Developmental Medicine and Child Neurology*, 22(1):2, supp. 42 (1980).

27. H. L. Needleman et al., "Deficits in Psychological and Classroom Performance of Children with Elevated Dentine Lead Levels," *New England Journal of Medicine*, 300(13):689-732 (29 Mar. 1979).

have been identified as having chronically excessive lead absorption.

In spite of the significance of this study, the threshold for lead's adverse health effects has yet to be determined. "It is reasonable to expect that future studies . . . will demonstrate effects at lower tissue levels."[28]

ENVIRONMENTAL REGULATION AND MANAGEMENT PROGRAMS

Progress has also been made in the area of environmental regulation of lead pollution. In 1972, for instance, widespread elevated blood lead levels were discovered among children living near an ore smeltery in El Paso, Texas. Lead dust particles emitted from the smelter were regarded as the primary cause. Since that time, installation of pollution control and other engineering improvements have substantially reduced lead emissions. An epidemiologic follow-up in 1977 found that children living in the same neighborhood had dramatically decreased blood lead levels. The results of this study, plus similar findings relative to smelteries in Idaho, Nebraska, and Belgium, "argue for the feasibility of attaining a national air lead standard"[29] that serves the interests of public health, especially those of young children.

In general, however, those federal agencies responsible for environmental lead regulation have failed substantially to reduce human exposure to lead. Scientists' warnings about the dangers of lead intoxication and public health officials' recommendations have often become "squelched in a regulatory process geared to political ambition and industrial greed."[30]

The long delay in regulating lead content in paint manufactured in the United States reflects an overall reluctance to assume an aggressive regulatory stance toward lead. Other industrialized nations—Germany, France, and Australia—began to regulate lead in paint early in the century.[31] In the United States, it was not until 1955 that a voluntary standard of limiting lead content of interior paint to 1 percent was established; exterior paints contained high concentrations of lead until even more recently. Prior to that time, the lead content in paint often exceeded 30 percent.[32] As a result of this delay in reducing the lead content of paint, an estimated 40 million housing units in this country are old enough to have been painted with high lead content paint. It is estimated, furthermore, that 7 million of these are immediate threats because of their dilapidated condition.[33] Even though the recommended lead content of paint has been revised downward to .06 per-

28. H. L. Needleman, "Lead and Neuropsychological Deficit: Finding a Threshold," in Needleman, *Low Level Lead Exposure*, p. 49.

29. D. L. Morse et al., "El Paso Revisited: Epidemiological Follow-up of an Environmental Lead Problem," *Journal of the American Medical Association*, 242(8):741 (24/31 Aug. 1979).

30. David Schoenbrod, "Why Regulation of Lead Has Failed," in Needleman, *Low Level Lead Exposure*, p. 259.

31. Mahaffey, "Environmental Exposure to Lead," p. 12.

32. Lin-Fu, *What Price Shall We Pay?*, p. 6.

33. J. S. Gilsinn, *National Bureau of Standards Technical Note No. 746* (Washington, DC: National Bureau of Standards, 1972).

cent, leaded paint in older dwellings is a persistent source of exposure for young children.

Recent legislation pertains directly to the hazards of lead-based paint. In 1971, the Lead-Based Paint Poisoning Prevention Act—P.L. 91-965—was passed by Congress. In addition to regulating the lead content of paint, prohibiting the use of leaded paint on toys, furniture, and food utensils, and establishing guidelines for paint to be used in residential buildings constructed or rehabilitated with federal funds, this act and subsequent amendments authorized federal assistance for community lead management programs.[34] The objective of these programs is twofold: (1) early detection and prompt treatment for children under six years of age with excessive lead absorption and poisoning and (2) elimination or abatement of lead-based paint hazards.[35]

The federal government currently supports lead management programs in 60 American cities. The Louisville-Jefferson County (Kentucky) Childhood Lead Poisoning Control Program,[36] the national training center, is a model of the comprehensive services these programs attempt to provide. Youngsters are screened by taking blood samples in several different settings—door-to-door in target neighborhoods, in Head Start classes, and in public health pediatric clinics. Based on the results of laboratory analysis of these samples, plus other confirmatory diagnostic tests, children are categorized according to their risk. Comprehensive medical and environmental management includes continued health monitoring, referral for medical treatment and neuropsychological assessment, parent education, housing inspection, and abatement of lead hazards. In addition to these lead-management activities, the Louisville program conducts a community health education project aimed at informing the general public about the causes and symptoms of childhood lead poisoning, with particular emphasis on the hazards of lead-based paint. The health education project includes publication and distribution of pamphlets, "resident awareness programs" for churches, community groups, and elementary school children, and contact with the local media to arrange news coverage and public service announcements. The Louisville program, "definitely one of the best in the nation,"[37] illustrates the scope of measures that must be taken to eliminate the risk of developing lead poisoning among America's young children.

Screening children, performing laboratory analyses, inspecting houses, and removing leaded paint are costly endeavors. In 1974, the State of Kentucky enacted legislation designed to establish a similar comprehensive lead-management program on a statewide level. Because of a lack of available funding, the Kentucky Department of Human Resources has never set

34. Lin-Fu, *What Price Shall We Pay?*, p. 4.

35. U.S. Department of Health, Education, and Welfare, Public Health Service, "Childhood Lead-Based Paint Poisoning Prevention Program Regulations," *Federal Register*, 44(44): pt. 91 (5 Mar. 1979).

36. Louisville-Jefferson County Department of Health, *Childhood Lead Poisoning Control Program Procedure Manual* (Louisville: Louisville-Jefferson County Department of Health, 1978).

37. Houk, quoted in Detjen, "Lead Poisoning," p. 16.

forth any regulations for implementation or enforcement of this law.[38]

POLICY IMPLICATIONS

One obvious implication is that further investigations are necessary. Since much of the lead research has been supported by federal grants, this need for continued research is itself a public policy issue. If the crucial question of whether chronic low-level lead toxicity produces subtle neuropsychological deficits in young children is to be answered definitely, there must in turn be continued support for research efforts. This is particularly crucial since so many young children have been found to have moderately elevated blood lead levels. Moreover, the very youngsters who are at highest risk for lead intoxication, preschool black children from urban slums, have also been identified as high risk for developmental difficulties and academic failure because of a variety of other factors. Social class, parental education, family income, or medical and nutritional status might also contribute to delayed or retarded development and poor school achievement. It is indeed important to determine at what level lead absorption, with no overt medical symptoms, can cause cognitive deficits or perceptual-motor and behavioral anomalies that impede intellectual development and school achievement.

Despite the need for further research, there are obvious practical implications of the evidence to date.

> Given . . . that it is possible . . . that impairment sometimes occurs at levels lower than 40 [μg. lead/100 ml. whole blood], it is necessary to ask what are the practical implications now? . . . it would seem not only reasonable but highly desirable to reduce the risk of lead exposure as far as possible. This means, for example, that it is necessary to ensure that lead content in paint is kept very low; that the lead content in foodstuffs (especially for babies and young children) should be severely limited; . . . that industrial pollution from smelters and other sources should be strictly controlled.[39]

It also means that lead additives to gasoline should continue to be phased downward; that vehicles that move in and out of contaminated areas should be thoroughly washed before traveling on public streets; that workers in lead industries should be provided the opportunity to change clothes and shower at the work site; and that consumer products containing lead should be labeled as potentially hazardous.

As the Reagan administration withdraws federal intervention from environmental and health areas, it is not likely that any new regulations will be established. In fact, existing and proposed standards are in jeopardy. For instance, bowing to the complaints of the lead industry concerning the cost of implementation, the Occupational Safety and Health Administration (OSHA) has eased requirements for worker exposure to lead.[40] While relaxing these standards does not directly impact young children, with the probable exception of the children of lead workers, it does reflect an apparent lack of concern

38. C. Colwell, "Concern About Lead Paint Rises But Enforcement Doesn't," *Courier-Journal and the Louisville Times*, 251(25):16 (2 Nov. 1980).

39. Rutter, "Raised Lead Levels," p. 21.

40. R. J. Smith, "OSHA Shifts Direction on Health Standards," *Science*, 212(4502): 1482 (26 Jun. 1981).

for environmental and health issues in general and for lead toxicity in particular.

Furthermore, if regulation is returned to the states, as the present administration intends, there may be little or no enforcement. Although federal agencies—the Food and Drug Administration (FDA), the Environmental Protection Agency (EPA), and OSHA—are held responsible for most sources of human lead exposure, the Lead-Based Paint Poisoning Prevention Act of 1971 regulates control of housing with lead paint to the states and cities.[41] The situation in Kentucky and Louisville-Jefferson County illustrated the problems inherent in giving this regulatory authority to state and local agencies. Because of the lack of available money, the 1974 Kentucky lead paint law has yet to be systematically implemented, and Jefferson County's housing code that requires the removal of lead paint is not being adequately enforced. Ironically, even though the state law has never been enforced, its very enactment created a legal loophole that impeded local enforcement of lead paint regulations. A ruling from Jefferson District Court maintained that the local health department had no authority to require the removal of lead paint from the homes of youngsters identified as high risk for developing lead poisoning because according to the 1974 statute, the Kentucky General Assembly had given that authority to the state Department for Human Resources, which had never even drawn up regulations for implementation.[42] This decision has recently been reversed, but for more than a year the Louisville-Jefferson County Department of Health was unable to initiate court action to remedy hazardous sources of lead exposure.[43]

As long as environmental sources of lead remain a threat to the physical and mental health of the nation's youngsters, early diagnosis and case-by-case hazard abatement are crucial for the prevention of disabling neurological sequelae. There should be continued federal support for childhood lead poisoning control programs. Yet the future of these community programs is uncertain in light of proposed budget cuts. The shift from categorical grants that directly finance local programs to block grants that will be dispersed by the states may well reduce the funds available for lead management. To date, 75 percent of the federal funds that had directly supported lead poisoning control has been rechanneled to state agencies that are still in the process of allocation.[44] As state and local governments face their own budgetary crises, it is unlikely that funds will become available at these levels to develop and enforce legislation aimed at diagnostic screening of youngsters and removing immediate lead hazards from their homes and surroundings.

41. Schoenbrod, "Why Regulation of Lead Has Failed," p. 259.

42. Colwell, "Concern About Lead Paint," p. 16.

43. Henry Wilson, Chief Environmental Services, Louisville-Jefferson County Childhood Lead Poisoning Control Program, personal communication, 5 Aug. 1981.

44. Kent Gray, Chief Technical Support Section, Environmental Health Services Division, Center for Disease Control, personal communication, 12 Jun. 1981; James Simpson, Environmental Health Services Division, Center for Disease Control, personal communication, 3 Dec. 1981.

At present, the safest methods for lead hazard abatement often involve major and expensive renovations, such as installing new wallboard or aluminum siding and replacing woodwork.[45] In the past Community Development and Comprehensive Employment and Training Act (CETA) funds have been used to remove lead hazards from the homes of high risk youngsters;[46] budget restrictions for these programs will probably reduce or terminate their contribution to hazard removal. Other measures designed to ease this financial burden for property owners should be maintained. For example, the Department of Housing and Urban Development (HUD) should intensify its evaluation of newer, less costly techniques for removing lead paint; owner occupants should continue to be allowed the expense of hazard removal as a medical deduction.[47]

Preventing pediatric lead toxicity and its pernicious consequences must be given priority in the public policy arena. Too many young children have already been disabled because of the nation's failure to assume an aggressive regulatory position toward lead, especially lead paint in older housing. In spite of the expense involved in comprehensive lead management, can this country afford to continue to allow its most valuable natural resource, its children, to be wasted by this debilitating yet entirely preventable illness?

45. Lawrence Chadzynski, "Finding the Source of Lead," in Needleman, *Low Level Lead Exposure*, pp. 239-47.

46. V. N. Houk, "Implications of Newer Data for Screening and Evaluation of Children," in Needleman, *Low Level Lead Exposure*, pp. 231-7.

47. Ibid, p. 235.

ANNALS, *AAPSS*, **461**, May 1982

Evidence Supporting Comprehensive Early Childhood Education for Disadvantaged Children

By DAVID J. IRVINE, MARY D. HORAN, DAVID L. FLINT, SUSAN E. KUKUK, and THOMAS L. HICK

ABSTRACT: A trend toward providing educational experiences for preschool children has been evident in recent years. The trend raises a number of policy issues. Who should be served? What kinds of programs are most effective? Should preschool programs be administered by the public schools? An evaluation of the New York State Experimental Prekindergarten Program provides evidence of the effectiveness of one early childhood education program in improving performance of disadvantaged children and in increasing the likelihood that effects will persist over time. Major components of the program are an instructional program for 4-year-olds, comprehensive noninstructional services, involvement of parents, and staff development to increase continuity of learning experiences of children from prekindergarten through the primary grades. It was found that (1) prekindergarten favorably affected children's cognitive and noncognitive performance; (2) involvement of parents augmented the favorable impact of prekindergarten; (3) prekindergarten reduced the possibility that a child would repeat a grade or would require special education; and (4) increasing the continuity of learning experiences of children helped maintain the effects of the prekindergarten program in the primary grades. The results indicate that a comprehensive early childhood education program, operated by the public schools, can improve the performance of disadvantaged children.

David J. Irvine is a specialist in education of the gifted with the New York State Education Department. At the time of the study described here, Irvine was coordinator of the Prekindergarten Evaluation Unit of the New York State Education Department. The other coauthors were staff members of that unit.

Mary D. Horan is an associate in education research with the New York State Education Department.

David L. Flint is associate personnel examiner with the New York Department of Civil Service.

Susan E. Kukuk is data processing coordinator for the examination development staff of the Regents External Degree Program.

Thomas L. Hick is an assistant in education research with the New York State Education Department.

IN recent years, interest has been growing in the possible values of providing educational experiences for children younger than the traditional school age. Many states now provide kindergarten programs for children. Even so, some specialists in child development and education believe that starting formal educational experiences at the age of five may be too late. The general public and state legislators have also shown an increasing interest in various kinds of programs for preschool children.

WHY THE INTEREST IN PRESCHOOL PROGRAMS?

A number of factors may account for this growing interest in preschool education programs. Evidence has been accumulating that shows that the potential for learning in young children is greater than was once believed. Even newborn infants show greater ability to perceive their environments than had been realized. Along with this is evidence of the deadening effect of unstimulating environments on the intellectual development of children between birth and the time they enter school.

The new interest in preschool education stems in part from the lack of readiness for learning on the part of some children when they enter school at the traditional age of five or six. Preschool education may help close the gap between the readiness of these children and the majority of children entering school.

Declining test scores have alarmed many people about the state of education. The decline comes in spite of increased spending for education. Another factor may be the enormous sums now being spent for remedial or compensatory education. The terms "remedial" and "compensatory" imply tacit acknowledgment that a deficit exists that must be overcome. Preschool education is proposed in some quarters as a way of heading off learning deficits before they occur. Over the long run, it is suggested, preschool education may be a better investment than remedial programs.

Finally, interest in preschool education has been encouraged by new evidence of the impact of Head Start and similar programs. A number of researchers have shown not only that preschool programs can have an impact on children's achievement, but that the impact can be long-lasting. Children have been studied in some instances from age three until high-school graduation. The bulk of the evidence shows that children who attended preschool programs outperform similar children who did not. The graduates of preschool programs outperformed control-group children on test scores, were less likely to need special treatment, and were more likely to graduate from high school.[1]

QUESTIONS OF SOCIAL POLICY

If early childhood education programs should be made widely available, a number of policy questions are still to be answered. The answers will not be the same for all states or localities, but the questions should be addressed.

Who should be served? Decisions will need to be made about ages of children to be served and, within the age range, what segments of the population should be served. Should

1. Consortium for Longitudinal Studies, *Lasting Effects After Preschool: Summary Report*, Final report, HEW grant 90C-1311 to the Education Commission of the States (Washington: U.S. Department of Health, Education, and Welfare, Sept. 1979).

all of a given age range be served, or will the programs be restricted to subpopulations, such as the economically disadvantaged or the handicapped?

What goals would the programs be designed to achieve? Will the emphasis be on broad intellectual development, noncognitive development, social skills and adjustment, preparation for school broadly defined, or development of basic skills narrowly defined? The goals of educational programs will need to be distinguished from day care programs, which have their own distinct goals as well as goals in common with preschool education.

What kinds of programs are most effective in reaching the goals set for early childhood education? Beyond this, which programs are most cost effective?

Who should operate the programs? How well-equipped are the public schools to administer such programs? Would early childhood education programs be better run by private contractors, eleemosynary organizations, or some other nonpublic facet of society? Would programs operated by other than the public schools provide continuity between preschool and regular school levels?

Finally, what is the role of the home? What are the respective responsibilities of the home and the school for the education of young children? How do these responsibilities fit together?

THE NEW YORK STATE EXPERIMENTAL PREKINDERGARTEN PROGRAM

In 1966, the State of New York began a program that may provide partial answers to some of these questions. That year, the legislature appropriated money for an Experimental Prekindergarten Program, which has operated since then under the aegis of the State Education Department. The program now serves approximately 6500 children in 48 local school districts and three boards of Cooperative Education Services.

In 1975, a longitudinal evaluation was started to determine the effects of the program on children while they were in the program and as they progressed through the primary grades. The evaluation was not designed specifically to answer the policy questions presented previously. However, it provides evidence bearing on a number of the questions.

Prekindergarten

The Experimental Prekindergarten (PreK) Program was designed to serve children who, because of conditions in their homes or neighborhoods, may not be able to receive the maximum benefit from school. Children are selected for the program on the basis of low economic status and special needs resulting from overcrowded housing, racial segregation, chronic illness in the family, or a family record of poor school achievement.

The PreK program has four components: in-school experience, health services, social services, and involvement of parents. The guidelines for the program call for a highly individualized, well-balanced program that recognizes each child as a unique human being and places emphasis on the total environment. The daily schedule is highly flexible and allows time to provide a transition between activities. Large time blocks are provided for small group activities and for individual interests.

Continuity beyond prekindergarten

There is frequently a discontinuity between educational experiences of children in PreK and their experiences after they enter the regular school program. Whether greater continuity would have positive effects on children's performance as they progressed through the primary grades was one focus of the evaluation.

Seven districts, designated as "in-depth districts," provided staff development designed to increase continuity. In each in-depth district, three children were selected for intensive study. For each child, a team was formed consisting of the child's past, present, and future teachers to develop their skills of observation, ability to identify children's individual strengths and needs, and skill in developing a personalized program for each child. The plan was for the team to stay together as the child moved from prekindergarten into kindergarten and then into the primary grades. This approach was based on the premise that by studying individual children, the teachers and teams could increase the degree of continuity for all the children they serve and as a result improve learning.

Design of the study

Effects of the program were assessed at the end of PreK, at the beginning and end of kindergarten, and at the end of grades one, two, and three. The children studied were those who entered PreK in the fall of 1975 and those who entered in the fall of 1976. They were compared with control groups made up of children who were eligible for the program but were not enrolled in the program.

Effects of PreK on three areas of cognitive development were examined: (1) general reasoning, (2) verbal concepts, and (3) school-related knowledge and skills. The third measure, which was intended for use as a preschool instrument, was discontinued after kindergarten.

Several dimensions of noncognitive and behavioral characteristics were studied. Of primary interest for assessing effects of PreK were: (1) task orientation, (2) extroversion, and (3) verbal facility.

A final criterion of effectiveness of PreK was the extent to which children maintained normal progress through the primary grades.

Effects of attending prekindergarten

Results at the prekindergarten level indicate that the program had a strong favorable effect while the children were in the program. The prekindergarten children scored higher than control-group children on general reasoning, school-related knowledge and skills, and knowledge of verbal concepts. The effects were found regardless of the child's age, family income, or level of ability upon entering the program. The program seemed to have the most favorable impact on the general reasoning of children whose mothers had the least education. The children who spent the most time in the program—determined both by being scheduled for more time and by attending more regularly—tended to receive higher teacher ratings on task orientation, verbal facility, and extroversion.

After the children left the prekindergarten program, efforts were made to determine how they performed as they progressed through school. The findings showed that former PreK children had an advantage over control-group children in general reasoning and school-related knowledge and skills at the time they entered kindergarten. No differences were found between the two groups in knowledge of verbal concepts.

At the end of kindergarten, children who had attended prekindergarten had maintained their advantage over control-group children in general reasoning. No consistent differences were found between the two groups on the other two cognitive measures.

Long-range effects of the prekindergarten program were assessed by examining the progress children made in the regular school program and by studying children's performance on cognitive measures. A very practical concern is the extent to which PreK helps children—who were selected for the prekindergarten program because of economic and educational deficits in their early experiences—make normal progress in school. The progress of the former PreK children was compared with that of children in the control group. The groups were compared on the percentage of children who repeated a grade or were placed in special education classes. Normal progress for the children at the time of the study would have found the children completing the third grade. Compared with the children who had not attended prekindergarten, 33 percent fewer former PreK children had made less than normal progress.

If the progress of the 1348 former PreK children in the sample had been similar to progress of control-group children, 355 could have been expected to make less than normal progress. Instead, 238 made less than normal progress. Thus 117 children in the sample are succeeding in the regular program who might otherwise have required special assistance.

The former PreK children were compared with the control group on two cognitive measures, first, without taking into account the children's experiences after entering the regular school program. At the end of the first and second grades, no differences were found between the two groups on the measure of general reasoning. In knowledge of verbal concepts, the effects of PreK on first-grade performance seemed to be determined both by the child's pattern of performance on tests at the beginning of PreK and by the extent of the parents' involvement in the program. At the end of the second grade, no difference between the former PreK children and the control group was found on knowledge of verbal concepts. These findings suggest that when children who have had a successful PreK experience move into a school that does not relate the program of its kindergarten and primary grades to what the children have already experienced, the prospect of maintaining the effects of PreK is unpromising. Attention must be given to the nature of the program into which the children move.

Effects of continuity

The efforts made in the seven in-depth districts to increase the continuity of children's learning experiences through staff development had a favorable impact on children's performance in the first grade. Comparisons were made between former PreK children in the in-depth districts and former PreK children in non-in-depth districts, where no special efforts were made to increase continuity. On both the measure of general reasoning and the measure of knowledge of vebal concepts, former PreK children in the in-depth districts scored higher than former PreK children in the other districts. The impact was not restricted to those children who had been studied most intensively but extended to the other former PreK children in the in-depth districts. These results provide evidence that effects of PreK can be sustained through the first grade by making a concerted effort to provide continuity in children's experiences during their early years in school.

Effects of PreK and continuity on children's performance were again studied at the end of the second grade. On the total score for the measure of general reasoning, no difference was found between the two groups. However, children in the in-depth districts scored higher than children in the non-in-depth districts and children in the control group on the subtest measuring quantitative concepts. These results indicate that children's understanding and use of quantitative concepts at the end of second grade can be improved by means of PreK and a program designed to provide greater continuity in the primary grades.

On the measure of knowledge of verbal concepts, a difference was found between the in-depth and non-in-depth children at the end of the second grade. However, the difference was related to the amount of time children spent in PreK. It appears that the effect of continuity on knowledge of verbal concepts, which was found in studying first-grade performance, persists at the end of second grade, but only for those children who spent somewhat more than 500 hours in PreK. For continuity to be effective in enhancing knowledge of verbal concepts at the end of the second grade, the PreK experience apparently must be of sufficient duration, that is, something beyond 500 hours.

Effects of parents' involvement

The districts operating prekindergarten programs were required to provide opportunities for parents to participate in the program. Parents' involvement included employment in the program, school visits, home visits by school personnel, group meetings, and incidental contacts, such as telephone calls. The results showed that parents' involvement had a favorable effect on all three measures of cognitive development at the end of PreK. Children tended to score higher when their parents spent more time participating in school activities. The effects were found regardless of the child's age, the mother's education, or the family income.

Conclusions

Some conclusions seem warranted by the findings obtained up to this point:

—Prekindergarten has a favorable effect on the cognitive development of disadvantaged children.

—Prekindergarten has a favorable effect on the noncognitive development of disadvantaged children.

—Parents' involvement, as a component of prekindergarten, is effective in enhancing children's cognitive performance.

—Children who attended prekindergarten begin kindergarten with advantages on cognitive measures over similar children who have not attended prekindergarten.

—Prekindergarten has a favorable effect in helping disadvantaged children maintain normal progress through the third grade. It could reduce the need for special programs, which are frequently quite expensive.

—Staff development activities designed to increase continuity in children's learning experiences reinforce the favorable effects of prekindergarten on children's cognitive performance.

Taken collectively, these conclusions provide evidence of the potential value of a comprehensive early childhood education program. Such a program would include: (1) a developmental prekindergarten program that offers a variety of services and encourages parents to involve themselves in their children's education, and (2) staff development activities for school personnel from prekindergarten through grade three in order to increase continuity of children's learning experiences. In short, a child's education from age four to age nine would be viewed as a whole, rather than as separate steps or grades. The school and the home would be viewed as mutually responsible for education. Finally, the many interests, abilities, and traits of a given child would be viewed as inseparable in the educational process.

IMPLICATIONS FOR SOCIAL POLICY

The evaluation of the New York State Experimental Prekindergarten Program was designed to evaluate the effectiveness of a specific program. For that reason, it did not address broad questions of social policy. However, it does provide indirect evidence on a number of important issues related to public policy for young children.

1. Who should be served? The study was limited to disadvantaged children. Results indicate that early childhood education can have a beneficial effect on those children. There is some indication that within this subpopulation, children whose mothers had the least education benefited most.

2. What goals would the program be designed to achieve? The findings indicate that a program with broadly defined and diverse goals can be successful.

3. What kinds of programs are most effective? The findings show that a developmental program, which gives attention to a wide range of needs of children, has a positive effect on several dimensions of development as children progress through the primary grades.

4. Who should operate the programs? It seems clear from the evidence that a program operated by public schools can be successful. A large part of that success seems to be in the creation of continuity between the prekindergarten level and the primary grades, suggesting that public schools may have an advantage over other potential sponsors of early childhood programs.

5. What is the role of the home? The findings dramatize the vital role of parents. Perhaps one of the most effective strategies a school district can undertake is to involve parents actively in the learning of their children.

Although this evidence is incomplete, it adds to the sum of knowledge about early childhood education and its effect on children's development. To that degree, it can contribute to determining social policy with respect to children in their early years.

ANNALS, *AAPSS*, **461**, May 1982

Head Start as a National Laboratory

By EDWARD ZIGLER and VICTORIA SEITZ

ABSTRACT: Project Head Start was initiated during an optimistic era when many believed that intelligence could be vastly improved through environmental input. This extreme position holds many dangers. The search for the brief periods in development when intervention will yield life-long benefits has also been misleading; all stages of life deserve their own program focus. Head Start has held a unique position as a national laboratory for the design of effective interventions for children and adults. The program has served as a base from which to experiment with various services and approaches such that those found to be successful can be expanded or can spawn related efforts. Ways to improve Head Start's orientation include the admittance of children from all socioeconomic levels and the use of social competence, instead of IQ score changes, as the criterion by which to evaluate the success of early intervention. A promising future direction would be to expand its Child and Family Resource Programs, where arrays of services are offered in one neighborhood center. With adequate funding, the evolution of Head Start is assured, since the program has been flexible, innovative, and a stable foundation from which to move forward in social programs for children and families.

Edward Zigler is Sterling Professor of Psychology, director of the Bush Center in Child Development and Social Policy, and head of the psychology section of the Child Study Center at Yale University. A member of the national planning and steering committee of Head Start, he recently chaired the presidential committee that assessed the development of the program. He was the first director of the Office of Child Development—now the Administration for Children, Youth and Families—and was chief of the U.S. Children's Bureau.

Victoria Seitz is associate professor of psychology, Yale University Child Study Center and Department of Psychology. After earning her Ph.D. in experimental psychology in 1968 at the University of Illinois, she has been a teacher and researcher focusing especially on the evaluation of long-term effects of early intervention programs.

NOTE: This article is based on a presentation by Edward Zigler at the symposium "Preschool Intervention Programs—The Accomplishments of Two Decades," chaired by Victoria Seitz at the Annual Meetings of the American Educational Research Association, Boston, MA, 9 April 1980.

SEVERAL years ago, in his presidential address to the American Psychological Association, Donald Campbell presented his vision of what he called "the experimenting society":

> The United States and other modern nations should be ready for an experimental approach to social reform, an approach in which we try out new programs designed to cure specific social problems, in which we learn whether or not these programs are effective, and in which we retain, imitate, modify, or discard them on the basis of apparent effectiveness on the multiple imperfect criteria available.[1]

Of the many social programs implemented in this nation in the past 20 years, Project Head Start stands out as an exemplar of the best of what Campbell was proposing. The rare and essential value of the Head Start program is that it has permitted an evolutionary approach to the problem of designing effective interventions for economically disadvantaged children and their families.[2] Head Start's viability as a continuing program has allowed it to serve as a stable base from which to experiment with a number of services and methods. Some of these have proven ineffective and have been discontinued; some have been demonstrable successes and have spawned further related efforts.

In considering what we have learned from Head Start and the implications of this knowledge for social policy, we must first realize that no program can please all the people all the time. The sheer size of the Head Start program has meant that it is under constant public scrutiny and that every dollar spent on it is being closely watched by some policymaker or taxpayer. Evaluations of every aspect of the program have been so numerous as to fill volumes, and interpretations of all these data have ranged from the blunt statement that compensatory education has been tried but has failed[3] to an analysis of its many successes.[4] Whatever position one takes, few would deny that Head Start has had a pervasive influence on our national efforts for young children.

Social scientists, who often feed at the government trough, also have an influence on and particularly great responsibility for the direction and future of Head Start. In choosing what evaluations to make and what to make of them, we must consider how our pronouncements may affect decision makers and what the consequences might be for children. Extreme positions may make for good headlines, but more moderate stances are most likely closer to the truth and do not risk the tearing down of what already has been built. This recommendation for caution may seem somewhat ironic, since Head Start was born in an era of extremism—extreme belief in the malleability of intelligence, extreme faith in the environment as the ultimate shaper of important psychological traits, and above all, extreme enthusiasm. Because versatility was built into the program,

1. Donald T. Campbell, "Reforms as Experiments," *American Psychologist*, 24:409 (Apr. 1969).

2. For an annotated history of this immense social experiment, see Edward Zigler and Jeanette Valentine, eds., *Project Head Start: A Legacy of the War on Poverty* (New York: Free Press, 1979).

3. Arthur Jensen, "How Much Can We Boost IQ and Scholastic Achievement?" *Harvard Educational Review*, 39:2 (Winter 1969).

4. Edward Zigler, "Project Head Start: Success or Failure?" *Learning*, 1:43-47 (May 1973).

it has withstood numerous attacks and about-faces in political and social attitudes.

THE PENDULUM-LIKE NATURE OF IDEAS

The entire history of ideas, both in science and in the social policy arena, often resembles a swinging pendulum. Invariably, the pendulum swings too far in one direction, generating excesses that almost inexorably give rise to excesses in the opposite direction. Unquestionably, this has been true in terms of our conception of the developing child. Earlier in this century, the work of Arnold Gesell and others popularized maturational theories of development. That is, physical and cognitive growth were viewed as predetermined processes over which we could exert little control. This rather pessimistic stronghold was shattered in 1961 with the publication of J. McV. Hunt's book *Intelligence and Experience.*[5] Hunt may have been arguing against the concept of "fixed intelligence," but he certainly went to the exact opposite pole. For a time he convinced almost everybody that intelligence, as we measure it with our standard tests, can more or less be moved around at will, depending upon the experiences of the child. Hunt continued into the 1970s to argue that IQ changes of 50 to 70 points could be obtained through one intervention effort or another. By denying the importance of genetic and biological factors in human development, Hunt's position represented environmentalism gone astray.

Preschool power

How did this affect Head Start? While the program planners were not necessarily apostles of Hunt's ideology, a naive trust in environmental benefactions was part of the mood of the nation. This was a quite different time—a period of optimism and hope. We started thinking about Head Start in 1964, and by the middle of 1965 there were 560,000 children in the summer Head Start program. To give you some sense of the optimism of the time, there was a ceremony in the White House Rose Garden when President Lyndon Johnson announced that Head Start would become a full-year program. Referring to the 560,000 children who had spent eight weeks in summer Head Start, President Johnson concluded: "Thirty million man years—the combined lifespan of these youngsters—will be spent productively and rewardingly, rather than wasted in tax-supported institutions or in welfare-supported lethargy."[6]

The president was not the only optimist among us. The mass media were certainly responsive to the notion of easy IQ changes through environmental manipulations. One issue of the *Reader's Digest* had emblazoned on its cover, "How to raise your child's IQ 20 points." There was also an early journalistic report of the Deutsches' findings that, over the course of a 10-month program, children's IQs went up 10 points. By a little simple division, the headline came out, "Program Raises Children's IQs a Point a Month." The infa-

5. J. McV. Hunt, *Intelligence and Experience* (New York: Ronald Press, 1961).

6. Lyndon B. Johnson, "Remarks on Project Head Start, May 18, 1965," in *Public Papers of the Presidents of the United States* (Washington, DC: U.S. Government Printing Office, 1966).

tuation with raising IQ scores was one reason why IQ changes became the ultimate criterion of the success of Head Start and other early intervention efforts. When reports piled up that children's IQs increased by 10 points after Head Start experience, the nation was elated. Then came the Westinghouse report[7] that this IQ advantage disappeared in the early school years, and the enthusiasm for Head Start waned.

When we consider the overexuberant spirit of the 1960s, it is not difficult to see why a pessimistic reaction was bound to follow. Jerome Kagan's neomaturationism[8] became the antidote for Hunt's environmentalism. We read that Head Start had died. Somewhere between the hopes and the cynicisms, a more reasonable view is forming of what intervention can in fact accomplish, and how much IQ can in fact be modified.[9] Using the standard behavior genetics concept, the reaction range of the genotype for intelligence is probably somewhere around 20 to 25 points.[10] This is a far cry from Hunt's expectations of enormous IQ changes, but it is far less likely to provoke extreme counterclaims that IQs are virtually unchangeable. This more realistic opinion is also the basis for a surprisingly optimistic stance regarding intervention efforts. A widely accepted standard in educational circles is that a change of half a standard deviation in a group's scores is of practical value. By that criterion, IQ changes of only eight points would be a worthwhile outcome. Thus we do not need extreme expectations of 50-point changes to justify an intervention program. Actually Head Start was never mounted for the purpose of raising IQ scores, but since it has so ofen been evaluated on that basis this more moderate justification is of value.

Magic periods

One particularly serious error that emanated from the overoptimism of the 1960s continues to be pervasive today. This is the search for the so-called magic period, the answer to the question, Where can society spend as little money as possible to get the biggest possible payoff? To some extent, this obsession arose because psychology was overwhelmed by the ethological concept of critical periods, a notion more useful as a metaphor than in direct translation to human development. When we examine the voluminous literature on magic periods, we see that the long search has gotten us nowhere.

For a time there was an entire *Zeitgeist* within psychology that early experiences were terribly important. For example, in the very influential book *Stability and Change in Human Characteristics*, Benjamin Bloom[11] asserted that half

7. V. G. Cicirelli, *The Impact of Head Start: An Evaluation of the Effects of Head Start on Children's Cognitive and Affective Development* (Washington, DC: National Bureau of Standards, Institute for Applied Technology, 1969).

8. J. Kagan, R. B. Kearsley, and R. E. Klein, *Infancy: Its Place in Human Development* (Cambridge, MA: Harvard University Press, 1978); J. Kagan and R. E. Klein, "Cross-cultural Perspectives on Early Development," *American Psychologist*, 28:947-61 (Nov. 1973).

9. Edward Zigler, "The Environmental Mystique: Training the Intellect versus Development of the Child," *Childhood Education*, 46:402-12 (May 1970).

10. Lee Cronbach, "Five Decades of Public Controversy over Mental Testing," *American Psychologist*, 30:1-14 (Jan. 1975).

11. Benjamin Bloom, *Stability and Change in Human Characteristics* (New York: John Wiley, 1964).

the learning of the child is over by the age of four. Now just on the basis of logic, since we have no idea when all learning is over, how could we possibly know when half of it is over? Bloom based his argument on correlations between IQ scores at various times during development. He pointed out that IQ scores at about age four correlate a respectable .70 with later IQ scores. Yet this accounts for only about half the variance, not half the learning! Furthermore, we must heed the statistical dictum that correlations do not imply causation. Applying Bloom's logic to the fact that parents' and children's IQs also correlate about .70, we could make the assertion that half the learning of the child is over before the child is born.

There were other champions of magic periods. Infancy became a very popular critical period after Burton White professed that the solution to many problems in child development might lie in putting mobiles over infants' cribs. His work on the first three years of life[12] convinced him that the critical period was the first three years. On the basis of that belief he declared that Head Start could not possibly be a success because it came too late in the life of the child. Now there are signs of a new swing of the pendulum to the view that the critical period is later, not earlier, in development. Two outstanding English workers, A.D.B. and Ann Clarke, propounded this opinion,[13] but then went a step further[14] to assert that Head Start is inefficacious because it is targeted too early in life. Most recently other learned workers have heralded adolescence as yet another critical period.[15] What all of this fanfare will mean to the future of early childhood intervention is unknown, but we can only hope that social scientists heed the warning advanced previously to use great care and responsibility in how they choose to expound their views.

The literature on critical periods may be taken as hopelessly confusing, or it may be interpreted as evidence of a simple and basic fact that any parent could have told the "experts." All of these magic periods are wrong, and all of them are right. Life is continuous. There are certain environmental nutrients that optimize development at each and every stage. If social programs are to respect the continuity of development, what will be needed is a series of efforts to provide the particular nutrients that dovetail with the needs of each age period. This would range from prenatal care for pregnant women to special programs for adolescents to efforts that address the needs of the elderly. We should quit the magic period game and recognize that it is never too early; it is never too late. Our social policy should encourage the design of programs appropriate for each developmental stage. Here again, Head Start has been a model of this type of commitment.

12. Burton L. White, *The First Three Years of Life* (Englewood Cliffs, NJ: Prentice-Hall, 1975).

13. Ann M. Clarke and A.D.B. Clarke, *Early Experience: Myth and Evidence* (London: Open Books, 1976).

14. A.D.B. Clarke and Ann M. Clarke, "Prospects for Prevention and Amelioration of Mental Retardation: A Guest Editorial," *American Journal of Mental Deficiency*, 81:523-33 (May 1977).

15. Reviewed by Edward Zigler and Victoria Seitz, "Social Policy Implications of Research on Intelligence," in *Handbook of Human Intelligence*, ed. R. J. Sternberg (New York: Cambridge University Press, forthcoming).

HEAD START AND THE EVOLUTION OF SOCIAL INTERVENTIONS

Against this brief historical backdrop, let us now consider the accomplishments of Head Start. First and foremost, Head Start has always been an educational and service program for economically disadvantaged children and their families. Beyond that, the Head Start program in America is of great importance to social scientists because it comes so close to being a national laboratory for social intervention programs. The story of Head Start has been one of constant experimentation with the development of new programs. For example, this national laboratory produced a short-lived program called Health Start. On the other hand, it produced the Home Start program, which focuses on parental education and involvement and is now in some 400 communities around the country. Head Start aided the development of the Education for Parenthood Program, a curriculum for adolescents of all socioeconomic classes. Head Start gave rise to developmental continuity efforts, including Project Follow Through and a systematic program of planned variations amenable to evaluation.[16] It gave rise to the Head Start Handicapped Children's Effort, an attempt to deal sensitively with mainstreaming handicapped children even before they reach school age. And Head Start produced the Child Development Associate Program, Parent and Child Centers, Parent and Child Development Centers, and the Child and Family Resource Program. Let us examine a few of these in somewhat more detail.

Education for parenthood

The purpose of the Education for Parenthood Program is simply to teach the fundamentals of the developmental process to young people before they become parents. The value of such an effort is terribly clear when we consider that of the one million cases of child abuse that occur each year, many can be traced to parental lack of knowledge about children's vulnerabilities and capabilities. If parents only knew some of the reasons behind the "terrible twos," or that it is impossible to toilet train a 6-month-old, many of these tragedies could be avoided. The point of Education for Parenthood is to supply this type of information.

While students have been very enthusiastic about the program, it has been somewhat controversial for several reasons. Some see it as yet another instance of governmental infringement into private family life. Another critic worried that the plan was ultimately to substitute Education for Parenthood for Head Start.[17] When we look at the facts, however, we see that parenting education is not an alternative to anything, but rather a relatively cheap supplement. The whole program, now in 3000 schools and several countries, costs less than $1 million. It is true that we have not done as much research as we should have concerning its effectiveness. Yet it would be difficult to assess how many children were not abused

16. A. M. Rivlin and P. M. Timpane, *Planned Variation in Education: Should We Give Up or Try Harder?* (Washington, DC: Brookings Institution, 1975).

17. S. L. Schlossman, "The Parent Education Game: The Politics of Child Psychology in the 1970s," *Teacher's College Record*, 79:788-808 (1978).

or how many parents better enjoyed the task of child rearing as a result of Education for Parenthood. Furthermore, it would probably cost more to evaluate the treatment than the treatment itself costs!

Child development associate

The Child Development Associate (CDA) Program is based on the assumption that competency in caring for young children can be formally recognized though a credentialing process. Given the economic facts of inflation and the increasing numbers of young mothers entering the work force, the number of children being placed in day care in our nation is skyrocketing. Both parents and professionals have a strong concern that such day care be of high quality. Yet the concept of quality, if not carefully defined, could lead to pricing day care out of the affordable range.

Ten years ago, the CDA Program was experimentally launched as an attempt to establish a recognized group of highly competent child care workers to help meet the nation's need for quality day care. After several years of pilot work, often conducted within Head Start settings, a well-defined, competency-based evaluation of child care skills was established. This effort involved thousands of parents in the process of analyzing the quality of day care, defining essential skills for day care workers, and evaluating their children's Head Start teachers.[18] Since 1975, when the first CDA credentials were awarded to individuals whose skills had been assessed by trained teams of observers, the Child Development Associate has become a nationally recognized credential and has created a new professional category. More than 6000 individuals have earned the CDA credential, and an additional 6000 persons are in CDA training in over 350 programs. Fifteen states and the District of Columbia have recognized the significance of the CDA credential, and some have incorporated it into their child care licensures. As Sharon Kagan and Edward Zigler have noted, "The existence of the CDA credential [has] confirmed what many child care specialists knew for years—that elements of quality child care could be specified and evaluated."[19]

From its laboratory base in Head Start, the CDA program has expanded to influence many institutions, both directly and indirectly. For example, in a number of college programs for prospective teachers of young children, heavier emphasis is now placed on field-based training.[20] Considerable further development and promotion of the CDA program is desirable if it is to have its fullest possible impact in meeting the day care needs of our country. Yet in the few years since its conceptualization, the CDA effort has made much progress toward this aim.

Making Head Start better

From the first summer of Head Start until today, there has been a

18. M. M. Smith, "CDA: Evolution of a Viable Program," in *Resource Readings for C.D.A. Candiates*, ed. L. M. Hatfield and R. Weigand (Indiana Association for Education of Young Children, forthcoming; hereafter cited as *CDA*).

19. Edward Zigler and Sharon L. Kagan, "The Child Development Associate: Has the 1970 Challenge Been Met?" in *Conference Proceedings, CDA Day at NAEYC* (Washington, DC: University Research Corporation, 1980), pp. 7-8.

20. Smith, *CDA*, p. 7.

crying need to change the perception of what makes an intervention program successful. Although the vast majority of evaluations have focused on changes in IQ test performance, many have argued forcefully against this narrow and simple-minded approach. Few interventions were initiated for the sole purpose of raising IQ scores—such a task is not as easy as once believed—and there is little evidence that a gain of a few IQ points guarantees the individual success in life. As outlined in the initial plans for Head Start,[21] the appropriate goal and criterion for an intervention program's success is social competence, broadly defined. The problem is that while we have many reliable tools to assess intelligence, the construct of social competence lacks basic definition and therefore lacks easy measurement. This difficulty is being addressed by some very competent workers, but the need is so pressing that Penelope Trickett and Edward Zigler[22] advanced an interim definition and suggested a choice of available measures.

Specifically, they defined social competence as having only three components. The first is physical health, a component psychologists tend to omit, although it is clearly a mistake to do so. We can all accept on faith that a healthy child is more competent than one who is frequently ill. With respect to this criterion, Head Start has never gotten the credit it deserves for being the single largest deliverer of health services to poor children in this country. The second component is formal cognition and the highly correlated variable of academic achievement. Obviously, the intellectual phenomena that psychometricians and Piagetians measure are important to human adaptation and unquestionably play some role in overall social competence. The third component—also one that has been vastly underevaluated—encompasses the motivational factors we know have profound influence on performance. Over the past 15 years, our research[23] has demonstrated that a great deal of the attenuated performance of poor children is due not to cognitive inadequacy but to a variety of motivational factors, for example, fear of the test and the examiner, low self-esteem and an "I can't do it" attitude, and an attenuated desire for personal efficacy. Alleviation of such factors has been found to result quickly in the common 10-point IQ increase that proponents of intervention rave about. In short, children who are healthier, happier, and have a richer background of experiences are bound to be more socially competent. This is the basis on which we should rate our intervention programs.

Another problem with Head Start that was not necessarily caused by the program planners is the unsolved issue of socioeconomic mix.[24] It is unfortunate that, back in

21. Office of Economic Opportunity, *Head Start: A Community Action Program* (Washington, DC: U.S. Government Printing Office, 1968), pp. 2, 4.

22. Edward Zigler and Penelope K. Trickett, "IQ, Social Competence, and Evaluation of Early Childhood Intervention Programs," *American Psychologist*, 33:789-98 (Sept. 1978).

23. Reviewed by Victoria Seitz et al., "Effects of Place of Testing on the Peabody Picture Vocabulary Test Scores of Disadvantaged Head Start and Non-Head Start Children," *Child Development*, 46:482 (Jun. 1975).

24. See Deborah Stipek, Jeanette Valentine, and Edward Zigler, "Project Head Start: A Critique of Theory and Practice," in Zigler and Valentine, *Project Head Start*, pp. 477-94.

1964, we did not argue more vehemently against any policy that tends to establish a tracking system in which poor children go to one set of centers while more affluent children go elsewhere. In the early days of Head Start, the best we were able to win was the 90-10 principle—that 10 percent of the applicant children did not have to be poor to qualify for the Head Start program. This formula, which was rather slavishly adhered to for years afterward, was simply symbolic to show that we recognized that we did not want to track children along socioeconomic class lines. The problem continues to exist for Head Start, and it is a very tough one because money is limited. Should we reserve the money for children who most need it by some specified criterion of neediness, even though this excludes slightly less needy children or those who might desire to pay their own way? It is a very difficult problem, and we are still thinking on it.

And now to the future. There is a continuing story to Head Start. One forceful criticism it has begun to address is the general practice in which experts make a program and then try to fit families to that program. It is time for a new model, a commonsensical one in which we construct not programs but neighborhood centers with arrays of programs. Such centers would have Head Start; they would provide inoculations; they would have play groups, day care, and emergency services that might keep children out of our deplorable foster care system. They would end the magic period era and offer programs for families with children of all ages. In short, the neighborhood centers would have a cafeteria of services. Families themselves would decide which of those services they wished to employ, instead of government officials telling them which ones they ought to have.

We have the beginnings of this model. While not as advanced as they should be 15 years after the beginning of Head Start, Child and Family Resource Programs (CFRPs) are based on this general concept. Even the Government Accounting Office, whose purpose is usually to delineate what is wrong with programs, released a very favorable report on the CFRP model.[25] Their recommendation to increase this type of family support services is both feasible and economical, and this approach can capitalize on the strengths of other forms of intervention we have already refined.

Head Start currently appears to be in the good graces of both important decision makers and the citizenry. In the final year of his presidency, President Carter voiced his own commitment to the Head Start program and commissioned a new Head Start committee to assess Head Start on its fifteenth anniversary and to make recommendations regarding the future of this program.[26] The White House enthusiasm for Head Start has now been extended to the Reagan administration, which has included the Head Start program as one of the safety net programs under the poor. While a number of other social programs will be cut, the Reagan administra-

25. Comptroller General of the United States, *Report to the Congress: Early Childhood and Family Development Programs Improve the Quality of Life for Low-Income Families*, Document no. (HRD) 79-40 (Washington, DC: U.S. Government Accounting Office, 6 Feb. 1979).

26. Administration for Children, Youth, and Families, *Head Start in the 1980's: Review and Recommendations* (Washington, DC: U.S. Government Printing Office, 1981).

tion has made the decision not to cut the Head Start budget. At this time, the best prediction is that Congress, consistent with Reagan administration recommendations, will authorize a three-year budget for Head Start that will include some modest increase in the funds for this program.

It is hoped that the argument about whether or not Head Start works is over. Rather, the question is for whom does it work best and with what kinds of specific programs. Regardless of its exact direction in the future, we can be certain that Head Start will not wither on the vine or remain stationary. We have kept Head Start alive for 15 years because we have been willing to be innovative. We have followed Donald Campbell's very good advice on being an experimenting society: we tried many programs, expanded those that worked, and tried something else for those that failed. Whatever else the future holds, we must do our very best to protect and keep in place what is best and solid in the Head Start program as it now exists in this country, and use that as a base to move forward in services for children and families, the poor and the not-poor.

ANNALS, *AAPSS*, **461**, May 1982

Day Care: Short- or Long-Term Solution?

By ELIZABETH JONES and ELIZABETH PRESCOTT

ABSTRACT: With the rapid increase in maternal employment, out-of-home care for young children is being actively promoted as a social necessity in a changing society. The trend is toward group care, in centers of increasing size serving children from infancy up. However, the needs of young children for sensory experience, flexibility in timing, and a sense of the future are very difficult to meet in institutionalized settings. Day care serves, at present, as a necessary form of welfare, provided to rescue the child and parent victims of the system. In the long run, however, it will be important to develop social policy in support of alternatives that are good for children and families. Several seem to show promise: (1) flexibility in time and place of work, that is, flexible hours, job sharing, part-time work, work-site care, and work at the child-rearing site; (2) redefined "families" as support networks, that is, extended families that include unrelated as well as related members, shared housing, and neighborhood family day care; and (3) choice of childless life-styles by some adults.

Elizabeth Jones is a member of the faculty in human development at Pacific Oaks College, Pasadena, California. She earned an M.A. in child development from the University of Wisconsin and a Ph.D. in sociology from the University of Southern California. Dr. Jones and Elizabeth Prescott have been engaged in research on day care for nearly 20 years and have served as consultants to public and professional organizations in this field. Their joint publications include: The Politics of Day Care; Assessment of Child-Rearing Environments: Who Thrives in Group Day Care?; *and* Dimensions of Teaching-Learning Environments: Focus on Day Care.

Elizabeth Prescott has an M.A. in psychology from California State University, Los Angeles, and is a member of the faculty in human development at Pacific Oaks College, Pasadena, California. She has coauthored numerous works with Elizabeth Jones.

OUT-OF-HOME care for young children is being actively promoted as a social necessity to meet the needs of families in which parents work. We agree with its present necessity; however, we question its viability as a widespread, long-term approach to child rearing in this society.

In this article we will review, briefly, the recent history and status of day care and the social conditions in which it is proliferating. Then we will look in somewhat more detail at the factors that seem to make for quality child-rearing environments, drawing on our own research as well as others'. We will examine conditions and trends in day care to assess the likelihood of these factors being present. Finally, we will suggest that day care advocacy and child advocacy may not, in the long run, be altogether synonymous—that it may be necessary to develop a variety of other options to make quality child rearing possible.

As of 1979, 50.3 percent of women were in the labor force; 43 percent of mothers with children under six were working.[1] The fastest-growing group of mothers coming into the labor force have children under three, and 70 percent of these work full time. More than half of all mothers who work outside the home cite money as their reason for working. At least one child in six is being raised by a single parent—mother or father.[2] If current forecasts are correct, by 1990 the preschool population is expected to be 23.3 million. Nearly 10.5 million of these children are projected to have mothers in the labor force—an increase of more than 50 percent over 1978.[3]

Increasingly, day care is being provided by nonrelatives outside the child's own home. In 1970, 35 percent of care for children under age six took place in someone else's home—family day care—and 11 percent in day care centers.[4] In 1962, there were 4,426 day care centers nationwide;[5] by 1976 the number had increased to 18,300.[6]

Several general social trends are affecting day care. The first is the issue of scale. Industrialized societies are committed to the notion that bigger is better—and certainly more efficient.[7] In day care centers, as in schools, there is constant pressure to eliminate or consolidate smaller programs in order to maintain an optimum size defined in terms of economic efficiency.

Second, not only are day care centers getting bigger but they—or rather the children they serve—are getting younger. A decade ago, few served children under two, and many states forbade group care of children so young. Now both custom

1. U.S. Bureau of the Census, *Statistical Abstract of the United States*, 101st ed. (Washington, DC: U.S. Government Printing Office, 1980), p. 403.

2. Beatrice Glickman and Nesha Springer, *Who Cares for the Baby?* (New York: Schocken, 1978), pp. 11-12.

3. Elizabeth Waldman et al., "Working Mothers in the 1970's: A Look at the Statistics," *Monthly Labor Review*, 102(10):39-49 (Oct. 1979).

4. Lois Hoffman and F. Ivan Nye, *Working Mothers* (San Francisco: Jossey-Bass, 1974), p. 104.

5. Seth Low, *Licensed Day Care Facilities for Children* (Washington, DC: U.S. Department of Health, Education, and Welfare, Children's Bureau, 1962), p. 3.

6. Craig Coelen, Frederic Glantz, and Daniel Calore, *Day Care Centers in the United States: A National Profile 1976-1977*, Final Report of the National Day Care Study, vol. 3, (Cambridge, MA: Abt Associates, 1979), p. 103.

7. E. F. Schumacher, *Small Is Beautiful* (New York: Harper & Row, 1973), p. 64.

and law have changed, and infants and toddlers appear in group care in rapidly increasing numbers.[8]

Day care exists not primarily as a service to children but as a service to parents. For this reason it seems important to look closely at the fit between the characteristics of the service provided and the children's needs.

WHAT CHILDREN NEED

The child development literature suggests that there are three aspects of day-to-day experience that are critical for children: (1) sensory experience, (2) flexibility in timing, and (3) a sense of the future.

Sensory experience

Infants, toddlers, and preschoolers learn through direct sense experiences. They need to be in touch with skin and with water, dirt, grass and wood, and with varied tastes and smells. Urban living has tended to limit such experiences; and it was partly in response to these limitations that half-day nursery schools were invented. However, teachers working an eight-hour day may be reluctant to allow messes that have to be cleaned up; there is too much to do already.

Centers may look as if they provide large amounts of play equipment, but often, when the amount available is divided by the total number of children and the short-term interest of many toys is taken into account, there is not a great deal to do.[9] The rules of safety necessary in a large group also limit exploration and risk taking.[10] Homes inadvertently provide many opportunities for sensory experience in the kitchen, the bathroom, the yard, or the park; there is soft furniture in the bedroom and living room, and perhaps a dog or a cat. When family day care permits free-ranging use of the home, these needs often are well met.[11]

Flexibility in timing

A young child is not efficient, in adult terms. The immediacy of here-and-now experience and the compelling need to figure out everything for the first time—their own physical functioning as well as the workings of the physical and social world—require children to pursue their own questions in an egocentric fashion, relatively free from interference. To meet children's needs, adults must provide time periods without severe constraints.

If children must conform to their parents' work schedules, the natural rhythm of their day is often disrupted. In many day care centers children seldom have control over the initiation and termination of their activities, and the amount of time spent in transition from one

8. Richard Ruopp et al., *Children at the Center*, Final Report of the National Day Care Study, vol. 1 (Cambridge, MA: Abt Associates, 1979), p. 253.

9. Sybil Kritchevsky and Elizabeth Prescott with Lee Walling, *Planning Environments for Young Children: Physical Space* (Washington, DC: National Association for the Education of Young Children, 1969), pp. 12-14.

10. Elizabeth Prescott and Thomas G. David, "The Effects of the Physical Environment of Day Care" (Concept paper prepared for the Office of Child Development, U.S. Department of Health, Education and Welfare, Washington, D.C., 1976), pp. 92-96.

11. Elizabeth Prescott, "Is Day Care as Good as a Good Home?" *Young Children*, 33(2):13-19 (Jan. 1978).

group activity to another eats into focused play time.[12]

Flexibility appears to be associated with questions of scale. The National Day Care Study found that in smaller groups, children were more consistently involved.[13] We have found that in family day care, where the social unit is small, measures of flexibility are much higher than in centers.[14]

In our research,[15] we found that sheer size of a day care center was inversely related to program quality. In centers that served over 60 children, compared with those enrolling 30 to 60 children, there was significantly more emphasis on rules and routine guidance. The teacher's manner was often rated as neutral or distant and almost never as sensitive. Although large centers had better-trained teachers and an absence of crowding, both predictors of sensitive teacher interaction, this prediction did not hold for large centers, where "meeting the schedule" must be given priority. Often this necessity interferes with meeting the needs of individual children.

A sense of the future

Children need to receive from their surroundings the message that there will be a place in the world for them, and that the place will be good. This message appears to be communicated in a variety of ways. One way is through experience with adults who remain in the setting long enough to know the child as unique and special and to become known by the child as distinct, comprehensible persons. Learning is an incremental process; each new understanding requires the assimilation of many experiences that "fit" the learner's mental picture. Only from such a solid base of knowing is the child ready to accommodate new pieces of discrepant experience—to take the risk of building new understandings.

The stability necessary for this growth is particularly hard to achieve in day care because of the very high rate of staff turnover in all types of care. The organization of day care creates a series of conditions that make it difficult to create a community where adults have a clear sense of purpose and fulfillment. Because of low wages and low status, many caregivers feel trapped in the "housewife syndrome" of daily drudgery and lack of stimulation. Administrative controls remove decision making from the level of action, creating another set of morale problems. But even if these conditions were improved, a factor at least as important would remain: the mobility patterns of contemporary Americans. For most of its workers, day care is a job, in a particular place and time. Americans change jobs a lot, just as they change houses and, increasingly, spouses. This pattern may represent a healthy ability to take risks, to test ourselves in new situations. But it makes it remarkably difficult for children to depend on us.

When families move, they generally take the children with them. When a day caregiver moves, she says goodbye. And the child mourns—or learns not to care.

12. Elizabeth Prescott and Elizabeth Jones et al., *Assessment of Child-Rearing Environments: Who Thrives in Group Day Care?* (Pasadena, CA: Pacific Oaks College, 1975), pp. 16-17, 63.

13. Ruopp et al., *Children at the Center*, pp. 95-96.

14. Prescott, "Is Day Care as Good as a Good Home?" pp. 13-19.

15. Elizabeth Prescott, "The Large Day Care Center as a Child-Rearing Environment," *Voice for Children*, 2(4):1-4 (May 1970).

As working conditions have improved in some segments of day care, fewer staff leave the system altogether. However, they frequently change jobs within the system, which is increasingly designed to accommodate these changes. A bureaucracy—and most group day care is becoming bureaucratic in design—is organized to promote efficient task accomplishment through clear definition of roles, so that individuals in the system can be replaced without interrupting the task. A well-trained teacher or administrator can offer competent care for these children in this center this month, and for a different group of children in another center next month, if enrollment declines in the first center. And the care is competent—safe, healthy, and developmentally appropriate. Staff turnover is not just an accident; it is built into the system. But what is necessarily missing in large centers with high staff turnover is someone who is keeping track of each child's growth.

A further complication is the length of the day in full-day group day care, which makes it inevitable that the children will be in the center longer than the teachers. The child has a series of teachers every day. This is, of course, a predictable regularity that the child can learn to anticipate. But it adds substantially to the disconnectedness of a young child's experience.

The child's peers may in fact become more dependable and meaningful for him than the adults. While relatively few outcomes of day care have been identified, one finding that recurs consistently is that children in day care appear to be more oriented to peers than to adults.[16]

16. Jay Belsky and Laurence D. Steinberg, "The Effects of Day Care: A Critical Review," *Child Development*, 49(4):929-49 (Dec. 1978).

Peers are able to give children a sense of the present—but not of the future.

To gain a sense of the future children need role models—older children and adults who can be observed doing the world's work. In day care children may see only adults who spend the day watching and providing activities for children. This is a context markedly different from that of traditional child rearing. Except in family day care, the child experiences a rather artificial environment where adults are called teachers but the setting is not a school.

Problems of lack of stability and paucity of strong role models both contribute to and stem from the difficulty of creating a coherent sense of community, in which adults can act with purpose and commitment, and children can absorb and internalize this mode of being in the world. Integrity in adult behavior is based on commitment to a set of values, a belief system that makes life meaningful. These values, whatever they are, are handed on to children. They need not be articulate, and they need not even be consistent, but they need to be experienced directly by the child: "We do it this way." Young children need to learn who they are, in the context of a community. They learn this by experiencing themselves—trying out behaviors and getting reactions from both the physical and the social worlds—and by observing models of who they might become.

A community implies both loyalty to values and loyalty to people; each person in it matters and will be cared for. The adult's response may not always be appropriate, from the point of view of the child development expert, but adults do care what happens to this child—to satisfy their own needs if not the child's. The feeling of mattering to other people, of being able to exert an influence on them, and of having a future is what the child gets in such a community.

Day care staff are expected to show fairness to all children and professional detachment, rather than to share their own passionately held values, if any. And so the models for adult behavior available to children in day care are likely to be characterized by a blandness that gives children no roots, no vision of a future, no set of values to adopt or to rebel against—and no access to power. Children need a fair share of power vis-à-vis adults if they are to feel sturdy enough to take initiative in their activities; according to Erikson,[17] initiative is the critical developmental task of the preschool years. A child in a family matters, as a person, to the adults in it; their emotional involvement gives the child a power base. In a large group, few children are able to exert enough initiative to get adult notice as individuals.

WHAT FAMILIES NEED

The traditional family had three primary functions: (1) it was the basic economic unit of the society, with division of labor among its members, (2) it provided personal support for its members, and (3) it socialized children into the economic and interpersonal systems.

The first function, and much of the third, have been lost. When the personal support function breaks down, therefore, there is nothing to hold the unit together. Our society has few controls—legal or moral—over the family; anyone can rear a child. But child rearing is a long, demanding, and complex process in which the active, caring involvement of more than one adult is needed. Single parenting requires an even more active support system. When families get pushed into corners—by their personal circumstances, or the economic system, or racism, or other factors—their capacity for competent child rearing is reduced. Families need an income, a place to live, interesting things to do, time to be together, and spaces in their togetherness. They need ideals and people they can believe in. The family in its traditional form is no longer a dependably available option; its adult members show more tendency to reject it than to stick with it. For many people the family has become impossible.

Impossible social structures, as we define them, are those that have undesirable outcomes and/or that tend to break down in process. In those social structures that involve both adults and children, undesirable outcomes and breakdowns may include the following:

—antisocial acting-out by children and/or adults, for example, delinquency or child abuse;

—apathy, seen in children and/or adults;

—adult exhaustion;

—high turnover of adult group members; adults can choose to leave; children usually cannot;

—lack of involvement in activities and relationships;

—lack of pleasure, awe, and wonder;

17. Erik Erikson, *Childhood and Society* (New York: Norton, 1950), pp. 224-26.

—failure to keep track of the development of individual children; and/or

—failure to provide a congruent context within which the child's experience of the world makes sense.

Many families are making use of day care as a support system. But our observations lead us to believe that full-day care is also very likely to be impossible. Much day care is characterized by all the outcomes and breakdowns just listed.

WHAT THE ECONOMY NEEDS

To maintain itself, the economy needs workers and consumers. People who happen to be parents fall into both categories. Because this is a large-scale society, the majority of them work in large-scale, bureaucratic organizations. Such organizations are designed so that workers are interchangeable parts in the efficient production process; for this purpose, they should be unencumbered and mobile. Until recently, our society has left child rearing to women and economic responsibility to men. Now that women are increasingly sharing economic responsibility, no one is free to mind the children.

At the same time, our technological, consumption-based society is rapidly approaching limits that cannot safely by ignored. Our excessive use of energy has created excessive pollution. Our demand for material goods is reflected in spiraling inflation. For the health of the environment and its inhabitants, it may be necessary that we produce less and consume less. If quality of life, rather than efficiency of production, became our primary criterion for work, we would take the needs of children and families into account in designing work conditions. Rather than increase the number of day care spaces indefinitely, in order to free all parents to join the work force as now defined, we need to consider redefining times and places of work.

SOME SOCIAL POLICY OPTIONS

It is possible, but very difficult, to provide quality day care that takes young children's needs into full account. We should be trying hard to do so. At the same time, it seems shortsighted to advocate the relegation of great numbers of our children on a long-term basis to what is essentially a welfare system. We need to be looking for alternatives that are good for children. We have chosen to discuss several that seem to show promise: (1) flexibility in time and place of work, (2) redefined "families" as support networks, and (3) choice of childless life-styles. To become a reality, each will need institutional support as well as personal choice and initiative.

Work flexibility

Children are not threatened by having working parents; they are threatened by extended, inflexible separations from them. On the family farm both parents worked hard; child care was no one's sole function. But much of the work took place in the presence of the children, who thus had access to parents when really needed, as well as continual models of adult behavior. In our modern economic system, possible options that would benefit children include:

—flexible hours;

—job sharing;

—shorter hours;
—child rearing at the work site; and
—work at the child rearing site.

All presently exist on a small scale.

Although flexible hours may not reduce total separation time, they do offer limited possibilities for meeting families' particular needs. "Flex-time," a fast-spreading innovation, permits workers to choose their arrival and departure times for an eight-hour day.[18] Two parents on flex-time might reduce the hours for which they needed child care to four or five per day, if that were their choice.

The sharing of one job between two people, three jobs among five people, and so on is a practical means of increasing work flexibility without revising job definitions. Many families that cannot make it on one income might do so on one-and-a-half incomes. Some job-sharing arrangements have been devised to support family or other needs of workers, others to minimize layoffs during periods of lower employment; California is the only state to offer work-sharing unemployment insurance.[19] All have the potential of support for families with children, particularly when the job sharing and the hours worked are matters of worker choice. There is evidence that the cost to employers of benefits that cannot be prorated is more than offset by gains in productivity and by decreases in absenteeism, turnover, and overtime pay.[20]

Some jobs can be accomplished on a part-time basis. In any job in which the worker is selling performance rather than time,[21] adjustment of on-the-job hours may be possible. Half-time workers typically maintain a faster pace, getting more work done, than those on the job for eight hours.

Women have a much easier time than men in securing part-time work;[22] however, there are fathers as well as mothers who would like to spend more time with their children. In Norway, all major political parties have called for reduced work time for parents of young children: "It makes no sense whatever to bring the mother into the one-sided occupationally absorbed and stressed work role the father is already into."[23]

Advocates of day care are promoting work-site care, sponsored by employers. Their argument is that parents who have dependable child care will be more dependable workers, and thus employer investment in day care is worth the cost. Work-site care can reduce, by travel time, the length of parent-child separations. It can also be planned to give nursing mothers time with their babies, to enable parents to eat lunch with their children, and even to take an occasional day—with pay—to participate in the day care program. Children may have opportunities to observe their parents at work. Such programs have potential

18. Glickman and Springer, *Who Cares for the Baby?* p. 63; James A. Levine, *Who Will Raise the Children?* (Philadelphia: J. B. Lippincott, 1976), p. 95; Alvin Toffler, *The Third Wave* (New York: Bantam, 1981), pp. 246-47.

19. Beth Ann Krier, "When One Job Equals Teamwork," *Los Angeles Times* (30 Nov. 1980), pp. 1, 16-17.

20. Levine, *Who Will Raise the Children?* p. 95.

21. Ibid., p. 88.

22. Ibid., p. 75.

23. Glickman and Springer, *Who Cares for the Baby?* p. 62.

for reducing the isolation of children in this society from the adult work world and perhaps for making work places more responsive to the needs of people.

Homes are good places to raise children and, in some instances, to work for an income. Toffler describes "the electronic cottage," in which new technologies will permit large numbers of people to work at home, communicating by computer and avoiding commuting, as the wave of the future.[24] A result could be a "home-centered society," with greater community and family stability and decreasing urbanization.[25] The latter trend has already appeared; the new census shows that rural and small-town America is growing faster than the cities, for the first time since 1820. There is evidence that many people are putting family and community values above economic and career advancement.[26]

Redefined families as support networks

Extended "families" that include unrelated as well as related members have potential for shared child care and mutual support. Definitions of family have become, of necessity, more flexible in recent years. An effective family may be a father and child; a grandmother, mother, and children; several unrelated people living together—not just the tidy nuclear family, which seems to be getting untidier every year. If we have lost our commitment to the nuclear family, we need to be creative in devising alternatives. Aldous Huxley in *Island*[27] described that particular utopia's invention of Mutual Adoption Clubs—groups of people of all ages who had agreed to "adopt" each other and to share responsibility in an "inclusive, unpredestined, and voluntary family." Children in trouble at home could go to one of their other "homes." In our society some people do still have extended families and rely on them; others may need to invent them.

The scarcity and costs of single-family housing are likely to pressure more families into experimentation with shared space, an innovation that builds in both the difficulties of cooperation and the advantages of shared care of children. Single parents, especially, need to explore ways of sharing housing and care, and government needs to support their efforts.

Some early childhood professionals might well be devoting their energies to networking—helping families become resources for each other, identifying the range of alternatives open to them—not just to automatically providing day care. Some parents who put their children in full-day care are simplifying their own lives at the cost both of their children and of the day caregivers, who are subsidizing care through their low wages.

Another approach to the issues of both scale and stability in providing care for children who must have it, might be to develop neighborhood family centers offering subsidized, professionalized family day care. Family day care offers small

24. Toffler, *The Third Wave*, pp. 194-99.
25. Ibid., pp. 204-7.
26. Tom Morganthau et al., "America's Small Town Boom," *Newsweek* (6 Jul. 1981), pp. 26-37.

27. Aldous Huxley, *Island* (New York: Harper & Row, 1962), pp. 102-4.

numbers of children and adults the setting of a home; its primary problems are quality control, limited income, and turnover. It is usually provided by grandmothers or by mothers at home with their own children, who are not solely dependent on their earnings for their support. Could it be made an attractive career choice by subsidizing qualified couples—not necessarily married couples, just pairs of people—by offering them a big, old house? Given the state of the housing market, that might be a real incentive to stable child care. Their income would be lower than salaries in publicly supported group care, but their autonomy would be much greater.

Neighborhoods with no one at home during the day are particularly vulnerable to crime.[28] A family day care center on every block, peopled by wide-age groups of up to a dozen children with two adults, and a floating substitute, would make neighborhoods safer and child care more like a family. Toffler has suggested in *Future Shock*[29] that it may become appropriate, in a highly specialized society, for people with special competence in child rearing to assume a large share of that responsibility. In small, stable units this can be done while meeting children's needs and families' needs for support as well. A day care home staffed by people qualified to give advice and a listening ear to parents, as well as care to their children, could become the heart of a "mutual adoption club" for the families it serves.

28. Jane Jacobs, *The Death and Life of Great American Cities* (New York; Vintage, 1961), p. 152 ff.

29. Alvin Toffler, *Future Shock* (New York: Random House, 1970), pp. 215-17.

Choice of childless life-styles

Parenting is a very long-term commitment. Young people who have adopted the cultural goals of material comfort and personal fulfillment and who accept mobility, both geographic and interpersonal, as necessary to the realization of these goals, may not have room for children in their lives. In a specialized society that choice needs to be an acceptable one; and it is, in fact, one that is increasingly being made. Children will not be cherished unless they are functional. Their historical functions include real work in the community, such as tending animals and gardens, running errands, baby care, and housework, carrying on the family name and status, and providing loved objects for adult nurturance. There is little work for children in contemporary society, family stability is not valued, and not all adults have high nurturance needs, nor need all nurturance be directed toward one's own children. There are too few jobs and the world is overpopulated. If there are fewer children, perhaps we can better care for those we have.

PUBLIC POLICY IMPLICATIONS

Federal day care policy has been primarily concerned not with quality of life for families and children but with the regulation of maternal employment. Works Project Administration (WPA) nurseries were created during the Great Depression to relieve unemployment of teachers. During World War II, day care was provided to free women for the labor force. In the past decade, federal day care moneys have been available to move mothers from the welfare rolls into gainful employment.

At this time it is clear that any hopes for massive federal funding of child care are unrealistic. Attempts to mandate a federal policy in an area in which there is still much ambivalence may be impossible except in the form of incentives through tax credits and enabling legislation. The next few years may be a fruitful time to work on a smaller scale at the local level. In fact, the availability of federal money for day care may inhibit creative approaches; the recipient of federal money must also accept the paper work that accompanies requirements for accountability and that single-mindedly focuses on numbers of slots for care, rather than on quality of care. Public funds and small, creative, idiosyncratic programs do not make good bedfellows.

Child rearing is one of society's most important functions. It needs a supportive climate. Public policy, including that on a local level, which supports efforts to rebuild neighborhoods; business practices that give parents more work options; school attendance policies that include the flexibility to enable young adolescents to learn about parenting and about themselves by working in day care; and experiments with varied family structures and housing arrangements may also support quality child care.

SUMMARY

Good full-day care in settings whose structure is institutional rather than personal appears to be an unrealizable objective on a large scale, unless we are willing to accept definitions of "good" child rearing very different from those that have been held in our society. Bureaucratic child rearing will inevitably move us toward a brave new world quite different from that which Americans have valued. There is at the same time little evidence that lack of support for day care will keep mothers at home, under current economic and social conditions. It seems essential, then, that we examine a wider range of options for shared care of children.

ANNALS, *AAPSS*, **461**, May 1982

Natural Helping Networks in Alleviating Family Stress

By EUNICE L. WATSON and ALICE H. COLLINS

ABSTRACT: As they have for generations, natural helping networks act as family support systems in many different social and cultural settings. The value of natural helping networks in assisting working parents with young children to find and maintain family day care has been documented. The resources these networks provide in alleviating or intervening in family stress that otherwise might lead to neglect and abuse is beginning to be recognized, explored, and utilized. We pioneered a method for professionals to identify and recruit natural helpers in these networks, to collaborate in the matching of needs and resources in neighborhoods, and to link with the formal agency system as needed. In this article, the method is described with mainland and Hawaiian applications. It is suggested that policymakers should recognize the value of natural helping networks as a financially feasible method of reaching parents in ways that prevent or ameliorate child abuse and neglect and that offer ongoing social support to families.

Eunice L. Watson, after receiving her Master of Social Work (MSW) degree from the University of British Columbia, had a range of experience in the child welfare field, from direct service to research, before becoming social work consultant in the Day Care Exchange and Day Care Neighbor Service. She is at present administrator at Child and Family Service, Honolulu, and is consultant to a number of professionals developing natural network projects elsewhere in Hawaii.

Alice H. Collins has had a broad experience in social work since receiving a degree from the New York School of Social Work, now Columbia University School of Social Work. In addition to practice and research, she has taught at the masters level and has written several texts. She was director of the Day Care Exchange and the Day Care Neighbor Service Project and at present is in private consultation practice, specializing in work with natural networks projects.

THE damaging lifelong consequences of abuse and neglect suffered by young children is of serious concern today to laymen and professionals alike. Whether or not more children are affected than in the past, or whether society has become more sensitive to the problem, are questions best left to historians. However, the literature on victims and perpetrators of abuse suggests that it follows on the heels of intolerable stress, a pervasive aspect of modern life.

Intervention that interrups family violence and reduces stress on the victimized child is often impossible because knowledge of the young child's plight is kept almost exclusively to the family. Thus intervention is not undertaken when parents are most accessible to help—before the stress in their own lives has resulted in permanent physical and emotional damage to their children. Paradoxically, this problem has worsened because of changes in professional development. As diagnostic skills and treatment became more sophisticated, the volunteers, who formerly interrupted or prevented child abuse and neglect, have been relegated to the single role of informer, a role of low esteem. Informants tend to be viewed with thinly veiled suspicion and subjected to the kind of cross-examination that discourages further reporting. At the same time, protective agencies often have such heavy caseloads that even those referrals readily accepted may not receive investigatory attention for frustratingly long periods of time. The informant waits helplessly for an agency intervention that may never be forthcoming if evidence is insufficient and parents are resistant to service. Thus families may not receive early treatment, and it may be virtually impossible to prevent borderline abuse and neglect from flaring up in the future.

HELPING NETWORKS

Fortunately, there is increasing understanding of the existence of a social phenomenon that holds real promise for positive intervention on a large scale at a feasible cost. Existing social networks are being rediscovered and studied, and the findings are being applied. Attempts are being made to develop typologies of networks, including for example, those offering mutual aid, volunteer linking, community empowerment, and natural neighbor help. Although it is yet too early in the research on networks to establish a definitive classification system, it is possible to describe the type of network with which this article is concerned.

Natural helping networks

Natural helping networks are defined as those sets of linkages among relatives, friends, and acquaintances who interact at many different levels.[1] These networks appear to revolve around a "central figure," "natural neighbor," or "gatekeeper," who acts as an exchange agent or a matchmaker for needs and resources, and also offers direct advice, support, and practical help to members of the network. When the operation of natural networks is understood and the place of the central figures in them appreciated, it can be seen that they can become invaluable allies in the efforts of professionals to protect children, help parents, and support family life.

1. Alice H. Collins and Diane L. Pancoast, *Natural Helping Networks* (Washington, DC: NASW Press, 1976), pp. 18, 19.

Role of natural helpers in the past

The role of natural networks and the ways that the central figures in them identify and intervene in child abuse and neglect are by no means new phenomena. A few generations ago, neighbors and members of extended families saw themselves as their brothers' keepers. They had little inhibition about implementing that belief. Relatives, noting that some family members were not acting as responsible parents, did not hesitate to discuss their behavior with them and to insist on change. Family histories were well known to the community and repetitious problem behaviors understood, so that effective interventions were naturally designed and executed. Information came to natural neighbors not only through their own direct observation but also from reports of other network members, such as children who might note inadequately fed and clothed classmates, or shopkeepers and service providers who might discreetly gossip[2] about their clients.

These neighborhood central figures did not visit merely to reproach neglecting parents. Their genuine concern and sympathy for parents and their young children overshadowed any fear of invasion of privacy. Not only did they offer advice but they gave support and ongoing contact with themselves and others in their network whose help they mobilized. Most importantly, perhaps, they offered what is today called respite care—taking on the care of the children for varying periods of time to give parents an opportunity to resolve their problems under lessened daily stress and to recoup their energy for resumption of their family responsibilities. However, they did not hesitate to invoke legal protection for the children, where they deemed necessary, although their methods today might be labeled kidnapping.[3]

These lay people were unquestionably more judgmental and directive in thier advice and actions than would be considered advisable by most modern professionals. Of course, professional understanding about underlying motives and the influence of this knowledge on professional methods are important. It could be conjectured, however, that the network approach was—and still might be—more familiar and generally acceptable than a series of interviews aimed at examining deeply buried and painfully confessed feelings and actions.

The neighborhood today and natural neighbors

Some years ago it was assumed that networks had disappeared with the shift to urban life and that there were no such things as neighborhoods any longer. A number of studies refute this notion.[4] Moreover, the alert observer will become aware of the existence of natural networks, although they may not be located in what are usually thought of as geographic neighborhoods. All or part of an apartment house, a trailer park, an office, or a factory

2. Arthur C. Emlen and Eunice L. Watson, *Matchmaking in Neighborhood Day Care* (Corvallis, OR: DCE Press, 1971), p. 18.

3. Solon Robinson, *Hot Corn: Life Scenes in New York Illustrated* (New York, NY: De Witt & Davenport, 1854), pp. 50-73.

4. Diane L. Pancoast et al., *Natural Helping Networks and Service Delivery an Appraisal of 30 Programs,* Final Report (Portland, OR: Regional Research Institute, 1981).

division may give every evidence of being a true natural neighborhood with an identifiable central figure. Such networks are unobtrusive because they are characteristically small and un-self-conscious, although they have many connections to other networks that make up the enormous web of society.

Social agencies and civic bodies have begun to recognize the importance of natural helping networks in a variety of settings.[5] They have begun to develop methods whereby partnerships between professional consultants and central figures can be of mutual advantage in reaching the many people who are in need of help but are not now served by the delivery system of public and private agencies.

THE POWER OF NATURAL HELPING NETWORKS

Is such a partnership just described feasible in dealing with the stresses of family life that express themselves in the abuse and neglect of young children? If so, how can it be established and maintained in the light of the attitudes toward informants mentioned previously, as well as the strong professional and political inhibition against offering unsolicited service.

Identification and recruitment of central figures as day care neighbors

As with many other discoveries, we received insights into these questions from a project with a different goal. The Day Care Exchange and the Day Care Neighbor Service[6] was a demonstration-research project, funded by the Children's Bureau, to study family day care and to establish a service that would train and certify family day care givers. Very little was known about the extent or quality of family day care when this project was funded in 1964 except from the few agency-sponsored programs based on a foster care model. In general, group day care was the only formally recognized service and was offered solely to families whose mothers worked out of absolute necessity. In contrast, the Day Care Exchange Project was based on the recognized increase of working mothers in society in general. Statistics of use indicated plainly that the great majority of preschool children were being cared for in unrelated family homes under informal arrangements made by those directly concerned. Consequently, it seemed imperative to discover what kind of care they were receiving and to improve it, if that appeared to be necessary.

Preliminary surveys showed that contrary to widely held opinion, family day caregivers needed and wanted very little training; most of them gave good care and needed no central exchange to become known as good givers to parents seeking care. In fact, the best of them were already functioning very much as the projected official exchange would have done. They cared for children themselves and brought together people looking for care with those they judged capable of providing it well. They saw themselves as helping people in their networks. We recognized their central-figure role, gave them the title "day care neighbor," and recruited them as partners in the on-going demonstration-research on the Day Care Neighbor Service. The helping function

5. Charles Froland et al., *Helping Networks and Human Services* (Beverly Hills: Sage, 1981).

6. U.S. Department of Health, Education and Welfare, Children's Bureau, Grant no. D-135, R-287.

was seen to be an integral part of their daily lives, assumed voluntarily and carried on with competence. They were found to be discriminating and proficient in judging the quality of child care they might recommend.

One day care neighbor expressed this succinctly and vividly when she told the professional consultant:

> Mae, downstairs, (in the large apartment building which was the natural neighborhood network) is mad at me because she wants to babysit and I don't send her any of the kids I can't take because I am full up. She was working and paying only $2.50 a day for her two kids so she couldn't get a sitter. Now, she's staying home and wants me to find her some kids to sit for. . . . I'm not going to give her the names of any with babies. She's asked for babies. . . . But, you can't put a little one there. I think babies need the most loving, you know, and she can't be bothered. She'd give them a sandwich or a cookie, you know, but I don't think she's the kind that could love a baby. I might be wrong, but I've just got that feeling. And until it changes, I won't find her anyone, no matter how much she bugs me.[7]

Another day care neighbor, through her knowledge of network resources and her use of good judgment, recruited someone that she knew would be especially skillful in infant care and kindly helpful to a young mother. This careful match assured the infant of a stable arrangement that was mutually satisfying to mother and caregiver.

The partnership of natural helping networks and the formal agency system

The Day Care Neighbor Service provided a vehicle that enabled us to observe and describe such privately made arrangements for young children at all socioeconomic levels, which far exceed those made through the formal agency system. The discovery of these natural helping networks and this informal delivery system led us to develop a method whereby the central figures in the networks might be identified, recruited, and supported as partners. The goal was to continue to learn how the natural system operated and to help the day care neighbors enlarge their circle. In effect, it returns to an earlier mode of intervention: helping those who do not ask for help they obviously need.

The first steps focused chiefly on the efforts of the day care neighbor in carrying out the exchange functions—for which the project had been funded—to assure that young children are provided with the kind of experiences that are considered essential for them—good physical care, continuing contact with nurturing adults, increasing socialization, and an opportunity to explore the world around them. The day care neighbors were seen to understand and work toward those goals, as expressed in various, often nonverbal, ways.

Day care neighbors' sensitivity to child abuse and neglect

In the course of the research-demonstration we observed and were impressed with the extent to which the day care neighbors recognized and tried to deal with child abuse and neglect. They often described, with much concern, the behavior of young, immature, and very anxious parents whose expectations of their little children resulted in unrealistic demands and harsh discipline. The day care

7. Alice H. Collins and Eunice L. Watson, *Family Day Care* (Boston: Beacon Press, 1976), pp. 105, 106.

neighbors functioned as interested relatives or friends might once have done, offering advice and information, and perhaps most important, demonstrating enthusiastic acceptance of the children. There seemed little doubt that this gentle intervention was effective, not only for the child in care, but also for the other children in that family and even for those children of their friends, neighbors, and relatives.

In more serious cases, the central figures were frequently the primary observers of grossly neglectful and abusive behavior against very young children. A characteristic day care giver response to neglect was termination of the child care arrangement, which obviously was contrary to the best interest of the child. There is some evidence[8] that parental neglect was one of the main reasons for termination of good family day care arrangements, due to the distress and frustration of the day care giver.

When a day care neighbor reported a prospective termination to the professional partner, it was often possible to convince the day care neighbor to help the child care giver not only to understand the value of the care but also to continue it. At the same time, the professional, who had gained the trust of the day care neighbor, could support the reporting of the situation to the proper authorities and could facilitate the intervention necessary to successfully protect the child. These situations clearly call for all the professional's skill and patience to deal with these sensitive relationships.

8. Arthur C. Emlen, Betty Donoghue, and Quentin D. Clarkson, *The Stability of the Family Day Care Arrangement: A Longitudinal Study* (Portland, OR: Tri-County Community Council in cooperation with Portland State University, DCE Press, 1972) p. 232.

TRAILER COURT PROJECT: A FOCUS ON CHILD ABUSE AND NEGLECT

The extent to which the day care neighbors recognized abuse and neglect and intervened in it had not been anticipated when the Day Care Neighbor Service began. Now it seemed important to study this aspect of family day care with the limited funds still available.[9] A survey of neighborhoods with the greatest numbers of abuse and neglect referrals enabled us to identify two trailer courts that housed highly transient, poverty-level families. Both the trailer court managers functioned as central figures. They were both known and unpopular with the protective service agency because of their frequent demands that the agency "do something" about parents whose children were poorly cared for. These middle-aged women had received public welfare from time to time, knew the ropes, and used their knowledge of the system to get what they believed was needed to protect the young children in their trailer courts.

Professional consultation-collaboration

Indeed, the consultant, at times, had to persuade the managers to moderate their protective behavior when they felt the public agency was moving too slowly. There was, for example, the occasion when an angry manager announced that she was going to wait with a shotgun for an alcoholic father, observed from her front window. This father continuously failed to provide adequate food and threatened to kidnap and

9. Eunice L. Watson, "Trailer Courts" (Unpublished monograph, Portland, OR, 1971).

disappear with the children if his wife complained or went to the authorities. Here, as in similar situations, the professional's advice on better ways of handling the situation prevailed because the manager had come to trust the professional's judgment and ability to mobilize community resources.[10]

Feasibility and cost effectiveness

The trailer court experience convinced us that consultation with natural helping networks not only could effectively reach abused and neglected young children but also could serve to increase the quality and quantity of family day care; and all at a feasible cost. One professional consultant was able to recruit and collaborate with about 15 central figures at a time, each of whom were apt to be in active touch with 50 families in the network in one year. The next question concerned the applicability of this approach in places with diverse populations, unlike the more homogeneous urban neighborhoods of the original project.

CHILD AND FAMILY SERVICE'S MULTI-ETHNIC PROJECT IN HAWAII

An opportunity arose to test the transferability of this project in Hawaii, a state with a variety of ethnic groups and extremes in socioeconomic levels. Child and Family Service, a private agency serving Oahu families, recognized that there was a high incidence of child abuse and neglect on the Waianae Coast of the island. An office of the parent agency had been established there with the stated purpose of decreasing the incidence of child abuse and neglect and lessening family stress. It appeared that the need for such service far exceeded the availability of the staff resources. Even if more outreach and counseling were provided, many of the potential or actual perpetrators of child abuse and neglect would still remain inaccessible by virtue of cultural, ethnic, psychosocial, economic, or language barriers that hinder the use of the formal agency system.[11] A limited project was undertaken on the model of the Day Care Neighbor Service, but with the stated objective of improving family life in a community with a very high-risk population that encompassed native Hawaiians, Portuguese, Asians, Samoans, Filipinos, and Caucasians, all with many young children.

Helping hands (lima kokua)

The question of what to call the central figures was felicitously resolved by a community leader. When the project was explained to her, she suggested that the central figure be called *Lima Kokua,* the Hawaiian term for "helping hand." The position was so well recognized in the community by professionals, volunteers, and clients, that there was almost an oversupply of nominees. Six were selected as prospective partners to the part-time professional, who was engaged to be their consultant-collaborator. Although this person was a well-trained social worker, she had had no experience with this new way of using her skills and knowledge. She had to shift to an anthropological

10. Alice H. Collins, "Helping Neighbors Intervene in Cases of Maltreatment," in *Protecting Children from Abuse and Neglect,* eds. J. Garbarino and S. H. Stocking (San Francisco: Jossey-Bass, 1980), pp. 133-72.

11. Sharon Hayashida, *Report on Kokua Lima Project* (Honolulu: Child and Family Service, 1980), prologue, p. 1.

approach to identify the helping hands; she had to learn enough of the customs to successfully recruit and work with them; and she had to refocus from a provider role to one of consultative and collaborative exchange and partnership.

Training and ongoing consultation were provided for the professional, but training was not offered to the Helping Hands in accordance with the firmly held belief that the contribution of central figures in any setting depended upon their intimate knowledge of the idiosyncratic customs of their own unique networks. Training, which implied a single "right" approach, or a lack of professional skills on their part, was strongly contra-indicated.

Consultation-collaboration in a multi-ethnic community

The Lima Kokua Project was organized to deal with the high incidence of problems related to family stress and instability on the Waianae Coast. It identified and utilized natural helping networks to learn how these networks functioned in supporting and maintaining family stability, and it provided consultation-collaboration services to the central figures of the selected networks.[12]

During the identification and recruitment stages the professional explored the targeted neighborhoods and interviewed a broad spectrum of people to learn about local customs and interest in order to obtain names of those who were known to be helpers, and to give information about the project's goals and objectives.

> The general reaction to the Lima Kokua Project and to the concept of natural-helping networks was quite positive, although with varying degrees of enthusiasm. There were some questions regarding the violation of confidentiality and possible negative effect of interference with a natural phenomenon. These appeared to be satisfied with the explanation that names would not be used and that the Helping Hands would not be asked to do anything new or different from what they were presently doing.[13]

People who identified with the formal agency system, especially direct-service providers, tended to doubt the feasibility and/or value of the project, while those closer to the natural helping networks easily understood and were excited about the recognition of these neighborhood-based resources.

Similarities between Hawaii and mainland projects

The response of the helping hands to the consultant-collaborator, and the insights they provided into the real life of the community, closely parallelled the experience of the earlier mainland programs and of similar projects that were reported in a variety of settings.[14] As it had been on the mainland, the frustrating failure of the central figures to keep records and their tendency to view appointments with the consultant-collaborator as having no special priority resembled the earlier experiences of the Day Care Neighbor Service. The many ways in which the helping hands supported their friends and neighbors, listened to their problems, and provided advice and practical assistance were also similar, as was the opportunity for the consultant-collaborator to learn how the natural helping networks functioned.

> The Consultant-Collaborator was made aware of, and monitored the progress of a wide range of people who would not

12. Ibid., p. 1.

13. Ibid., pp. 1, 2

14. Froland et al., *Helping Networks.*

ordinarily have sought professional services. In this way, intervention at an earlier stage of potentially serious problems was made via the Lima Kokua. . . . [Where indicated] the person in need of additional service was helped to get to the right resource and prepared for entering the formal agency system. . . . the Consultant-Collaborator was able to make suggestions to improve service delivery.[15]

CONCLUSION

The power of natural helping networks was discussed positively, extensively, and as a promising innovation in the President's Commission on Mental Health Report on Community Support Systems.[16] Further public recognition came in the form of a grant made to the Regional Institute at Portland State University to study the relationship between agencies and natural helping networks.[17] Recent publications[18] reiterate earlier statements about the importance of city neighborhoods and their potential in human terms to make urban life safer and more satisfying, especially to children.

As yet, the projects that have made use of natural helping networks and other support systems have been chiefly funded on an experimental basis, often for research purposes, and therefore only involve a small staff and limited private or public funding. The crucial policy steps that would incorporate this new method into common practice have yet to be taken. This is not surprising when it is recognized that major changes in the mode of operation in bureaucratic organizations are always slow. Even agency people who have enthusiastically supported natural helping networks have sometimes failed to incorporate it into agency practice, often pleading lack of time. In actual fact, working with natural helping networks is a way of saving expensive professional time to make what is available go farther, since it has the capacity of reaching many more families in the time now spent on counseling.

Value of natural helping networks in human service delivery system

While it is true that in this model a professional's time can reach more hard-to-serve clients than can traditional direct services, and therefore is more cost effective, this argument may be dangerous given the contemporary cost-cutting policy. Those with the power to determine budget allocations may ask, If the model is so natural and so money-saving, why fund the professional as consultant-collaborator? Why not fund a training program for the natural neighbors to carry out these traditional agency services? Such an approach would be similar to the less desirable aspects of the programs using paraprofessionals that were undertaken a decade ago. It would fail to implement the unique and potentially important aspect of

15. Hayashida, *Report on Kokua Lima*, p. 7.

16. President's Commission on Mental Health, *Report on the Task Panel on Community Support Systems*, vol. 2 (Washington, DC: U.S. Government Printing Office, 1978), pp. 14-40.

17. Department of Health and Human Services Contract no. 18-P-00088.

18. Ann W. Spirn, "The Role of Natural Process in the Design of Cities," *The Annals* of the American Academy of Political and Social Science, 451:98-105 (Sept. 1980); Donald Appleyard, "Livable Streets: Protected Neighborhoods," ibid., pp. 106-13.

the new mode of service delivery—the partnership that supports and strengthens the natural helping networks without altering them.

Nor should it be assumed that individual services should be abolished in favor of working solely in the more economically rewarding natural network method. This method should be added to, and integrated with, the range of services of the formal agency system—not substituted for those proven effective. The greatest value of this model is its ability to maximize effectiveness of both the natural helping networks and the formal agency system through the dynamic linkage made possible by the consultation-collaboration relationship.

Evaluation and recommendation

There are, however, several problems that must be addressed if the new service delivery system is to be widely adopted. Just to establish the service requires the professional to explore the customs of the designated population and to identify the central figures. This is time consuming. Administrators must allow for this "tooling-up" period, which is unproductive in terms of service statistics. Indeed, data collection in general presents problems. Central figures are unaccustomed to keeping records on their contacts and, in fact, usually are resistant to what they view as the documentation of gossip. They have contacts so often and so naturally in the course of their everyday lives that they are not even aware of what they do, much less able to record it. Professionals must devise ways of collecting data that are both acceptable to the central figures and meet the needs of the agency—not an easy assignment.

Another issue that needs to be addressed promptly if consultation-collaboration with natural helping networks is to succeed is the need for training the professionals who are to function as the consultant-collaborator. Fortunately, a beginning has been made in this direction. Some seminars have been held, and courses are beginning to be taught as part of professional curricula.

How should success be measured in this model? The partnership that links natural helping networks and the formal agency system may result in more or fewer referrals for agency services. It may increase or decrease the intensity of the intervention of central figures. The clearest measures of success are when a central figure interrupts child abuse, helps a family resolve disputes, or provides necessary information and referral. But how do consultants evaluate their role in supporting helping hands in their efforts to encourage, for example, a mother to devote more time toward the caring of her own young child, as opposed to meeting the demanding expectations of her extended family? Or how should a mother be persuaded that her baby needs her presence more than the household needs a color television? Throughout such demands the central figure should be free to function autonomously. This freedom may cause discomfort in sponsoring agencies that feel a sense of responsibility or a need to control the behavior of their staff and volunteers.

There is no doubt that natural helping networks exist and that their resources can be utilized to a greater extent. Ideally, government should recognize these natural helping networks as both efficient and effective in reaching families under stress, a major cause of child abuse and neglect. But first the initial tooling-up will take money. And second, success will be best assured if professionals and the community indicate an interest in this new approach. No sweeping executive order could accomplish as much.

ANNALS, *AAPSS*, **461**, May 1982

Child Care and Working Mothers in Puerto Rican Families

By MARSHA HURST and RUTH E. ZAMBRANA

ABSTRACT: This article focuses on child care arrangements, mothering attitudes, and family support systems as they affect the labor force participation of urban Puerto Rican mothers. In general, for women in the United States, paid work outside the home has become a normal part of life and, for most women, a necessary aspect of existence. Puerto Rican women, particularly those in the New York City area, however, have declining, not rising, rates of labor force participation. Our study looked to child care factors for a partial explanation for this work pattern. The study method used in-depth interviews with a sample of 40 Puerto Rican mothers stratified by occupational status. All these mothers have worked outside the home, but not all are currently working. Cultural values toward family care were strongly expressed by the mothers and were found to significantly affect work patterns, particularly for women with erratic work histories. The social policy implications of this study relate to the need to recognize and act on the connection between participation in the labor market and cultural attitudes toward child care for a significant low-income urban minority population.

Marsha Hurst, a political scientist, earned her doctorate at Columbia University in 1972, taught government at John Jay College of the City University of New York for five years, and was an NIMH postdoctoral fellow in community medicine and medical sociology at Mount Sinai School of Medicine in New York City. Currently she is an adjunct assistant professor of community medicine at Mount Sinai, researching and publishing in the area of women's health.

Ruth E. Zambrana, a sociologist, received her doctorate from Boston University in 1977. She has been at the Mount Sinai School of Medicine, Department of Community Medicine, since 1975, and has worked in program development and health services delivery to the East Harlem community. Currently she is on leave as assistant professor of community medicine at Mount Sinai, and is dean of the Graduate School, Wright Institute, Los Angeles.

UNTIL recently, women's role in industrialized economies has been defined as being outside the labor force, except in unusual family circumstances or during temporary strong demand in certain sectors of the economy. One of the most striking and significant characteristics of the post-World War II labor force, however, has been the consistent increase in women's labor force participation. Most of this increase has been among women with children under age 18, and the fastest growth has been among women with children under 6, almost 50 percent of whom were in the labor force in 1981 compared with slightly over 10 percent in 1950.[1] These trends are reflected less dramatically in changes in the New York City women's labor force. In New York City, as in the entire United States, the most notable increase in women's labor force participation has occurred among mothers with preschool children, whose participation went from 20 percent to 32 percent in the first six years of the 1970s.

The increases in labor force participation rates are true for women in almost all regions, from almost all groups. For all women in the United States, paid work outside the home has become a normal part of life, and for most women, a necessary aspect of existence. There is one exception to this trend. Hispanic women, particularly in New York, have declining, not rising, rates of labor force participation. Puerto Ricans, alone among all groups of women, appear to be either leaving or not entering the labor force.[2]

The purpose of this article is to identify the characteristics of a sample of Puerto Rican women who function in a dual role as workers and mothers, and to explore the ways they manage their child care needs. This article focuses on working and parenting commitment and on the social support systems and cultural attitudes that affect the Puerto Rican woman's child care decisions. The study is intended to provide an insight into child care arrangements among working Puerto Rican mothers and to suggest considerations important to the formulation of family policy.

BACKGROUND

A mother's decision to work outside the home is usually related to the age of her children and the availability and acceptability of child care arrangements. Any attempt to understand the labor force participation of Hispanic women, however, must recognize the importance of other factors relevant to this population. First, the demographic characteristics of the Hispanic women in the United States are important. Second, attention must be paid to the characteristics of the Hispanic labor force as a whole in relation to larger labor force participation needs of the economy. Third, indications of labor force participation barriers due to racial and gender discrimination must be included. The focus of our study is on the relationship between sociocultural attitudes, maternal roles, and child care responsibilities.

In many respects, the majority of Hispanic women are in a poorer position to compete for better jobs

1. U.S. Department of Labor, *News* (Nov. 1981): Table 2.

U.S. Government Printing Office, 1979).

2. M. J. Newman, "A Profile of Hispanics in the U.S. Workforce," *Monthly Labor Review*, 101(12):5 (Dec. 1978).

than are other women in the population. Hispanic women, particularly Puerto Rican women, tend to be younger, less educated, and more frequently heads of families than other women. In 1978, the median age of Spanish-origin women in the mainland United States was 22.8, compared with a median age of 31.2 years for other women. While two-thirds of the women in the country have completed four years of high school or more, only 40 percent of Hispanic women have had this much schooling, and the percentage is less (35 percent) for Puerto Rican women, who comprise the vast majority of Spanish-origin women in New York.[3]

The characteristics of Spanish-origin women that may be most important in relation to work at home and in the marketplace are those connected to the proportion of Hispanic women who are heads of family. In 1978, the Hispanic woman was twice as likely to be married with husband absent than a woman in any other group. The overwhelming majority of these families (92 percent) were in metropolitan areas, and two-thirds of those were in central cities.[4]

These figures are even more startling for Puerto Rican women, who are more likely to be divorced (11 percent) or married with husband absent (including separated, 16 percent) than any other Spanish-origin woman. In New York City, 40 percent of all Hispanic families are single-parent families. Among Puerto Rican families, the percentage is even higher.[5]

Nationwide, women of Spanish origin are overrepresented among blue-collar workers (28 percent compared with 15 percent of all women), and underrepresented among white-collar workers (48 percent compared with 64 percent of all women). Only 9 percent of employed Spanish-origin women are professionals, while 16 percent of employed non-Spanish-origin women are professionals. The occupational status of Puerto Rican women tends to be even more heavily weighted toward blue-collar work (31 percent in 1978), particularly in the garment industry. In New York City, Puerto Ricans are "concentrated in declining [manufacturing] sectors of the city's economy."[6] Manufacturing jobs in New York City were cut by over one-third between 1960 and 1970, forcing thousands of Puerto Ricans out of the employed labor force completely.[7]

In addition, because of discriminatory practices, Hispanic women may end up in poorer job situations than other women. An analysis of the earnings of white, Puerto Rican, and black graduates of the same vocational school found that even when the training and school achievements of the women graduates were held constant, earnings of white graduates were higher than

3. U.S. Department of Labor, *Women and Work: A Databook* (Washington, DC: U.S. Government Printing Office).

4. U.S. Bureau of the Census, "Persons of Spanish Origin in the United States," *Current Population Reports*, series P-20, no. 34 (Washington, DC: U.S. Government Printing Office, 1979).

5. T. W. Lash, W. Sigal, and D. Dudzinski, *Children and Families in New York City: An Analysis of the 1976 Survey of Income and Education* (New York: Foundation for Child Development, 1979), p. 4.

6. L. L. Gray, "The Jobs Puerto Ricans Hold in New York City," *Monthly Labor Review*, 98:16 (Oct. 1975).

7. R. S. Cooney, "Intercity Variations in Puerto Rican Female Participation," *Journal of Human Resources*, 14(2):222-35 (1978).

those of black and Puerto Rican graduates.[8]

On the whole, given the family status, educational attainment, and job potential of Spanish-origin women, it is not surprising that they are underrepresented in the labor force. In fact, the labor force participation rate of Hispanic women in 1976 lagged behind white women by 3 percent and behind black women by 8 percent. Among Puerto Rican women, there was a 12 percent lag behind all Hispanic women.[9]

In New York City, where most mainland Puerto Ricans are concentrated, women's labor force participation is lower than it is nationwide. Indeed, many of the same factors that decrease Puerto Rican women's job opportunities, especially the high proportion of female-headed families and the city's declining lower-level job sectors, have affected other groups of city residents.[10]

For women as a whole, labor force participation tends to decrease as role strain intensifies, causing both work overload and role conflict.[11] The demands of child care for preschool-age children make those years the hardest for working mothers, and make that the period when women are most likely to leave the labor force. Puerto Rican mothers do not follow this pattern, but instead have generally lower but more consistent labor force participation rates over the child-rearing years. This may relate to particular patterns of child care and to a different effect of role conflict on these arrangements. Although the structural attributes of employment have been examined in relation to Puerto Rican women, researchers have not yet looked at work and child care together to find explanations for the uniqueness of this group.

Clear explanations do not emerge from the literature on female role conflict. Kupinsky points out that "much of the evidence to validate the role conflict hypothesis is inferential in nature" because of the difficulty of measurement and evaluation.[12] Some aspects of role conflict, such as time conflict and financial conflict, are fairly concrete and involve relatively tangible conflicting allocations. The convenience of work conditions as well as the number of children at home are clearly related to female labor force participation.[13]

The assumption that the mother's employment adds to family income must be reexamined. When there are young children at home the increased income brought in by the wife is substantially decreased because of the cost of acceptable

8. S. H. Baker and B. Levenson, "Earning Prospects of Black and White Working-Class Women," *Sociology of Work and Occupation*, 3(2):123-50 (May 1976).

9. U.S. Department of Labor, *Women and Work*.

10. Lash, Sigal, and Dudzinski, *Children and Families in New York City*, p. 92.

11. J. B. Herman and K. Gyllstrom, "Working Men and Women: Inter- and Intra-Role Conflict," *Psychology of Women Quarterly*, 1:319 (1977); E. Robeson, "Strain and Dual Role Occupation Among Women" (Ph.D. thesis, City University of New York Graduate Center, 1977); L. Bailyn, "Family Constraints on Women's Work," *Annals of the New York Academy of Sciences*, 208:161 (1973).

12. S. Kupinsky, "The Fertility of Working Women in the United States: Historical Trends and Theoretical Perspectives," in *The Fertility of Working Women: A Synthesis of International Research*, ed. S. Kupinsky (New York: Praeger, 1977), pp. 188-249.

13. M. Hurst and R. E. Zambrana, *Determinants and Consequences of Maternal Employment: An Annotated Bibliography, 1968-1980* (Washington, DC: Business and Professional Women's Foundation, 1981) gives a complete review of this literature.

child care and the decreased increment to the husband's income. For a women who must pay for full-time child care and other home-making services, there is little financial gain from employment unless her income is substantial. For many women substantial financial gain is never realized because time spent in child rearing decreases the value of prior training and experience and increases the likelihood of a discontinuous work history with little or no accumulated seniority, thus decreasing earning power.[14]

Role conflict studies have generally focused on the work role rather than on the parent role. Some researchers have tried to take a fresh look at the role of mothering,[15] but the commitment to mother has generally been assumed to be equivalent to the measure of time spent with children. The commitment-to-mother variable may be most responsive to the influence of cultural norms and expectations. Because research to date has not systematically focused on the cultural proscription of minority groups but has dealt almost exclusively with the dominant American family structure,[16] little is known about the nature and importance of this variable in other cultural groups. For this reason, our study will pay particular attention to the attitudes and cultural values related to child care decisions and work, as well as to the role of family support systems.

The ability of a woman to combine these dual commitments successfully may be influenced by the existence and maintenance of support systems and attitudes congruent with her dual roles. Conflict between the roles may be related to inadequate support systems and negative or incongruent cultural attitudes. In sum, we suggest that the commitment to work and to mother are mediated by social and cultural factors, and that the most significant focal point for these concerns is the issue of child care.

METHODOLOGY

In-depth interviews were conducted with 40 Puerto Rican mothers. The criteria for selection of our sample were: formerly or presently married; 25 to 45 years of age; parenting responsibility for at least one dependent child; and residence in the New York metropolitan area. Network sampling procedures were used to identify interviewees within three broad occupational categories.

A semistructured interview guide was used to conduct our interviews, which took an average of two hours. Interviews were conducted in Spanish or English, depending on the preference of the interviewee. The guide was used to conduct interviews with both currently working and currently nonworking Hispanic mothers. This instrument was geared to examine work history, commitment to work, attitudes toward parenting, and the availability and use of support systems and child care options.

One major framework for analysis of data was the definition of continuous and discontinuous work history. Continuous work history was determined for the sample as steady adult labor force participa-

14. P. M. Hudis, "Commitment to Work and to Family: Marital Status Differences in Women's Earnings," *Journal of Marrige and the Family,* May 1976, pp. 267-78.

15. J. T. Fawcett, ed., *The Satisfaction and Costs of Children: Theories, Concepts and Methods* (Honolulu: East-West Population Institute, 1972).

16. See, for example, J. Bernard, *Women, Wives, Mothers: Values and Opinions* (Chicago: Aldine, 1975).

tion with breaks of one year or less, related only to the birth of one or more children.

CHARACTERISTICS OF SAMPLE POPULATION

Forty urban Puerto Rican mothers were interviewed; the majority (62 percent) were between 30 and 39 years of age, and 20 percent were between 25 and 29 years of age. At the time of the interview, 78 percent of the respondents were living with a spouse or partner in the household. Of the entire sample, 75 percent had been married once and 25 percent had been married more than once.

Roughly equal numbers of respondents from blue-collar (30 percent), white-collar (35 percent), and professional (35 percent) groups were interviewed. Women's occupational status was based primarily on last or present job held.

All the women had worked during their adult life. However, 65 percent had a discontinuous work history. By occupational status, the most discontinuous work history was among blue-collar workers (100 percent), and the most continuous work history was among the professional women (64 percent).

By educational status, 27 percent had an average of nine years of schooling; 30 percent, 13 years of schooling; and 43 percent, 18 years of schooling. Women who had less than eight years of schooling had an average of five children, and professional women (16 years or more of schooling) had an average of one child. Average age at the birth of the first child for the three occupational groups was: blue-collar workers, 22 years; white-collar workers, 21 years; and professionals, 25 years. The data suggest that the more education a woman has, the fewer the number of children. The only exception are women with college degrees but no graduate education, who have more children (2.5) than high school graduates (2.3), but our sample was too small to determine any level of significance.

The average combined income for blue-collar families was $12,400; for white-collar families, $16,700; and for professional families, $32,000. Women's income alone for blue-collar workers averaged $4,905; for white collar, $10,333; and for professionals $12,914. These averages include part-time workers and women receiving supplemental income. All blue-collar and white-collar workers were working full time, while more than half of the professionals were working part time.

The mothers interviewed all held primary responsibility for child care, either by caring for the child or children themselves, or by finding acceptable alternative child care. The respondents used a variety of child care resources, including parents only; relatives, such as grandparents, aunts and sisters, husbands, and older siblings; unpaid nonrelatives, such as neighbors and friends; paid nonrelatives, for example, babysitters and housekeepers; and institutional care, for example, day care and foster care.

Table 1 clearly shows that type and use of child care resources varied by occupational status. Blue-collar mothers most often took care of their children themselves (62 percent). White-collar mothers predominantly used relatives (68 percent) for child care. Professionals utilized almost twice as many types of resources in combination as did either the blue-collar or white-collar mothers, with greater use of

TABLE 1
CHILD CARE RESOURCES USED BY OCCUPATIONAL STATUS OF MOTHER (in percentages)

OCCUPATIONAL STATUS	CHILD CARE RESOURCES		
	SELF	RELATIVES	NONRELATIVES
Blue collar	62	10	19
White collar	21	68	11
Professional	21	38	41

nonrelatives, both paid caretakers and institutions.

MOTHERING ATTITUDES AND CHILD CARE

Two groups of mothers had strong and overriding commitments to work and had the most continuous work histories: women with clearly perceived financial need because of inadequate family income and women with high educational attainment or advanced job training. For women without these commitments, labor force participation was more erratic and appeared more responsive to second-level factors, particularly attitudes toward exclusive mothering and the availability of acceptable—mainly within the family—child care. Women rarely identified a cultural value that would inhibit them from working during child-rearing years, but rather stressed the importance of their own expectations and the spouse's attitude toward women's employment. The higher the family income, the more likely that egalitarian decision-making patterns and congruent husband and wife attitudes supported maternal employment. Women did not feel that their families, especially their mothers, disapproved of mothers working, but rather that family traditions disapproved of a nonfamily member taking care of family children.

We found that the critical breaking points in and out of the labor force for most of these women revolved around family events that pivoted on activity of the spouse or parent. Frequently, women who continued to work after the birth of their first child pulled out of the labor force at some point when their children were older or when they bore a second child. Generally this breaking point corresponded with a break in child care arrangements, as the mother or mother-in-law became too old or too sick to care for the children, or when the presence of more than one child made child care a difficult burden for a family member. In these instances, the unavailability of acceptable family child care combined with a strong cultural value of mothering—"the way I would do it"—pulled the woman out of the labor force until another breaking point pushed her back in.

A common theme of the interviews was the strong internalization of sex-linked family roles experienced by many women. This is characteristic of other lower-income ethnic groups.[17] Twelve women in

17. J. Dowdall, "Women's Attitudes Toward Employment and Family Roles," *Sociological Analysis*, 35(4):251-62 (Winter 1974).

our sample discussed their early life expectations in terms of traditional home and mother roles, some explicitly attributing a cultural context to their early socialization. In some cases, women had a strong early identification with a full-time mothering role based on feelings that their own family life was incomplete:

I always looked forward to being married and having a family, and I think that had a lot to do with my own childhood. I wanted a home with children—two kids, a boy and a girl. I always wanted to stay home with the children. It was like a fantasy for me, this type of thing, because I didn't have a regular home or a mother and father.

For many women recounting these early expectations was tinged with sadness or bitterness because teenage pregnancies or divorce rudely interrupted their dream. "After a certain age it was expected . . . to be married and have kids and, like the fairytale goes, live happily ever after, which doesn't necessarily happen," said one woman who slipped a .45-caliber pistol into her bag and went after her teenage boyfriend when he refused to marry her.

Parental expectations, even when they included educational attainment, emphasized marriage and family. The work expectations of women who expressed strong internalized mothering commitments generally ended at marriage. The vision of family "perfection" dependent on being a full-time mother and wife was the pinnacle of personal expectation and the only goal of everyone these women knew. "Well, I just wanted to get married and have babies; I never thought much about the future. . . . Everyone was brought up that way." "I wanted to have a family, a home and kids. I guess what every woman wants." Lack of working-mother role models reinforced the limited visions of most women interviewed and made later desires for an identity outside that of wife and mother difficult. "At 18 I knew that if I wanted to have children my children would really need me at home. I didn't know how you could be a career person and be a mother at the same time."

The husband's attitude often reinforced this orientation toward exclusive mothering. As has been found in other ethnic groups, the lower the socioeconomic status, the more likely that the husband forbade the woman to work outside the home and the more likely he was to believe that the woman should be the primary child care person.[18] For women who had erratic work patterns, the husband's attitude toward child care was a particularly critical determinant of their break with the labor force.

It was common across all occupational groups for the mother or mother-in-law of the respondent to be the primary care person, along with related individuals. In general, the lower the socioeconomic status, the more conflict the women felt in not taking care of the childen themselves. For these women, mothering was an overriding source of personal identity and self-esteem. The availability of social support networks in the white-collar group was reflected in their use of relatives for child care. Their commitment to work was facilitated by the stability of the arrangement and their perceived

18. N. A. Eiswirth-Neems and P. J. Handal, "Spouse's Attitudes Toward Maternal Occupational Status and Effects on Family Climate," *Journal of Community Psychology*, 6(2):168-72 (Apr. 1978).

economic need. Professionals could be more flexible with their schedules and could better afford paid caretakers. Many of the professionals were combining part-time work with study, which may explain the relatively high percentage (21 percent) that said they themselves provided child care.

Frequently women felt they would not have gone back to work if they did not have their mother or mother-in-law to care for their children. The child's grandmother was clearly seen as the ideal substitute caretaker. A woman who went back to work when her second child was 10 months old, leaving both children with their grandmother, believed that her first born had gotten sick because he was left with a strange babysitter. With her mother, her children were getting the kind of love she had received as a child; and although she had to work on her mother not to be overprotective, she still felt good about her boys being brought up with love "shared by three generations."

Women who had mothers or mothers-in-law to care for their children characterized their return to work after childbearing as "easy." "Who is better than my mother?" The most comfortable situation was clearly when the child was taken care of by the grandmother in the child's own home. One grandmother took care of her first two grandchildren in her home and then when the third child was born did the caretaking in her daughter's home. "My mother used to do everything. . . . She used to make my dinner and everything, no problems." Not only convenience but confidence and love were characteristics of the grandmother-as-caretaker relationship. "I trusted her and I know everything she did was the right thing. And they were attached to her so they never cried when I left." "You never know how they're really going to take care of them [the children] unless they're family." My mother-in-law is "very affectionate, very loving. There was a family there." The quality of this family child care relationship was so important that respondents would move close to their mother "so that the worry from nine to five would be minimized."

Not infrequently, conflicts erupted between the woman and her mother regarding child-rearing approaches. These types of issues arose more frequently among women who were highly educated, and thus suggest some differences that may be due to intergenerational mobility. The conflicts were usually minimized during the children's younger years. When the children reached an age at which the mother felt they could attend day care or a nursery, or when the mother was financially able to afford a nonfamily system of child care, the grandmother became a secondary or back-up support. Occasionally, very close friends who were familiar with the children would be used, but in all instances if she lived in the area, the mother of the woman continued to be important for child care. A common theme among the working women regarding their mothers was, "She didn't do such a bad job with me, so I guess she'll do O.K. with my kid."

In general, the women felt most comfortable leaving their children with relatives at least until they were old enough for day care or nursery school (generally three years old), when they were transferred to the school. One woman had her stepmother take care of her child, but the woman was also caring for her own two young children and two of her daughter's children. The respondent believed that there was no discipline in the house, and children were being given bottles at the age of six. The lack of discipline, along with overprotectiveness, were the most common complaints women had about their in-family caregivers, and these, they often felt, were worth tolerating for the security of knowing the child was with family.

If a mother or other relative were not available for child care, women would go to great lengths to make sure that outside child care was not needed. One trained nurse went back to work nights and during the day took care of her preschool son, the house, and herself until she became very ill with mononucleosis related to exhaustion. Not only did she not "believe in babysitters or day care," but her husband did not give her support with her need to work. "He felt that if I wanted to work, then I had to pay the consequences of taking care of the house, doing the cooking, taking care of the child. I was still responsible for everything." Now, although she believes she was a much better mother when she was working, she will wait until her youngest child is of school age to go back to work.

As the respondents' children grew older, child care became easier to arrange. As with other populations, beginning around nine or ten years of age children were frequently left on their own after school or were occasionally enrolled in after-school programs. Exceptions tended to be preadolescent girls, who more often were still left with relatives if their mothers were working.

Women who worked part time almost invariably cited child care logistics as part of the reason for choosing part-time rather than full-time work. This was particularly true of women with school-age children who could "attend" to their own children if they worked during school hours only. School attendance also made it easier for full-time working mothers who had grandmother support to rely on these relatives without feeling they were overburdening them, or for husbands who worked night shifts to do after-school child care.

Child care by a babysitter is seen by women who use family members as being fraught with unknowns. The paid service relationship is regarded as being incompatible with loving child care. "I don't think they're interested in taking care of your child. They just want the money you are going to pay them at the end of the week." The data clearly showed that availability and use of family support systems for child care were important determinants of employment status.

CONCLUSION AND POLICY IMPLICATION

To date, most research on women's labor force participation has focused on structural variables that inhibit or facilitate maternal employment, especially opportunities in the labor force, job qualifications of women, family income, and number and age of children. Little attention has been paid to a second level of explanatory factors: intrafamilial and intracultural attitudes, and particularly those related to the availability of acceptable child care resources for working mothers.

Since mobility and improved quality of life in the United States are largely attained through the economic system, Puerto Rican women, more than other American women, are missing opportunities by being outside this system. In order to equalize the life opportunities of these women, they need to have equal access to the opportunities of labor force participation. Thus understanding the reasons for declining participation or lack of access is critical in terms of any policy that strives toward equity. The results of our study showed the pattern of labor force participation to be highly discontinuous, characterized by erratic movement in and out of the labor force, rather than by a dichotomous working or nonworking pattern. The classic breaking points of dominant population groups—marriage and child bearing—were less significant for this group than the availability and acceptability of child care. For the majority of women, family continuity in child care was the most important facilitator of employment patterns.

Clearly, the low level of education and training among this ethnic sector coupled with a strong family orientation, particularly in the area of child care, does not allow the women to adapt easily to contemporary employment demands. In light of these identified needs, a comprehensive employment policy should be geared toward increasing education and training within the work environment, as well as toward facilitating the use of compatible child care arrangements.

Current policies to support child care services are unlikely to help most Puerto Rican families. Direct subsidies to support child care services are part of the cutbacks in government support for social services. Indirect subsidies in the form of tax credit for up to 20 percent of child care costs affect very few Puerto Rican women. The working poor earn too much to qualify for the meager direct subsidy programs and too little to take a tax credit. New legislation is being proposed to make the tax credit meaningful for working-class families, but for most middle- or low-income Puerto Rican families who use a family member for child care, either cultural attitudes prohibit the acceptance of payment for that service or the payment must be in the form of undeclared income to be useful.

Women in our sample were most concerned about being able to trust the child care given and with knowing the child was in a warm and loving environment. In their perception, it was mainly relatives who inspired this trust. Therefore policy should be directed either toward restructuring the work situation so that parents themselves can provide their own child care—job sharing, flex-time, or part-time work opportunities, particularly for blue-collar and white-collar workers—or toward facilitating care by other relatives, for example, allowing paid care by relatives without jeopardizing their public assistance status. In addition, widespread on-site day care for infants and preschoolers would allow parents to have regular daytime access to their young children and would reinforce, rather than break, the close family bond. In most other societies, women resume work almost immediately postpartum, but children are kept nearby in order not to interrupt the maternal-infant bond.[19] To date

19. M. H. Jimenez and N. Newton, "Activity and Work During Pregnancy and the Postpartum Period; A Cross-Cultural Study of 202 Societies," *American Journal of Obstetrics and Gynecology,* 135(2):171-76 (Sept. 1979).

there has been little support from employers, unions, and government in providing essential support services, such as on-site child care services, although women's satisfaction with child care arrangements[20] as well as availability and use of support systems[21] have been positively linked to participation in the labor force. The development of child care policy based on perceived need of these women will certainly improve the quality of life among both children and their parents.

20. J. E. Harrell and C. A. Ridley, "Substitute Child Care, Maternal Employment and the Quality of Mother-Child Interaction," *Journal of Marriage and the Family*, 37:556-64 (Aug. 1975).

21. F. L. Paltiel, "Supportive Measures for Working Women" (Unpublished paper prepared by Women: Resources for a Changing World, Radcliffe Institute, Cambridge, MA, 1972).

ANNALS, *AAPSS*, 461, May 1982

Parents' Choice of Day Care Services

By JOHN C. MOORE, Jr.

ABSTRACT: In this article, findings are summarized from a multivariate analysis of types and amount of child care used by a national sample of parents with children under 14. Findings and policy implications are presented in four areas: a comparison of type versus hours used as alternative indicators of child care need, an analysis of the importance of location versus caregiver relatedness among users of home arrangements, the relationship between household structure and use of care, and the importance of household income as related to cost of child care. Based on the results of the study, it is concluded that the traditional link between employment status and use of formal group care is misleading, since being employed is critical to the amoung of care used, but not to the type chosen. It is emphasized that the complexities observed among the several household characteristics and the use of care strongly suggest that parents are in the best position to judge the amount or type of child care arrangements needed by their families. Based on this conclusion, public policy that rationalizes involvement in day care on the basis of support for family child rearing and economic functioning should permit maximum latitude to the range of choices available to parents.

John C. Moore, Jr. is an independent researcher and consultant to contract research firms, government agencies, and advocacy organizations. Recent projects include preparing a manual for using the 1980 Census data for local-level advocacy, serving as statistical consultant for a study of school desegregation from a Hispanic perspective, and providing management support for a project to develop a skill-based English-language curriculum for Hispanic adults. Dr. Moore is a contributing editor to American Family, *an independent national newsletter covering current events on families and public policy. Formerly, he was project director for the National Child Care Consumer Study.*

NOTE: This article was supported in part under a grant to the Day Care Council of America from the Office of Economic Opportunity Community Services Administration (grant no. 30079-D- 9-01). It is solely the work of the author and does not necessarily reflect the views or opinions of either the Day Care Council of America or the Community Services Administration.

DAY care for young children has been recognized as a social policy issue for nearly 100 years. Prior to the 1960s, however, the federal government did not support service delivery, except as a crisis reaction during the Great Depression and World War II.[1] Since 1965, government expenditures for day care and early education programs have risen from $12.3 million in 1965 to an estimated $3.0 billion in 1981.[2] Major federal programs include Title XX (the social services portion of the Social Security Act), income disregard in the Aid to Families with Dependent Children (AFDC) program, Head Start, the Department of Agriculture's Child Care Food Program, work-related income tax deductions, and preschool programs funded under the Elementary and Secondary Education Act.

Several rationales have been employed to justify federal involvement in the provision and regulation of services. Day care and early education services have been linked to reducing the welfare roles (with subsidized day care as a work incentive), enhancing equal opportunity (as in the Head Start program), and fostering the development of children (as in Head Start and the Child Care Food Program). With respect to regulating subsidized care, justification is made both in terms of child development and to protect the health and safety of young children.[3] Finally, in the attempts to pass comprehensive service legislation during the 1970s, all the above were involved, as well as the broader rationale of supporting the economic and child-rearing functions of all families with young children.[4]

PURPOSE AND METHODOLOGY

If government involvement in day care services is to be truly supportive of family functioning, it is essential that there be an empirical understanding of parents' decision making. We need to examine their choices in relation to reasons for using care, characteristics of the care used, household structure (number, age, and relationships among household members), and various economic and demographic characteristics. In the past 15 years, several studies at the national level focused on parental need for day care have been undertaken. Unfortunately, the sampling methodologies and approaches taken in the analysis have considerably limited their usefulness in guiding federal policy, or in clarifying many of the assumptions underlying the policy

1. For historical accounts, see Margaret Stenfels, *Who's Minding the Children?* (New York: Simon & Schuster, 1973); Bernard Greenblatt, *Responsibility for Child Care* (San Francisco: Jossey-Bass, 1977); and Wendy Gray, *The Social Work Profession and Day Care Services: Social Policy Issues, 1890-1990* (Wellesley, MA: Wellesley College Center for Research on Women, 1980).

2. Margaret Malone, *Child Day Care: The Federal Role*, Congressional Research Service Issue Brief no. 1 (Washington, DC: Library of Congress, Congressional Research Service, 1981), p. 1.

3. For a thorough discussion of rationales, see Karen H. Dunlop, "Rationales for Government Intervention Into Child Care and Parent Education" (Unpublished manuscript, Vanderbilt University, Institute for Public Policy Studies, 1978). For a discussion from an economist's perspective, see C. Russell Hill, "Private Demand for Child Care," *Evaluation Quarterly*, 2(4):323 (Fall 1978).

4. For a review of attempts to pass comprehensive legislation during the 1970s, see Gilbert Y. Stener, *The Futility of Family Policy* (Washington, DC: Brookings Institution, 1981).

debates. They are not very useful because they fail to examine the interconnections among employment status, types and hours used, and level of household income. Several of the major studies have been based on samples limited only to working women[5] or low-income families,[6] thus excluding critical variables from the analysis and limiting the generalizability of the results. Other studies, while comprehensive in their sampling strategies, have failed to use multivariate statistical methods of analyzing simultaneously the many possible predictors associated with the use of care. These latter studies also did not adequately draw theoretical or policy interpretations from the descriptive results presented.[7]

5. Greg J. Duncan and C. Russell Hill, "Modal Choice in Child Care Arrangements," in *Five Thousand American Families: Patterns of Economic Progress*, vol. 3, eds. G. J. Duncan and J. N. Morgan (Ann Arbor: University of Michigan, Institute for Social Research, 1975); and Richard L. Shortlidge and Patricia Brito, *How Women Arrange for the Care of Their Children While They Work: A Study of Child Care Arrangements, Costs and Preferences* (Columbus: Ohio State University, Center for Human Resource Research, 1977).

6. Mordecai Kurz, Phillip Robins, and Robert Speigelman, *A Study of the Demand for Child Care by Working Mothers* (Menlo Park, CA: Stanford Research Institute, 1975); Barbara Devaney, *Final Report: The Demand for Day Care Services* (Olympia, WA: Department of Social and Health Services, 1979); Seth Low and Pearl Spindler, *Child Care Arrangements of Working Mothers in the United States;* and U.S. Bureau of the Census, "Daytime Care of Children: October 1974 and February 1975," in *Current Population Reports*, series P-20, no. 285 (Washington, DC: U.S. Government Printing Office, 1976).

7. Unco, Inc., *National Child Care Consumer Study* (Arlington, VA: Unco, 1976)] and Westat Research, Inc., *Day Care Survey—1970: Summary Report and Basic Analysis* (Rockville, MD: Westat Research, 1971).

Results reported in this article are based on data collected under a federally sponsored, national area probability sample of 4609 families in which the only sampling restriction was that there be at least one child under 14 living in the household.[8] The data base thus incorporates full variability to support analysis of the relationships between the use of care, as measured by hours and main type used, and the following four characteristics:

—household structure: age of youngest child, presence of children in designated age groups, number of children under 14, presence of a handicapped child, presence of a child aged 14 to 17, presence of a nonspouse adult, whether respondent is married;

—work and income: respondent's employment status, annual household income, annual income earned by other than the respondent, whether government supported;

—demographics: race/ethnicity, education, region of the country; and

—child care usage: main reason for using main method, whether care is paid for, hourly cost for main method among those who pay, distance care is from home in minutes, schedule of care such as time of day, days of the week, whether fixed or irregular.

In the analysis, models were developed drawing upon an economic theory of household decision making that considers both the time and

8. For complete discussion of methodology, see Unco, Inc., *Current Patterns of Child Care Use in the United States* (Arlington, VA: Unco, 1976), ch. 2.

money resources available to families. Multiple regression and discriminant function analysis were the principal statistical methods used.[9]

For the analysis of hours used, the sample consisted of families reporting use of at least one hour of care per week and for whom complete data sets were available (n = 2149). For the analysis of main method chosen, the sample was restricted only to families with at least one child in the 2- to 6-year-old age range, with their main method of care being used at least 10 hours per week (n = 737). The analysis was limited to families with at least one preschool child so that centers and nursery schools would be feasible alternatives to home arrangements. The hours limitation was imposed in order to focus the analysis on families of greater relevance to policy. The sample for both analyses included only respondents who were women. Of all 4609 respondents, less than 1 percent were men, one-third of whom used no child care from outside their immediate families.

This article presents selected findings and implications pertinent to issues in four areas: comparison of hours used and main method chosen as alternative indicators of need for services; the importance of location versus relatedness of the caregiver among types of home-based care; household structure—marital status and age of youngest child—and the use of care; and the relationship of household income to the cost of care. Finally, conclusions are presented on the use of child care as a support service for family functioning.

9. For interpretation of results with respect to the economic theory of household decision making, see John C. Moore, Jr., *Parent Decisions on the Use of Day Care and Early Education Services: An Analysis of Amount Used and Type Chosen* (Ann Arbor, MI: University Microfilms, 1980), pp. 33-34.

AMOUNT AND TYPE OF CARE NEEDED

Whether or not a mother works is important for the hours of care used, but not for the type chosen. For four of the six types of care analyzed, the proportions of parents who used care for work were nearly identical, as shown in Table 1. In describing the need for care, therefore, employment statistics are valuable in showing the growth in need for full-time care, but not necessarily in pressing for a certain type of care.

People using full-time care do not appear to be constrained by inadequate household income or by the cost of care. Virtually no relationship was found between the family's annual income and the amount of care used. Also, after controlling for employment status—that is, when analyzing separately those who work full time, part time, or are not employed—increase in hours of care used made no difference in whether or not care was paid for at all, though it was related to a decrease in the hourly cost.

In contrast, the family's choice of the main method of care was found to be more related to values than to economic considerations. As indicated in Table 1, parent user groups, defined according to type used, were found to be more strongly differentiated on whether care was used for child development—such as school readiness, socialization, or fostering independence—rather than whether it was used for working. User groups also differed in their child care preference, as measured by race/ethnicity and level of formal education, even after controlling for

TABLE 1
PERCENTAGE DISTRIBUTION OF MAIN REASON FOR USING MAIN METHOD OF CARE

	MAIN METHOD OF CARE					
	OWN HOME		OTHER HOME		GROUP CARE	
MAIN REASON FOR USING CARE	Related Caregiver	Unrelated Caregiver	Related Caregiver	Unrelated Caregiver	Day Care	Nursery School
Employment-related	70	64	64	86	65	50
Child development	5	1	10	4	17	36
To go out socially	10	9	12	3	2	3
Other reasons	15	26	14	7	16	11
All reasons	100	100	100	100	100	100

ability to pay, price of care, and receipt of government support.

The principal economic differentiation among user groups was whether or not care was paid for, this difference being associated almost entirely with caregiver relatedness among home users. While relatives were found to be a far less expensive source of child care, the rather modest differences in household income indicate that parents' use of relatives may be only secondarily motivated by differences in cost.

Another important finding was the lack of relationship between type of care and number of hours used. Among the six percentage groups, the number of hours used per week ranged from a low of 26.5 for own home by nonrelative to 35.6 hours for center users.

An important conclusion to be drawn from the study is that hours of care used should be recognized by policymakers and researchers as a separate indicator of need for child care. Most policy issues are debated on the basis of differences among users of different types of care, with hours of care considered as but one of several descriptive characteristics of the type chosen. Also, almost without exception, major policy research studies of family needs for care have not focused on hours of care used as an important dependent variable, despite the important technical advantage of being able to add hours across all types used.

When considering the importance of child care to family functioning and effect on children, hours of care may well be more important than the type chosen. For a family using 40 hours of care per week, regardless of type chosen, the care is certain to be more important to the family's functioning than would be the case if the family used care for only a few hours per week. The same may be said for children: full-time care of any type or mixture of types may have a greater potential impact on children compared with part-time care.

What can be inferred from the study's findings about the traditional approach to describing the need for child care services, in which maternal employment statistics are linked to number of slots in licensed facilities?[10] Being

10. See, for example, the National Commission on Families and Public Policies, *Families and Public Policies in the United States* (Columbus, OH: National Conference on Social Welfare, 1978), pp. 46-47.

employed is clearly critical to the amount of care needed, but neither employment status nor hours of care used are principal determinants of a family's main method of care. Findings from the study suggest that particular support for center care—the preferred type for many traditional child care advocates—should be based on the need for child development services, as viewed from the parent's perspective. More generally, however, the overlap observed between reason for using care and type chosen is clearly more important than the simplistic associations that link centers with work-related care, nursery schools with child-oriented services, and home care with casual babysitting needs.

TYPES OF HOME CARE

A major finding from this study is that relatedness of the provider is more important than the location of care in distinguishing among parent user groups. This has important policy implications because home day care is generally defined on the basis of location, and policy concern over relatedness has generally been considered as an afterthought. More often than not, use of relatives is simply disregarded on the basis that related care givers are from within the user's extended family and thus beyond the purview of governmental involvement.

What are the principal differences between users of relatives versus unrelated providers? Without question, the major difference is whether or not care is paid for. Users of relatives are about half as likely to pay for the care and, among those who pay, the hourly cost is considerably less. Users of relatives tend to be less well educated, to have lower incomes, and to be from racial or ethnic minority groups. Also, relatives were used by parents who had a mixed schedule of times when care was needed, though there were no strong differences in the number of hours used or the reason why care was used.

Regarding location of care, the most important difference between users of their own home versus the provider's home is the number of children in the family. It is interesting to note that having a school-aged child was positively related to using care in the child's home, but presence of a child under three was not related to the location of care. The only other predictors of location of care were the presence of a nonspouse adult in the household and hourly cost of care, both of which were positively associated with using own home care.

The greater importance given to relatedness of the provider, compared with location of care, suggests that parents place more emphasis on who provides the care than on the surroundings in which care is provided. This emphasis on the provider is distinctly different from the government's usual focus on location of care. While it is understandable that location is highly relevant to the logistics of administering regulated and subsidized home care, the difference in perspective between parents and those concerned with policy is nevertheless significant. This difference is cause for questioning the extent to which government day care policies are indeed responsive to parental needs.

HOUSEHOLD STRUCTURE AND USE OF CHILD CARE

In describing the increasing need for child care, advocates often cite the rising divorce rate or increases

TABLE 2
PERCENTAGE EMPLOYED PARENTS AND MEAN HOURS OF CARE USED PER WEEK, BY AGE OF YOUNGEST CHILD

AGE OF YOUNGEST CHILD	PERCENTAGE EMPLOYED	MEAN HOURS OF CARE GIVEN			
		ALL GROUPS	EMPLOYED FULL TIME	EMPLOYED PART TIME	NOT EMPLOYED
0-2	35	19	39	22	11
3-5	50	24	39	21	13
6-9	56	18	29	16	9
10-13	58	15	22	12	7

in number of children living in single-parent families. In this study, being married was not found to be directly related to the amount of care used. While married respondents were found to use fewer hours of care per week, no difference in amount of care was found after controlling for employment status. Also, among two-parent families, there was almost no difference in amount of care used between families in which the husbands were employed versus unemployed. These findings indicate that the increase in numbers of single-parent families is only indirectly indicative of the need for child care, serving more appropriately as partial explanation for the increase in number of employed mothers with young children.

Not only is age of youngest child in a family frequently used as a predictor of need for child care, but it is also used to describe the developmental stage of the family itself and the amount of "household production" that adults in a family must generate. In this study, age of the family's youngest child was not related to hours used, without first taking employment status into account. Among families where the mother worked full time, very high amounts of care were used before the youngest child reached school age, with a second substantial drop in hours occurring when the youngest child reached the upper level of elementary school (Table 2). To describe need for care among young children, therefore, the statistics that show the rise in full-time labor force participation among mothers with children under six is a highly relevant statistical approach to take.

For advocates of school-age child care, it can be seen in Table 2 that families whose youngest child is of school age use about the same amount of care as families whose youngest is under two. While schools obviously reduce the amount of child care needed, the rise in the percentage of mothers employed results in a continuing need for before-and-after school care.

HOUSEHOLD INCOME AND COST OF CARE

As stated earlier, household income is not related to hours of care used, though income is somewhat related to type of care chosen. On the other hand, cost of care was found to be highly related to both amount and type of care. It appears that the variation in cost of different types of care—and arrangements within a type—can operate as a "safety valve" to make ends meet among families who have low incomes but need large amounts of care. When comparing low- and high-income families who use large amounts of care, the low-income families paid exactly half as much per hour, including those who did not pay at all.

While low-income families paid one-half the price of upper-income families, cost of care was found to be six times more important than household income in distinguishing among users of different types of care. Some might interpret this finding as indicative that parents are always interested in the cheapest type of care, but a more positive interpretation would be that parents prefer nonmonetized care more for the qualitative differences involved than for the cost savings realized. In other words, families might prefer using relatives for reasons other than an inability to pay for the care.

In considering the relationship of household income to use of care, it is important to appreciate the differences that can result depending on who in the family earns the income. When "other" income in the household is low, mothers are very likely to work and pay for care, though the hourly cost will be relatively low due to the high number of hours involved. When other income is high, mothers are less likely to work. They use fewer hours of care and are less likely to pay for care, though they will tend to pay more per hour.

These complexities among income, use of care, and amount paid for care provide evidence of the inadequacy of total household income, by itself, as the critical determinant of who should be eligible for subsidized care. The meaning of a given income level is quite different depending on whether the income is produced by one or two earners. By considering "other" income, as well as actual or potential wage-earning ability, subsidy policy would be more sensitive to the family's ability to pay.

CONCLUSION

In recent years, it has become increasingly popular to refer to child care as a family support service. Based on the findings presented in this article, it is concluded that the support relationship between child care and family functioning differs according to whether one considers the amount of care used or the main type chosen. Generally speaking, hours of care used is determined by the reason for using care. While the hours and schedule of work dictate much of the family's child care needs, choosing the type of care offers more leeway for exercising parental values as to the appropriate child care setting and provider characteristics.

It is concluded that child care is an important service in support of family functioning. The relationships observed among hours used, employment status, and need for income indicate that care of children by providers from outside the immediate family is an essential service in support of the family's economic functioning. Additionally, the association between type of care chosen and the use of care for child-oriented reasons, as well as the links with the parent's race/ethnicity and education, demonstrate that many parents regard child care as a supplement to their own child-rearing responsibilities.

An important conclusion to be drawn from the findings presented is that parents' decision making on the amount of and type of care used is a complex matter, subject to a range of household and individual characteristics. While there are two or three characteristics that bear outstanding relationships to amount and type used, there are several other family circumstances that influence decisions as well. Furthermore, several of the characteristics examined in the study were found to be interrelated in their relationships to the use of services. Not only is the connection between type used and reason for use weakly supported, but the traditional link between socioeconomic status and type of care used is not supported either.

If child care is to be truly a support service, and if we are willing to recognize the complexity of influences that affect choices parents make, it becomes essential that parents have control over decisions related to the amount and type of care to be used, as well as choice of specific arrangement within type. This conclusion is based on two assumptions that go beyond the scope of this study: parents are in a better position than professionals to assess their own individual situation in terms of child care needs, and they are concerned not only for their own well-being but also for the well-being of their children and their family unit as a whole.

This need for parental control over child care decisions is further substantiated under the assumption that parental preferences for certain aspects of care may well be different than those of social welfare and early childhood professionals, conceptions that certainly vary across groups of parents defined along racial, cultural, and social class lines. The potential difference between parent and professional attitudes is best exemplified by the long-standing prejudice against uncontrolled, home-based day care outside the purview of the professionals. In a 1975 editorial in *Child Welfare*, the editors proposed to upgrade family day care; by tying the home care in with "good" group care and then assaulting it with professionals: "The battery of professional health, education, and social work personnel in group day care can be brought to bear on the family day care homes."[11] Though no longer expressed as blatantly as in the golden age of day nurseries at the turn of the century, the bias of middle-class social workers and other professionals against lower-class family life still exists.[12]

Advocates who claim to view child care as a family support service must come to recognize that parents' control over services used is critical to retaining a sense of personal integrity and self-determination over their families' lives. By delegating decision making to parents, government therefore minimizes its intervention into family functioning and into relationships between parents and their children, an effect that should make government involvement in child care more politically palatable.

11. Editorial staff, *Child Welfare*, "What Is Family Day Care?" 54(9):613 (Sept. 1975).

12. For historically based discussion of the socioeconomic stratification in service delivery, see Greenblatt, *Responsibility for Child Care*, pp. 80-104. For a case study analysis of the influence of social class on parent-professional relations in day care, see Carole E. Joffee, *Friendly Intruders: Childcare Professionals and Family Life* (Berkeley: University of California Press, 1977). For a personal account of the day nursery experience and the biases evident in the early 1900s, see Ethel S. Beer, *Working Mothers and the Day Nursery* (Mystic, CT: Lawrence Verry, 1970).

Delegating decisions to parents does not imply a "hands off" policy to government financial support for child care, but it does unravel the politically conservative beliefs that parental authority is necessarily preempted whenever government supports child care and that government involvement would necessarily be tantamount to committing the "vast moral authority of the National Government to the side of communal approaches to child-rearing over against the family-centered approach."[13]

If the family support rationale were to be the principal justification for government involvement in child care, then government's actual role should emphasize disseminating consumer information, maximizing program alternatives from which parents may choose, and providing financial support in ways that permit full parental choice, such as through tax credits or vouchers.

Each of the several rationales identified contains different implications for the government's actual role in supporting child care. A good example of the effects of competing rationales on the role of government is the need to regulate child care. Government regulation of child care is generally rationalized as a means to protect the rights and well-being of dependent children (state licensing) or for the advancement of child development, as in care purchased with Title XX money. Regardless of the legitimacy of these rationales, the point here is that regulation of care tends to restrict the range of choice available to parents and thus is in danger of undermining the parent's sense of responsibility that comes with exercising freedom of choice.

It is important for child care advocates to see the conflict inherent in claiming that child care is a support service to parents, while at the same time supporting only regulated, "comprehensive" forms of care, and thus limiting the range of choices available to parents.

13. Excerpted from President Richard Nixon's message vetoing the Economic Opportunity Amendments of 1971, as reprinted in ed. Pamela Roby, *Child Care—Who Cares?* (New York: Basic Books, 1973), p. 737.

ANNALS, *AAPSS*, **461**, May 1982

From Child to Parent: Changing Conceptions of Early Childhood Intervention

By DOUGLAS R. POWELL

ABSTRACT: Many early childhood intervention programs have broadened their focus to include parents as well as children as primary clients. The intent is to maximize the long-term gains of early intervention programs by influencing the quality of family environments. This article examines critically the growing interest in programs that seek to train or support parents in the rearing of their young children. It investigates the rationale, scope, and effectiveness of parent programs. It also explores the critical policy issue of how standards of desirable behavior are established in programs that work with populations whose child-rearing practices deviate from those of program organizers.

Douglas R. Powell is an associate professor of human development at Wayne State University, Detroit. He has directed an experimental parent-child support program and has conducted research on the processes of professional intervention in family child rearing. Dr. Powell is a faculty member of the Bush Program in Child Development and Social Policy, University of Michigan, Ann Arbor. He holds a Ph.D. from Northwestern University.

In recent years, policy issues pertaining to early intervention programs for children from low-income families have undergone a marked change. Interest has shifted from a basic concern for whether early intervention is effective to a consideration of ways to increase the impact of intervention programs. Longitudinal studies now point to the positive effects of early intervention on school performance. Moreover, well-established programs such as Head Start enjoy strong support from policymakers of diverse political persuasions. The issue, then, is not whether there should be early intervention programs but how to achieve long-term benefits in an efficient way.

Parent involvement in intervention programs is being viewed increasingly as a way to maximize the child development gains of early intervention. The focus of many early childhood programs has broadened recently to include the family as well as the preschool child. This change is consistent with national concern about the welfare of families and with research evidence that suggests that the effects of early intervention are strengthened when parents are involved. Approaching parents as a primary rather than secondary client considerably alters traditional conceptions of early intervention and raises major policy questions about the ways in which programs attempt to work with parents.

This article offers a critical overview of programs that seek to train or support parents in the rearing of their young children. The intent is to examine significant dimensions of policy questions about the effectiveness and design of parent programs. This article reviews research findings on the effects of parent programs. It also examines the critical policy issue of how standards of desirable parental behavior are established in programs that work with populations whose child-rearing practices deviate from those of program organizers. As a preface to investigation of these two areas, the rationale and scope of efforts to enhance parent-child relations are explored.

PARAMETERS OF PARENT PROGRAMS

Arguments for programs aimed at parents of young children are based on such popular ideas as "parents are a child's first and most important teacher"; the early years are the most critical; many parents—especially poor ones—are in need of scientific child development information; and "every child has the right to a trained parent."[1] Rationales for parent programs also are based on a large domain of research findings that point persuasively to the importance of home and parental influences on early child development. The basic notion is that parent programs promote a family environment that is conducive to long-term gains in a child's social, cognitive, and physical development. What is more, when parent programs are compared with intervention programs for the child only, there is the argument that a parental focus is more cost effective in that it affects siblings other than the "target" child and may produce the unintended outcome of self-growth changes in the parent, for example, participation in job training.

1. T. H. Bell, "The Child's Right to Have a Trained Parent," *Elementary School Guidance and Counseling*, 9:271 (1975).

These general reasons for parent programs enjoy high regard in a society that presently has a deep concern about the health of American family life and an intense interest in strategies that promote the stability of families, especially as child-rearing systems. In fact, the propensity to support programs aimed at parents goes deeper than contemporary interests. Americans have long held that social problems are amenable to technological remedies,[2] hence the widespread and long-standing view of education as a panacea to societal ills. It appears that in the face of school failures with children from poor families, attention has turned to parent education as a means to improve home environments and, ultimately, underachieving children.

Parent programs are not a new idea, in spite of claims to the contrary by ardent advocates. The notion that parents need to be informed has a rich history. For instance, John Amos Comenius (1592-1670), the "father of education," wrote a handbook on the rearing of infants, dedicated to "Godly Christian Parents, Teachers, Guardians, and all who are charged with care of children," in which he proposed that children should remain in the School of the Mother until six years of age. He reasoned that children need more personalized care than a teacher of a group of children could provide. In the early 1800s there was a proliferation of pamphlets, tracts, magazines, and sermons on child rearing; in the 1820s, mothers' study groups—called Maternal Associations—were formed throughout the country; and in 1832, the first issue of *Mother's Magazine* appeared.[3] The work of G. Stanley Hall and the child study movement in the 1880s demonstrated great interest in the education of parents. The National Congress of Mothers, now known as the Parent-Teacher Association (PTA), was formed in 1897 as the first nationwide parent education organization. One of the major goals of the early PTA was to work with poor families. Mothers' clubs for poor women, supervised by PTA members, were formed to provide a forum for disseminating up-to-date knowledge on child care and family life.[4]

Today, parent programs reflect a diversity of assumptions about parents' needs and strengths, determinants of parental behavior, and methods of behavioral and/or attitudinal change. Programs vary considerably in terms of such factors as whether the focus is on the parent-child dyad or on the parent alone; specificity of instruction; one-to-one versus group discussion; concern for socioecological influences on the parent's life, for example, stress of unemployment; home- versus center-based setting; use of professionals and/or paraprofessionals; frequency of contact, for example, daily or weekly; duration of program, whether in weeks or years; and the existence and flexibility of a predetermined curriculum.

A group of programs has appeared recently that may be called parent support programs and

2. William Kessen, "The American Child and Other Cultural Inventions," *American Psychologist*, 34(10):818 (Oct. 1979).

3. Greta Fein, "The Informed Parent," in *Advances in Early Education and Day Care*, ed. Sally Kilmer (Greenwich, CT: JAI Press, 1980), pp. 157-62.

4. Steven Schlossman, "Before Home Start: Notes Toward a History of Parent Education in America, 1897-1929," *Harvard Educational Review*, 46(3):436-67 (1976).

may be distinguished from parent education programs in their emphasis on providing emotional support to parents. Whereas most parent education programs are interested primarily in the cognitive development of children, support programs tend to focus on parents' experiences in adjusting to parenthood and on the changing demands of rearing young children. Support programs often take the form of parents' groups that may function in ways that parallel self-help groups. There tends to be no established curriculum of lessons on child development; instead, the content of group discussion usually is determined by parents' interests.[5] Some support programs have been developed in response to the need for "ecological intervention in the form of family support systems"[6] and give considerable attention to forces in parents' environments—for example, neighborhoods—that influence child rearing.

The evolution of Head Start, the federal government's largest and most comprehensive early childhood program, reflects the reorientation of child-oriented programs to provide a significant focus on parents. In the 1970s, the consensus among reviewers of Head Start programs was that the more intensive the parental involvement, the more apparent the difference in children's performance.[7] In contrast to its 1965 beginning as a summer program for economically disadvantaged children, Head Start now mandates parental involvement and has become more differentiated programmatically to include several models that approach parents as primary clients. These include Home Start, the Parent Child Centers, and the Child and Family Resource Program. Home Start is a home-based program for parents of 3- to 5-year-olds that stresses the well-being of the entire family. Services emphasize health, nutrition, and use of community resources. The Parent Child Centers were created to provide low-income parents of children under three years with health, nutrition, social, and education services.

The Child and Family Resource Program is the most comprehensive Head Start demonstration model in terms of the emphasis on families. The program enrolls low-income families whose children are under eight years of age and deals with the entire family to promote growth and development. An assessment is made of each family's strengths and needs, and an individualized program is developed with the family for specific services.[8] A recent review of Head Start by a distinguished group of scholars and national leaders, chaired by Edward Zigler, recommended that features of the Child and Family Resource Program be incorporated into existing Head Start programs.[9]

5. Lois Wandersman, Abraham Wandersman, and Steven Kahn, "Social Support in the Transition to Parenthood," *Journal of Community Psychology*, 8(4):332-42 (1980).

6. Urie Bronfenbrenner, *Is Early Intervention Effective? A Report on Longitudinal Evaluations of Preschool Programs* (Washington, DC: Office of Child Development, Department of Health, Education and Welfare, 1974), pp. 48-50, 55.

7. Fein, "The Informed Parent," p. 170.

8. Ralph Turner, David Connell, and Arthur Reese, "The Preschool Child or the Family? Changing Models of Developmental Intervention," in *Life-Span Developmental Psychology: Intervention*, eds. Ralph Turner and Harry Reese (New York: Academic Press, 1980), pp. 250-74.

9. "Head Start in the 1980's: Review and Recommendations," mimeographed (Washington, DC: Office of Human Develop-

In addition to the parent-oriented Head Start initiatives, a variety of research-based programs has been developed to assist parents in rearing young children. One of the earliest efforts was the Florida Parent Education Infant and Toddler Program.[10] This program trained paraprofessionals to visit low-income mothers and their infants at home weekly to teach games based on research in child development. The mother was the main focus. In another program, in which the mother-child dyad was emphasized, home visitors served as "toy demonstrators" to encourage verbal interaction between mother and child as they played with toys and books.[11] Visits occurred twice weekly, starting when the child was two or three years old. From a research perspective, perhaps the most intensive effort to train parents is the Parent Child Development Center Program.[12] Three different models were developed, differing in participant characteristics and service delivery, in which in-depth education in child care and family life was provided. An array of support services was offered, including health care, social services, and transportation. Two recent programs reflect an interest in social forces external to the parent-child dyad that influence child rearing. One project initiates small clusters of parents to share information about child development and to take action on community issues pertaining to child care.[13] The other emphasizes the importance of support from neighborhood social networks in adjusting to the parenthood role.[14] In this project, groups of neighborhood parents meet twice weekly to explore common problems and interests related to early child rearing.

This brief overview of parent program activity is by no means representative of the field. It does, however, offer a glimpse of the scope of programs aimed at parents and points to the great variance represented by the label "parent programs."

RESEARCH ON PARENT PROGRAMS

What are the short- and long-term effects of parent programs? Are there significant changes in parents' behaviors and/or attitudes and in children's development? What dimensions of parent programs are the most influential? What is the relative impact of parent programs on children compared with child-focused intervention projects? These questions are addressed in the following pages.

Results of evaluations of a variety of parent programs are impressive

ment Services, U.S. Department of Health and Human Services, Sept. 1980).

10. Ira Gordon, Barry Guinagh, and R. E. Jester, "The Florida Parent Education Infant and Toddler Programs," in *The Preschool in Action*, 2nd ed., eds. M. C. Day and R. K. Parker (Boston: Allyn & Bacon, 1977), pp. 97-127.

11. Phyllis Levenstein, "Cognitive Growth in Preschoolers through Verbal Interaction with Mothers," *American Journal of Orthopsychiatry*, 40:426-32 (1970).

12. S. R. Andrews et al., "New Orleans Parent-Child Development Center," mimeographed (New Orleans, LA: University of New Orleans, Mar. 1975).

13. Moncrieff Cochran and Frank Woolever, "Programming Beyond the Deficit Model: The Empowerment of Parents with Information and Informal Support" in *Changing Families*, eds. Irving Siegel and Luis Laosa (New York: Plenum, forthcoming).

14. Douglas Powell, "Family-Environment Relations and Early Child Rearing: The Role of Social Networks and Neighborhoods," *Journal of Research and Development in Education*, 13(1):1-11 (1979).

in showing positive outcomes of a short- and long-term nature. There is little doubt that well-administered parent training programs have an immediate effect on children's intellectual performance and development; there are moderate to significant IQ gains for program children compared with control or comparison children. The evidence indicates that children experience gains in language ability, and several programs have demonstrated increases in personal security and in interpersonal cooperation. In terms of long-term impact, it seems that IQ gains are sustained for about two years and then gradually decrease, although several program evaluations have found significantly high IQs, in relation to control or comparison children, three years after the termination of program participation.[15] When global measures of program effectiveness are used, there are indications that such factors as elementary school grade retention or placement in remedial work are significantly lower for children whose parents participated in a training program.[16]

Changes in parents who participate in training programs have not been studied as much as children's gains, but the data suggest positive change is possible in such areas as use of more complex speech, less authoritarian child-rearing attitudes, and increased confidence in the parental role. Long-term effects are not clear.[17]

Research on the effects of parent programs has been done primarily on parent training programs. The effects of parent support programs are not known at this point.

It is important to note that there are enormous methodological problems in evaluating parent programs. Few evaluations have a randomly assigned control group, and efforts to approximate or compensate for this problem are questionable. There also are problems with possible effects from testing children repeatedly with the same instrument; with a lack of standardized or reliable and valid assessment tools, other than child IQ; and with the potential effects of participant attrition on overall sample characteristics. The great diversity among parent programs presents a hazard of comparing effects across programs. Because of the variance in program content and structure, a question of limited use is, What are the effects of parent programs? A more appropriate question is, What types of parent programs yield what types of outcomes? Moreover, evaluations of parent programs are far from uniform in their selection of variables and assessment instruments. Further, few evaluations have pursued the difficult job of longitudinal follow-up work. Most unfortunately, the vast majority of parent programs do not have evaluation components and where they do exist the design tends to be a simple pre-post test strategy.

While there is evidence of positive outcomes from parent programs, little is known from evaluation work about effective approaches to work-

15. K. Alison Clarke-Stewart, "Evaluating Parental Effects on Child Development," in *Review of Research in Education*, ed. Lee Shulman (Itasca, IL: F. E. Peacock, 1978), pp. 47-119.

16. Irving Lazar et al., "The Persistence of Preschool Effects: A Long-Term Follow-Up of Fourteen Infant and Preschool Experiments," mimeographed (Ithaca, NY: Community Services Laboratory, Cornell University, Sept. 1977).

17. Clarke-Stewart, "Evaluating Parental Effects on Child Development," pp. 47-119.

ing with parents. It seems easier to produce effects in intervention programs than it is to identify specific factors that contribute to success. For instance, an analysis of the effects of 28 programs designed to train parents to prepare their children for school achievement was unable to identify specific program factors that contributed significantly to success.[18] Evaluators have not examined program properties such as mode of instruction, specificity of goals, and frequency of contact in relation to program effects. Information about the dynamics of change within programs is essential to refined analyses of program effects. At present, as Alison Clarke-Stewart has argued, the presumed chain of influence in parent programs—from program curriculum to increased parental knowledge to changes in parental behavior to gains in child development—consists of unfounded assumptions.[19]

A major question regarding the overall effectiveness of early intervention programs is whether a parent-child focus has more impact on children than a child-only focus. This issue has not been explored thoroughly by researchers and to date there is not a definitive answer. It appears, however, that the child development gains are greatest when both parent and child are involved. Urie Bronfenbrenner's analysis of the effects of early intervention programs on children primarily from low-income families suggests that program strategies aimed at parent and child have more impact than child-centered programs.[20] This work has had considerable influence on the early intervention field and is cited frequently in justifications of parent programs. In terms of direct research on this topic, the limited available data are in conflict. Some studies indicate a greater effectiveness of parent-child programs while others point to the superiority of child-only interventions.[21] A comparative study of preschool curricula found recently that programs have more impact when parental education is involved.[22] Most of the research on this topic is confounded by important variables such as age of the child and frequency of program contact, limited in its examination of a range of variables over a long period of time, and post hoc.

CRITICAL PARENT PROGRAM TENSIONS

A critical question regarding the design and delivery of parent programs is the extent to which programs respect and support existing parental practices. Child rearing is a highly value-oriented process that reflects cultural traditions and socioeconomic factors. Parent programs entail a relationship between two or more parties—parent and program workers—who have their own ideas about how best to rear young chil-

18. Barbara Goodson and Robert Hess, "The Effects of Parent Training Programs on Child Performance and Parent Behavior," mimeographed (Stanford, CA: School of Education, Stanford University, 1976).

19. Clarke-Stewart, "Evaluating Parental Effects on Child Development," pp. 47-119.

20. Bronfenbrenner, "Is Early Intervention Effective?" p. 55.

21. Clarke-Stewart, "Evaluating Parental Effects on Child Development," p. 87.

22. David Weikart et al., *The Ypsilanti Preschool Curriculum Demonstration Project: Preschool Years and Longitudinal Results* (Ypsilanti, MI: High/Scope Educational Research Foundation, 1978).

dren. It is highly probable there will be major differences of opinion on appropriate child-rearing methods, especially where middle-class program workers deal with low-income parents. A significant problem is how programs deal with parents whose behaviors and attitudes are at variance with program values and curriculum intentions.

Whose standards of parenting should prevail in parent programs? Concern over the domination of program values has led some critics of parent education to question whether sociocultural diversity might "melt away" through intervention efforts.[23] While there are no systematic data on this topic, clearly there is great potential for conflict. Consider the sensitive matter of sex-role socialization. Middle-class professionals—the staffs of most parent programs—usually are uncomfortable with parental behavior that supports conventional gender stereotypes; it is perfectly acceptable, for instance, for boys to play with dolls. But what if parents abhor the idea of "sissy toys" for boys? How is this issue handled? Do staff assert their authority and make subtle comments of disapproval? Child development values—not scientific fact—are in conflict.

There also is the criticism that programs sometimes place parents in roles that indirectly show disrespect for parents' child-rearing behaviors and knowledge. For instance, there are serious questions about the practice of having parents serve as classroom aides to teachers in the hopes that parents will carry school expectations and curriculum into the home. Apparently the assumption here is that the teacher's behaviors are superior to those of the parent. Should the culture of the school reign in the home? There are other questions as well. First, might not the status of the parent be reduced in the eyes of the child if the parent is to function in the shadow of the teacher's authority?[24] Second, what are the benefits of attempts to encourage parents to act more like teachers? There are important distinctions between the functions of parenting and teaching,[25] and programs that fail to differentiate between the two may undermine valuable parental behaviors.

The context of these program practices—the extensiveness and effects of which are not known—is research done primarily in the 1960s that originally was interpreted as an indication of inferior child-rearing practices among low-income and ethnic minority parents. One of the research claims was that the communication style of low-income black mothers was of a restricted nature in that predetermined solutions often were given and few alternatives for thought and action were provided. This work was used to suggest that poor school achievement of low-income children was due to deficient parental practices and to argue that parental behavior should be modified through training programs. This line of research has been criticized heavily for its use of a white middle-class perspective to interpret a cul-

23. Luis M. Laosa, "Parent Education, Cultural Pluralism and Public Policy: The Uncertain Connection," in *Parent Education and Public Policy*, ed. Ronald Haskins (Norwood, NJ: Ablex, forthcoming).

24. Fein, "The Informed Parent," p. 172.

25. Lilian Katz, "Contemporary Perspectives on the Roles of Mothers and Teachers," in *Current Topics in Early Childhood Education*, vol. 3, ed. Lilian Katz (Norwood, NJ: Ablex Press, 1980).

turally based set of behaviors.[26] The extent to which parent programs currently adhere to this deficit model is not known.

The policy question remains: how might standards of parental behavior be established in parent programs? It is unlikely a program can exist for long without explicit or implicit understanding of what constitutes good parenting. Most social organizations do not function well when they attempt to embrace disparate values. The natural response of a program is to increase the level of congruence between the programs and the parents' child-rearing values. There are several ways to approach this goal, but each may lead to a new set of problems.

One strategy is to create program structures that guarantee parental input into the formation of program policies. This would place parents in the role of decision maker as well as learner. In child-oriented programs there is a history of attempts to give parents decision-making responsibility for staff selection and program policies. In Head Start, for instance, the original mandate was for "maximum feasible participation" of parents, and subsequent legislation added power and clarity to the roles of parents in making program decisions. In recent years, however, the emphasis on parent involvement in child-oriented Head Start programs has been in favor of parent education.[27]

The idea of parents as decision makers is highly controversial. A major problem is the threat of lay control over early childhood workers who have a fledgling professional identity. In parent programs this is intensified with a violation of a sacred tenet of professionalism: it is the professional, not the client, who defines the clients' needs and prescribes remedies.[28] A variant of the decision-making role is a "shared partnership" between parent and program worker. Several recent parent educational programs have attempted this approach.[29] More needs to be known about the negotiation process and power dynamics of such partnerships.

Another program strategy is to diminish the possibility of conflict by admitting only those parents who are sympathetic to the program orientation. A self-selection process among parents might accomplish the same end if program intentions are communicated clearly at the recruitment stage. This strategy is problematic for community-based programs that strive to serve population groups defined by geographic boundaries.

A third approach is to focus on staff behaviors by training workers to be sensitive to and accepting of divergent parental behaviors and attitudes, and/or to make use of paraprofessionals who have characteristics similar to the parent group. This latter strategy, which has

26. Sara Lawrence Lightfoot, *Worlds Apart: Relationships between Families and Schools* (New York: Basic Books, 1978), pp. 159-60.

27. Jeanette Valentine and Evan Stark, "The Social Context of Parent Involvement in Head Start," in *Project Head Start: A Legacy of the War on Poverty*, eds. Edward Zigler and Jeannette Valentine (New York: Free Press, 1979), pp. 291-313.

28. Douglas Powell, "The Role of Research in the Development of the Child Care Profession," *Child Care Quarterly*, in press (Spring 1982).

29. Weikart, *The Ypsilanti Preschool Curriculum Demonstration Project;* and William Kessen et al., "Variations in Home-Based Infant Education: Language, Play and Social Development," mimeographed (New Haven, CT: Yale University, Aug. 1975).

been popular in education and mental health fields in the last decade, assumes that paraprofessionals establish better interpersonal rapport with clients than do professionals. The paraprofessional role in parent programs needs to be studied. Is the expectation of effective relations with parents realized? Do paraprofessionals function as catalysts for program responsiveness to parents, or are they coopted by professionals to serve as messengers in a one-way communication channel from professional to parent?

A fourth strategy is to replace program goals for parents' childrearing practices with assistance to parents in carrying out their desires to enrich parenthood. Parents, not program staff, would generate their own standards of parental behavior. The parent support programs discussed earlier in this article fall within this approach. Selecting and preparing staff to function as value-free facilitators instead of intentional experts on child development are likely to be difficult tasks.

CONCLUSION

From a policy perspective, perhaps the greatest problem facing parent programs is that too much may be expected of them. Certainly they are not a panacea for solving societal ills; a generation free of poverty and crime is unlikely to be produced by these programs. In terms of gains in child development, however, the programs seem to have value. There may be other important benefits that have yet to be uncovered. Clearly the theory and research advanced to date justify further experimentation with alternative approaches to working with parents.

The form and content of parent programs increasingly need the attention of policymakers and program designers. The issues of cultural diversity and parent-staff roles are of too great a consequence to be left for fine tuning in the implementation stage of program development. These are policy decisions that shape the texture and substance of a program, not small program wrinkles in need of a little ironing. Interest in these issues should not stop once decisions on program design are made. We need to know how and why programs work. Efforts to enhance the lives of children through a focus on their parents will advance only to the extent that we unravel the sources and processes of influence in parent programs.

Book Department

INTERNATIONAL RELATIONS AND POLITICS

JAMES A. AHO. *Religious Mythology and the Art of War: Comparative Religious Symbolisms of Military Violence.* Pp. xv, 258. Westport, CT: Greenwood Press, 1982. $27.50.

Much has been written on the subject of war. Indeed much is yet to be written as mankind marches from one kind of war to another. Professor Aho, in this book, makes a noteworthy attempt to categorize the subject in both a philosophical and cosmological aspect—that is, the "art" and the "idea." The book is a challenging work for the scholar but a difficult book for the student or layman, especially because many foreign terms are quoted without being translated. For the scholar, the reference material is an excellent source for study and research. The Bibliography is categorized into divisions. The footnotes are very extensive and lead the reader into an in-depth background of the statements in the text. Many of the chapters have conclusions at the end, which seems to be an excellent way of coming to realize the aims of the author in talking about the various aspects of the subject.

At the end of his second chapter, Professor Aho indicates that war has a meaning to the society both for the victor and for the defeated. Even though he attempts to establish the connection between the religious symbolism of the society and its acts of war, he does admit that "all the combatants are not necessarily motivated religiously." The mythology may, on the one hand, be the philosophical stimulus from which the society drew its idea of getting involved in a war. On the other hand, the mythology may have been used by the society as a rationalization for its military endeavors. In either case there seems to be a connection between mythology and warfare. Professor Aho has attempted to establish this connection with many references to the literature of mythology and the historical records of the wars that have ensued among different societies. He further indicates the ethical requirements restricting the conduct of warfare among some of these societies. In general this book is not one just to be read. It should be thoroughly studied.

SAMUEL J. FOX

Merrimack College
North Andover
Massachusetts

ROBERT W. CHANDLER. *War of Ideas: The U.S. Propaganda Campaign in Vietnam.* Pp. xvii, 301. Boulder, CO: Westview Press, 1981. $28.50.

Lt. Colonel Robert W. Chandler, international political affairs officer in the strategy division headquarters of the U.S. Air Force, veteran of the Vietnam war, and former intelligence officer, in this book demonstrates his ability as a political scientist, international political communicator, and practitioner in propaganda strategies and tactics.

Chandler's book tells the story of propaganda employed by the United States in Vietnam between 1965 and 1972. Chandler says that Americans were trying in this propaganda effort to bring about national unity among the Vietnamese but that the effort was doomed from the start. Barry Zorthian, now of Time, Inc., was architect of the propaganda campaign and its director from 1965 to 1966. He summed up the activity by stating that the American people had had no previous experience in psychological operations such as this Vietnam one.

The book contains numerous quotations and illustrations of the leaflets employed in the propaganda war to prevent communist domination of South Vietnam. Nearly 50 billion leaflets—over 1500 for every person in North and South Vietnam—were distributed in this propaganda campaign. There were also posters, banners, newspapers, magazines, brochures, cartoon books, bumper stickers, matchbook covers, and other printed matter used in this war to win minds. TV and radio broadcasts were also used as were aircraft that flew over communist jungles to deliver word-of-mouth messages. The United States even had minstrels and drama groups carry the message to rural areas.

Chandler concludes that if the United States had in its propaganda worked through rather than on behalf of the Republic of Vietnam, many of the incongruities of the propaganda campaign could have been eliminated and the activity would have been in accord with the psychological patterns of the Vietnamese public. The United States, he says, should have been functioning in an advisory capacity in the propaganda campaign, rather than as the production agency. The South Vietnamese should have been the propagandists. The lesson learned, Chandler states, is that a nation should not try to conduct an unaccustomed communications effort as the United States tried to in Vietnam.

It is regrettable that the book is set in typewriter type, too light to be legible and with too little leading between lines. This makes it inordinately difficult to read. But the book gives so much to a reader that anyone interested in the subject matter will just have to struggle through these difficulties.

EDWARD L. BERNAYS

Cambridge
Massachusetts

EDWARD ANTHONY FESSLER. *Directed-Energy Weapons: A Juridical Analysis.* Pp. ix, 189. New York: Prager, 1979. $19.95.

Can "futuristic" (?) weapons developed by the major world powers be controlled by international law? Directed-energy weapons, a term that includes lasers and particle beam weapons, appear by Fessler's analysis to be beyond international control under the existing principles, definitions, and practices of arms control efforts within the existing U.N. and arms control negotiation systems.

Fessler's able and dispassionate legal analysis should not put the reader off regarding the significance of what he has done. He is alerting us to the fact that scientists and engineers of the modern industrial states under the insistence of military planners are developing new destructive weapons for terrestrial, near space, and space platforms that few of us understand, and that our legal agreements—in fact, the international legal community itself—cannot and probably will not be able to assert any control over them when, not if, they become operational.

But this is the dilemma of world citizenship: our political institutions lag events, and, too often, reality. Fessler, almost plaintively observes that, "one day, it may be possible to employ directed-energy weaponry as a means of arming an international enforcement agency for the purpose of maintaining peace." Fat chance!

That does not mean to say that negotiators should not make an effort to put these directed-energy weapons on the agenda of arms controls discussions when and if the present administration opens negotiations. After all, we have been fairly successful in outlawing the dum-dum bullet.

This is a serious and thoughtful volume that instructs us about many of the legal difficulties mankind constructs in order to maintain the military balances of terror. The successful development of these weapons threatens to tip that balance; hence, Fessler's concern, which should become ours.

JACK L. CROSS

Center for Strategic Technology
College Station
Texas

MICHAEL M. HARRISON. *The Reluctant Ally: France and Atlantic Security.* Pp. xvi, 304. Baltimore: Johns Hopkins University Press, 1981. $24.00.

A magistral study of the French role in the North Atlantic Treaty Organization (NATO), this book focuses chiefly on de Gaulle's policy of French "independence" within the alliance. Most scholars of western defense policy have felt de Gaulle substantially weakened NATO with his insistence on removing France from the military command organization, while retaining the basic alliance arrangement. Harrison comes to a different conclusion, one with important implications for present and future policy. The significant result of de Gaulle's policy, he finds, was to create a genuine national consensus in France on security and defense principles. This accomplishment, a rare thing in French history, not only contributes to the strength of French security, but the fact of French unity is of inestimable service to NATO.

The reasoning that leads to this conclusion is simply that NATO members are so diverse, their domestic politics so complex, and their national pride so touchy, that a "pluralist and tolerant alliance network" is probably the only one with much hope for support. It is also possible that such characteristics, together with enlightened self-interest, might contribute to a future European Defense Community, which both the United States and France have supported in the past.

Though the book was written before Mitterand's election as president, Harrison wisely included a close analysis of the left coalition's various foreign policy positions. These have often been purposely vague and ambiguous in order to achieve acceptance by socialist and communist rank-and-file membership, but over the past two decades have steadily moved toward the same broad national consensus that Harrison attributes to de Gaulle. This is illustrated vividly by official socialist and communist positions on the Strategic Nuclear Force (FNS), the vehicle for de Gaulle's *force de frappe.* In 1965, Mitterand declared simply that the force should be dismantled. In 1972, he merely pledged to interrupt the construction of the force by halting atmospheric nuclear testing. In 1974, he said only that the nuclear force was not his first priority but that he had no intention of disarming unilaterally without international guarantees of security. In 1976, the *Comité Directeur* of the socialist coalition found that the nuclear force was indeed an indispensable means of protecting the independence of a future socialist France. Communist policy, as is characteristic of the party, changed too, but more abruptly. From a position of vehement opposition to such a force before 1977, the Central Committee in that year decided that the FNS alone could protect France against external aggression, since her conventional forces were so weak!

Of more direct concern to Americans is the fact that as early as January 1978 Mitterand declared "the Americans ought to know that we will be loyal allies," a position consistently held since that time, although the communists have never quite abandoned their position that the Alliance is a vehicle for U.S. imperialism.

Thoroughly documented, the book is based on Harrison's doctoral dissertation done at Columbia, revised to take account of recent developments. The result is an excellent and timely review of French policy since World War II, which should be of the greatest value to all students of international and comparative politics.

OLIVER BENSON

University of Oklahoma
Norman

PAUL LENDVAI. *The Bureaucracy of Truth: How Communist Governments Manage the News.* Pp. 285. Boulder, CO: Westview Press, 1981. $24.75.

In the first third of *The Bureaucracy of Truth,* Paul Lendvai takes us on a guided tour of news East of the Elbe. It is an Alice-in-Wonderland world in which the newspapers are without news, planes never crash, and there are no mine disasters at home, only abroad. The rulers are all-glorious leaders.

For as the author points out, the main function of the media in the Soviet Union and its bloc countries "is not to inform the public, but to serve the ruling party. . . . Information is regarded as a state monopoly and any flow of information not subjected to control from above is seen as inherently subversive."

Lendvai does not spare the documentation in proving his proposition. Examples of news censorship, suppression, and secrecy tumble from his typewriter. There is a particularly apt case study of how the communist press treated the visit of Pope John Paul II to Poland in 1979.

While Lendvai's tour may leave the lay reader a bit foot-sore and weary, the journey is definitely worth taking. Our guide is right in believing that this is terrain that is little understood by nonspecialists in the United States and United Kingdom. (The book must have been first published in London in that it adheres to British-style punctuation and spelling.)

Parts 2 and 3 of the book detail the ways that the communist states attempt to maintain a closed society by jamming western radio broadcasts and intimidating foreign correspondents. The analysis may not be as "dispassionate" as Lendvai claims, but his occasional bursts of outrage are clearly justified.

According to the book's dust jacket, Lendvai came to the West in 1957 from his native Hungary, where he had been a journalist. He now lives in Vienna and covers Austrian and Eastern European affairs for the prestigious *Financial Times* of London. His writing style is quite serviceable and even eloquent at times.

Given the current history of the Soviet-backed attempts to impose a "New World Information Order" through UNESCO, and communist violations of the Helsinki Accords, this book is both useful and topical.

STEPHEN HESS

Brookings Institution
Washington, D.C.

J. ROLAND PENNOCK. *Democratic Political Theory.* Pp. xxii, 573. Princeton, NJ: Princeton University Press, 1979. $32.50. Paperbound, $6.95.

WILLIAM N. NELSON. *On Justifying Democracy.* Pp. ix, 176. Boston: Routledge & Kegan Paul, 1980. $16.95.

Over the past 30 years, American political thought regarding modern democracy has come nearly full circle. In the fifties and early sixties, pluralists, claiming that classical theorists had failed to measure how well citizens conformed to the behavioral assumptions of their theories, proposed revisions that attempted to reconcile democratic theory with the findings of scientific political research. In the last sixties and early seventies, their critics argued that the pluralists' revisions were inadequate: they misinterpreted some of the scientific findings, and they compromised traditional liberal-democratic concerns for the benefits citizens are supposed to derive from political participation. The critics of pluralism, however, subsequently failed to develop satisfactory restatements of democratic theory that were both behaviorally plausible and philosophically sound. As a result, since the mid-seventies we have witnessed a resurgence "neoconservative" democratic theory not greatly different from the pluralistic theories of the fifties and sixties. Reflecting this circular development, the analyses in both books reviewed here proceed from pluralist perspectives, even though the authors' main purposes are not to defend pluralism.

In *Democratic Political Theory* J. Roland Pennock provides us with a dispassionate thoroughgoing analysis of a variety of democratic theories. Indeed, he contends that there is no single viable democratic theory: rather, viable democratic theories will derive from a multiplicity of ethical and empirical sources. Accordingly, Pennock's primary aim is to develop an analytic scheme that will serve to clarify our thinking about these theories.

Pennock begins by classifying democratic theories broadly as justificatory and operational. The former deal with ethical questions like liberty and equality; the latter with explanation and prediction of the operations of political institutions or the behaviors of individuals. The two of course interplay, and Pennock is interested in wedding them as he discusses general problems of governance such as representation, responsiveness and responsibility, political participation, rules for decision making, and democratic leadership.

To facilitate this discussion he introduces two operational typologies, one based upon the distribution of political power in society, the other upon the motivations of citizens—human nature if you will. The power typology consists of elitism, populism, and variants of these depending upon the social and constitutional arrangements limiting the exercise of power. The motivational typology is a more complex admixture of normative and descriptive dimensions, but its main motivational categories turn out to be self-regarding individualism in various degrees, public interest, rights and duties—deontology, and collectivism.

In the penultimate chapter Pennock at last reveals something of his true colors. In this judgment the democratic system that has the best potential for meeting both democratic ideals and operational realities is one of functionally and geographically dispersed leadership accompanied by a system of relatively undisciplined political parties. The leadership processes Pennock has in mind, however, involve more than simply obtaining followers' consent by voting. He stresses ongoing intercommunication of feeling as well as ideas between leaders and followers, an "organic-pluralism" as he calls it. And in the last chapter he goes on to defend this sort of system against its critics, identifying it closely with liberal democracy.

On the surface, William Nelson's *On Justifying Democracy* appears quite different from *Democratic Political Theory.* Where Pennock's primary aim is to clarify our discourse, Nelson's aim is to develop a positive theory explicitly justifying democracy. Where each of Pennock's chapters is smoothly written albeit not necessarily connected to the next, Nelson's are more directly connected but written infelicitously with exasperatingly precise qualification. Where Pennock carefully tempers the ethical insights of justificatory theory with the empirical insights of operational theory, Nelson, a moral philosopher, tends to overemphasize the ethical—unintentionally—at the expense of the empirical.

Despite these differences, Nelson ends up defending a conception of democracy similar to that favored by the pluralists, whom he calls democratic revisionists. His justification differs, however: instead of defending his theory as an empirically accurate translation of justificatory democratic values, he provides a moral justification. A well-ordered society is (à la Rawls) a society in which all citizens mutually accept the same principles of justice, and in which the basic social and political institutions are known to satisfy these principles. It turns out the test a law must pass to be adopted in a constitutional democracy—namely, to be found mutually agreeable among the bulk of significant groups of citizens—is analogous to the first test that a moral principle must pass before it can become acceptable in a well-ordered society. Thus, a constitutional democracy tends to lead people to formulate mutually agreeable conceptions of fundamental constraints—morality, and leads them to adopt laws and policies compatible with such constraints.

While the above paragraph necessarily simplified Nelson's reasoning, his argument does not in my judgment adequately account for the fact that other systems of government besides democracy also strive to justify their laws and policies in terms of an agreed upon system of moral constraints. Pennock's warning that the realms of justificatory and operational democratic theory cannot be separated would be well taken here.

Despite the apparent inadequacy of his ultimate justification for democracy, however, Nelson manages to raise some difficult and interesting questions along the way. Why, for instance, is participation in politics good? Why should government follow the will of the people? What is the nature of procedural fairness, and what relevance do economic theories of democracy have to its justification? One cannot help but agree with Nelson's contention that in attempting to answer these sorts of questions democratic theorists have too often confused the definition of democracy with its justification. And if Nelson fails to provide satisfactory answers to his own questions, he nonetheless deserves good marks for raising them in a most provocative manner.

MICHAEL MARGOLIS

University of Pittsburgh
Pennsylvania

LLOYD I. RUDOLPH and SUSANNE HOEBER RUDOLPH, eds. *The Regional Imperative: The Administration of U.S. Foreign Policy Towards South Asian States Under Presidents Johnson and Nixon.* Pp. xii, 465. Atlantic Highlands, NJ: Humanities Press, 1980. $16.50.

This important collection of articles has been available in a different form for several years. Except for the Epilogue, an article by Christopher Van Hollen on "The Tilt Policy Revisited: Nixon-Kissinger Geopolitics and Asia" that appeared originally in *Asian Survey* in 1980, all of the articles were published by the U.S. Government Printing Office in June 1975 as Appendix V of Volume 7 of the report of the Commission on the Organization of the Government for the Conduct of Foreign Policy (the Murphy Commission), created by an act of the Congress in 1973. One wonders what "wider publics" were served by the publication of such a specialized series of articles by a commercial publisher in the United States. The Indian edition, also published in 1980 (by Concept Publishing Company in New Delhi), may make these papers available to an Indian audience that does not have ready access to U.S. Government publications.

An overview by Lloyd and Susanne Rudolph, the principal coordinators—entitled "The Coordination of Complexity in South Asia"—occupies nearly one-fourth of the book. There are 10 case studies, ranging from 18 to more than 60 pages, by competent scholars and government officials, past and present. Four deal with national security, four with economic policy, and two with people-to-people diplomacy. An annex of 30 pages provides "A Chronology of Events in South Asia Bearing on the Conduct of Foreign Policy."

The general tone of all the articles is rather critical of U.S. policy toward South Asia during the Johnson and Nixon periods, and of the attitudes and actions of the two presidents and the organization of the U.S. government for the conduct of South Asia policy.

According to the Rudolphs, "The 'government' for South Asia in Washington as well as in the region, lacks the means to coordinate functional complexity." "Global (or at least extra-regional) objectives were pursued at the expense of U.S. regional interests in South Asia and imperative coordination practiced in ways that isolated presidential level actors from the knowledge and goals of departmental professionals and cut off the professionals, in turn, from formulation of or knowledge about presidential objectives and plans." The most strongly criticized policies were made at the highest levels, with minimal consultation with more knowledgeable subordinates. Examples that are analyzed at length are Johnson's policies of "self-help and short-tether" regarding P.L. 480 assistance to India in 1965-68 and the Nixon-Kissinger "tilt toward Pakistan" in 1971. (On the latter question Christopher Van Hollen's observations are particularly devastating—and Van Hollen was Deputy Assistant Secretary of State for Near Eastern and South Asian Affairs at the time.)

It is saddening to reflect that many of the failures in U.S. foreign policy toward South Asia, and many of the deficiencies in governmental organization and operations that are documented for the Johnson and Nixon years in this volume are still prevalent today. A query posed by Stephen Cohen is still relevant: "Are bilateral ties ('good' relations with India and Pakistan) to be consistently sacrificed to extra-regional considerations?"

NORMAN D. PALMER

University of Pennsylvania
Philadelphia

JOSEPH A. YAGER, and RALPH T. MARBY, Jr. *International Cooperation in Nuclear Energy*. Pp. xxi, 226. Washington, DC: Brookings Institution, 1981. $17.95. Paperbound, $7.95.

International Cooperation in Nuclear Energy is a lucid, dispassionate assessment of two of this country's most consequential events, the global extension of civil nuclear energy and the subsequent horizontal proliferation of nuclear weapons. Yager and Marby examine the nuclear fuel cycle and forecasts developments in fuel use/supply and in proliferation potential for the next two decades under several economic and political constraints. While noting that proliferation is probably irreversible, they suggest market controls and international agreements on fuel supply that might at a minimum reduce incentives for greater dispersion of reprocessing and enrichment plants. These proposals could at least introduce some additional predictability into nuclear proliferation while reducing the probability of weapons development in countries motivated largely by the availability of fissionable materials.

This is among the first scholarly books to acknowledge two crucial facts: that horizontal proliferation cannot be prevented under current political conditions, and that there exists no known solution to the long-term storage problems posed by plutonium and uranium in general or by high-level radioactive wastes in particular. For reasons of immediate physical safety as well as fuel security and political-legal complications, even the better storage places and methods that come to mind are not very good: for an international reactor fuel bank, Colombia, with its long-term rural violence; for spent fuel, burial, such as was apparently implicated in the devasting Soviet chemical explosion at the waste disposal site outside Chelyabinsk in the 1950s. That no new institutional regime can necessarily resolve the dilemma of demand for nuclear power coupled with risks of proliferation does not diminish the usefulness of possible mitigating international arrangements such as those developed in *International Cooperation in Nuclear Energy*.

In later editions or new books, imaginable storage options call for the same rigorous treatment given the fuel supply problem here. The proliferation relevance of the distinction between civil and military nuclear facilities could also merit elaboration, since although reliable military nuclear program information may be restricted, there are societies in which this civil-military distinction may be insignificant and in which weapons development may precede electricity generation by nuclear reactors.

Marby's appendices on the current international nuclear regime and on the export policies of present nuclear materials and equipment suppliers are an integral part of the book and should not be ignored. To enhance the book's value to a general audience, Marby's sections should be read as an introduction to this thorough and highly enjoyable study.

Yager's and Marby's timely contribution will hold a place in the energy and proliferation literature because of its carefully reasoned economic arguments and its awareness of international political verities, including the discriminatory character of arms control to date. The authors' sobering final assessment of the low probability of even the most circumscribed success for horizontal nonproliferation, while a less comforting prognosis than pious hopes and good wishes, provides a firmer guide for the future. *International Cooperation* is a broad-ranging, vigorous interdisciplinary inquiry into an issue whose consequences are potentially unlimited across the lifespan of this planet. Everyone with a serious interest in understanding global nuclear energy politics, including the physical basis for proliferation, should feast their eyes on this book.

T. C. SMITH

Rutgers University
New Brunswick
New Jersey

AFRICA, ASIA, AND LATIN AMERICA

EMILY MARTIN AHERN and HILL GATES, eds. *The Anthropology of Taiwanese Society.* Pp. xi, 491. Stanford, CA: Stanford University Press, 1981. $30.00

Given its traditional focus on so-called primitive enclaves, western anthropology has tended to slight sinological studies. During the past two decades, however, a burgeoning literature on China has signaled the discipline's growing interest in large-scale societies. Most research has been done in Taiwan, the only part of China accessible to western scholars. This collection of essays emanates from a week-long conference held in August 1976 (at Wentworth-by-the Sea, New Hampshire) to provide a systematic assessment of that research.

The major issues and concerns of the conference reflected, often indirectly, throughout much of this volume are: a need to develop an integrated model of Taiwan's social organization and to relate findings to the broader field of anthropology; the problems and analytical implications of small-scale field studies in large-scale societies; the importance of internal versus external forces within social systems; the value of macro- over micro-level studies; the consequences of historical as opposed to ahistorical perspectives; and implications of approaching anthropological work as science or art. Several of these concerns are bound up in the fundamental question of Taiwan's relationship to China proper. There is, for example, general disagreement over the role of cultural traditions as opposed to Taiwan's position in the world political economy in influencing contemporary structures, behaviors, and belief systems. Although some of the articles take the "wider view," seeing social relationships within the Taiwanese society as being shaped significantly by its dependency on successive world powers, for example, Japan, mainland China, or the United States, most contributors approach their data in terms of cultural principles linked to a Chinese past. It is obvious that an integration of these approaches deserves top priority if this ethnographic field is to flourish and if work in this area of the world is to become fully incorporated into the broader social science field.

Essays in the book are—in keeping with the original conference's format—divided into six sections: political organization, local organization, economic organization, ethnicity, the family, and religion. The level of scholarship is uniformly high. Nonspecialists are likely to find the summarizing articles most useful—Edwin Winckler's analysis of political studies, Burton Pasternak's survey of literature on economics and ecology, Lawrence Crissman's review of local and regional studies, and Arthur Wolf's synthesis of kinship work. The articles by Hill Gates and Lydia Kung are of special interest. In the essay on social class and ethnicity, Gates provides a heuristic reconciliation of the work of Frederik Barth and Abner Cohen. Further, by placing Taiwanese class and ethnicity within a broad historical and world perspective, the contemporary social structure becomes dynamically related to modernizing societies elsewhere. The Kung article on young female factory workers raises significant questions about the debilitating impact of labor migration, industrialization, and "economic development" that beg comparative analysis. A final chapter by Sidney Mintz points out a number of methodological and theoretical problems inherent in the Taiwanese material in particular, and in anthropological approaches in general. Of special import to Mintz is the need for anthropologists dealing with the modern world to move beyond the level of "community: to interpret the impact of multilevel systems and extra-community forces."

In reading these works, one has the feeling that the underlying issues were addressed in rich detail throughout the formal discussions, informal interchanges, and seminars of the conference. None of this dialogue is included, but such inclusion would have done much to enrich the publication. It is, nevertheless, a very fine collection of essays, and should serve to bring anthropological sinologists closer to the legitimacy and recognition they deserve.

M. ELAINE BURGESS

University of North Carolina
Greensboro

ROGER BENJAMIN and KAN ORI. *Tradition and Change in Post-Industrial Japan: The Role of the Political Parties.* Pp. iv, 187. New York: Praeger, 1981.

In recent years, modernization theory has been criticized as an unsatisfactory tool in explaining political development. This theory, which holds that political institutions are shaped by socioeconomic conditions, has never been able to explain fully Japanese politics. The continued existence of "feudal" institutions as factions, *habatsu*, and personal support organizations, *koenkai*, for example, in a modern industrial society, is testimony to the shortcomings of this theory.

Benjamin and Ori argue in this volume that collective goods theory offers a better basis for explaining contemporary (and future) Japanese politics and the continued existence of traditional practices alongside modern political institutions. They do this by examining how these traditional forms, specifically factions and personal support organizations, function in contemporary Japanese political life.

Some problems arise, however, in their handling of these issues. In one section, for example, Benjamin and Ori argue that traditional forms have become institutionalized as substitutes for functions normally performed by political parties (such as recruitment), and as a result there is little chance or incentive for the parties to change. Yet the concluding chapter argues that political parties in Japan will have to change.

In another section, the claim is made that Japan began moving toward a multiparty system in 1967 with the "decline" of LDP strength. Yet the 1980 election results elicit the conclusion that LDP strength has been "fluctuating."

Finally, Benjamin and Ori contend that the party system in Japan has achieved and maintained a high level of stability in the face of rapid socioeconomic change, but conclude that we should reject the notion of stability in the system.

In addition to problems of contradictory findings, the volume also suffers from frequent misspellings, the inconsistent use of macrons, and an overreliance on jargon. Moreover, sections on the theory of collective goods in the first chapter and again near the end have little relevance to the main body of material.

To be sure, there are many salutary points to the book. Benjamin and Ori adequately summarize the current state of research on Japanese politics. They currectly make the distinction between mass (or "modern") parties and elite parties and how *habatsu* and *koenkai* function within them. There is an excellent model of factional politics developed from coalition theory as well as a valuable appendix listing faction membership. Most importantly, this volume asks questions that need to be asked. That the answers are often contradictory are perhaps due, at least in part, to the problem of being definitive in an age of transition to a postindustrial society. The conclusion drawn that it is unlikely that the Japanese party system will be able to absorb the demands of this new era presents a challenge to our understanding of Japanese politics in a changing world.

WAYNE PATTERSON

Saint Norbert College
West De Pere
Wisconsin

MARIUS DEEB. *The Lebanese Civil War*. Pp. xvi, 159. New York: Praeger, 1980. $24.95.

This book will attract readers who seek a systematic organization of facts, including the composition and political objectives of competing factions in each stage of the Lebanese civil war of 1975-76. It is divided into separate chapters that deal with the major belligerents'—the Conservative Lebanese Front, the National Movement, the Palestine Resistance Movement, and the Syrian Republic—roles at each stage of the conflict that raged between April 1975 and December 1976. To help facilitate understanding of what was a very complex political and military crisis, Dr. Deeb organizes his discussion of events around seven reasonably distinct phases in the civil war, each marked by some form of attempted settlement, subsequently rejected by one or another of the factions involved.

A key factor in analyzing expectations and disappointments in each of these stages, particularly after the promulgation of the National Movement's reform program in August 1975, is underlined prominently in this book: "Chehabism," on endeavors to achieve social and economic equity across sectarian lines by continuing essentially administrative and government planning reforms initiated in the period from 1958 to 1968 must, in the minds of most Muslim opponents of the status quo, be replaced by direct restructuring of Lebanon's top-level political apparatus. An essential part of such restructuring—after achieving direct legislative representation and doing away with the nearly 40-year-old "covenant" apportioning legislative seats according to "sectarian balance"—would be an executive system in which the powers of the president and prime minister, now Maronite Christian and Sunni Muslim, respectively, would be more clearly demarcated, with the latter more directly tied to the representative authority of a popularly elected assembly.

Dr. Deeb does an excellent job explaining how and why each faction in the 1975-76 civil war reacted to assumed "plots," either to impose general political reforms along these lines, or to evade the threat of change that such recommended reforms imply. There is however, a chief disappointment when he arrives at the compromise election of President Ilyas Sarkis and the establishment of the

Syrian-dominated Arab peace-keeping force at the end of "stage seven" of the civil war. One could expect a book published four years after the conclusion of the 1975-76 period of intense violence to offer at least a chapter indicating how new factors, or continuation of old ones, led the strife-torn republic to further "stages" of civil war after December 1976.

BYRON D. CANNON

University of Utah
Salt Lake City

GAD J. HEUMAN. *Between Black and White: Race, Politics, and the Free Coloreds in Jamaica, 1792-1865.* Pp. xx, 231. Westport, CT: Greenwood Press, 1981. $35.00.

This is a brief history of participation in Jamaican colonial politics by a tiny handful of male, upper-middle-class, free, creole politicos. The era covered [1792-1865] is important because it spans the years during which slavery was abolished in the British West Indies, and the group of men covered is important because they constitute the first nonwhites in Jamaican history to gain political and social standing of any substance.

Coloreds, as distinct from blacks, are a difficult group to isolate in historical documents because descriptions such as "men of color" or "people of color" traditionally have been used to describe blacks, mulattos, quadroons, and several other genetic combinations, including East Indians; the terms are thus as ambiguous as they are usually euphemistic. Thus, Heuman, who has ferreted out a distinct "brown" history and thereby expanded our knowledge of a subject heretofore largely untouched, has incidentally demonstrated his tenacity and his commitment to the pursuit of uncommonly challenging historical research. Happily, too, the results can be read and understood quickly, for Heuman writes in simple, jargon-free sentences with only rare grammatical mishaps. Furthermore, the actual amount of textual material amounts to only about 160 pages, with the remainder being devoted to prefatory material, bibliographies, and appendices.

However, the virtue of brevity may have been overdone in the case of *Between Black and White,* for one is sometimes left with the feeling that only the surface of certain critical events has been scratched. This shortcoming may be due to Heuman's apparent treatment of politics as that which concerns primarily electoral campaigns and the voting records or public statements of assemblymen or governors. A conception of politics as most contemporary political scientists and political sociologists see it, namely, as intimately tied to the social base of the culture, is not entertained here, despite the book's subtitle.

For instance, Heuman makes an excellent point in chapter 6 when he notes that race relations "became more strained after abolition than during slavery" due to a lacunae in formalized norms regulating black/white behavior. This observation provided an excellent entree for the exploration of postemancipation anomie within Jamaican society, including the probable flowering of informal and ultimately unacceptable coping mechanisms, and the impact of these social phenomena on subsequent political strategy and policy making. Unfortunately, however, later chapters provide us almost exclusively with the results of formal decision-making endeavors but deny us an adequate insight into the informal social conditions that spawned them.

In fact, there are enough unexplained situations throughout the book that one is left feeling somewhat the outsider, looking in on something very important but seldom being granted a full view of the meaning to the actors of their manifested behavior. We are told very little, for example, about creole occupations and virtually nothing about their wives, their families, or the general tenor of their domestic life, yet these nonpolitical realities frequently become major reasons why one does or does not take to the hustings, why one votes for or against a proposed public policy, or why certain members are willing to incur political risks while others are not. Thus, after having spent a whole book with Jamaican free coloreds, one is still left with the impression of actually not having met one.

Despite these drawbacks, there are things to learn from *Between Black and White*, not the least of which is that even in an age of rigid caste distinctions, white racial policy was not always based purely on racist ideology; policy in colonial Jamaica seems to have been as much a product of negotiated wrestling over solutions to complex social and economic conditions as of a stubborn determination to promote a particular philosophical position. As for the coloreds, we find described in these pages an emergent petite bourgeoisie that was desperately striving for social mobility and for the preservation of what property, position, and prestige they had in the face of resistance from economically beleaguered white planters and potentially dangerous usurpers arising from a black caste that was becoming socially too close for comfort. Although Heuman accepts the rhetoric of the day as evidence that most free coloreds were loyal to Britain and pursued their political campaigns out of respect for the moral position of the Colonial Office, the weight of the evidence provided in chapters 7 and 8 suggests that the preservation of personal privilege and of newly acquired business and authority interests rather than race, class, philosophy, or patriotism was the motivating force behind most free creole activities during the period under study.

DEAN W. COLLINWOOD

MacMurray College
Jacksonville
Illinois

HAROLD C. HINTON, ed. *The People's Republic of China 1949-1979: A Documentary Survey*. 5 vols. Pp. xv, 2994. Wilmington, DE: Scholarly Resources, 1980. $295.00.

This mammoth and beautifully printed work edited by Harold Hinton includes some 680 documents from the People's Republic of China grouped under various headings and covering the period from 1949 to 1979. The collection is basically chronological in arrangement beginning with Mao Zedong's "On the People's Democratic Dictatorship," 30 June 1949 and ending with "Yeh Chien-ying's Thirtieth Anniversary Speech, 29 September 1979." Volume 1, containing 100 documents, covers the period from 1949 to 1957, "From Liberation to Crisis." Volume 2, containing 112 documents, is devoted to the period from 1957 to 1965, "The Great Leap Forward and its Aftermath," and includes some documents, such as those that reveal the rise of Chiang Ch'ing in the late spring and summer of 1964 presaging the coming Cultural Revolution. Volumes 3 and 4 contain 301 documents and cover the period from 1965 to 1970, "The Cultural Revolution." Volume 5, containing 165 documents, deals with the period from 1971 to 1979, "After the Cultural Revolution."

The collection consists largely of translations previously published by such official agencies as the New China News Agency and Foreign Languages Press of Peking, the American Consulate General in Hong Kong, and the Foreign Broadcast Information Service in Washington D.C. Hinton has done some judicious editing of typographical errors and English grammar, but has avoided any major tampering with the original translations even where they could no doubt have been improved. There is also no indication that any attempt was made to check these translations against the original documents even when readily available.

To enhance the reader's understanding of the documents, Hinton has added a brief but valuable introductory comment to each. There is also a short two-page subject index containing some 58 headings which is repeated at the end of each of the five volumes. It is regrettable that this was not expanded to include, among other things, an index to names and organizations. It would have made the collection much more usable.

The biggest difficulty with a collection such as this involves the decision about what to include, and no two people could be expected to agree. As large as this collection is, it contains only a fraction of the translations of official documents that were spewed forth by various organizations during the period covered. Hinton elected to concentrate on political documents. Since there has been very little emanating from China since 1949 that did not at least have political overtones, this could cover a very wide range indeed. However, Hinton has chosen to interpret "political" rather narrowly. Thus while including such documents as the Labor Union Law and Agrarian Reform Law of 1950, he omits the Marriage Law. He also eschews "anti-American diatribes" as being of "little value or interest" and includes nothing specific on the Korean war, "which for all its importance produced virtually no major published Chinese documentation that was not almost pure propaganda." It is interesting how even in the post-Watergate era the Chinese charges of germ warfare and terrorization of prisoners of war can still be so easily dismissed as "pure propaganda."

Still, we can only be grateful to Professor Hinton for bringing us this extremely valuable collection of important documents. It is certainly a collection that no library can afford to be without. When used in conjunction with other collections such as Jerome Alan Cohen's and Hungdah Chiu's *People's China and International Law: A Documentary Study* (Princeton, NJ: Princeton University Press, 1974) and Mark Selden's *The People's Republic of China: A Documentary History of Revolutionary Change* (New York: Monthly Review Press, 1979), it provides the researcher with most of the important documents available in translation.

W. ALLYN RICKETT

University of Pennsylvania
Philadelphia

HERMAN KAHN and THOMAS PEPPER. *Will She Be Right? The Future of Australia.* Pp. xvii, 199. St. Lucia, Australia: University of Queensland Press, 1982. $18.75. Paperbound, $7.25.

This book deals with the costs and opportunities inherent in alternative Australian futures. Its relevance is heightened by the real-world Australian debate about developmental priorities and strategies that transcends the positions of contending political party groups.

Kahn and Pepper are by now established in this form of projective thinking. The present Australian study includes their model of world economic movements and categories of analysis. It posits futures—basically to the turn of the century—ranging from "more of the same," status quo policies to a substantially reoriented, economically "dynamic" approach. It fits in social, demographic, political, and Pacific basin/international context variables.

Kahn and Pepper conclude that, despite its exceptional natural wealth, even Australia cannot expect a free lunch. "Business as usual" will not produce disaster, but addiction to inefficiency, noncompetitiveness, and indeed, complacency will take its toll, politically as well as economically. To prosper, Australia should sacrifice short-term gains in favor of longer-term benefits. This shift would entail concentration on primary products, Australia's vast resources, and selected, mostly technologically based and comparatively advantaged manufacturing. This would require a stripping down of protectionism: in essence, a considerable rationalization of industry and of employment roles. The authors maintain that, despite some short- to middle-range inconvenience and dislocation, political will plus the judicious application of overseas earnings make this strategy feasible.

Kahn and Pepper conclude, however, that Australia will most likely not be prepared to bite any bullets, at least not very hard, or consistently. The ingrained, "she'll be right," underadventurous idom will probably stick, leading to a "premature" post industrialism well before sufficient and secure wealth has been generated.

However, the book's force of argument is simply not sufficiently elaborated, documented, and carried forward with adequate nuances. The book is simply too thin, and too often smacks of patchwork and superficiality. It is by no means an adequate "guide to action." Even if it were, the foundation on which sound prescription would need to rest would have to be made more solid.

While the present reviewer is inclined to accept much of the analysis, *Will She Be Right?* falls short of providing a sharp, cogent instrument for those who would arrange Australia differently. Nor will it dissuade those to whom the book's conclusions appear to be an assault on venerable Australian practices and prerogatives. In a fashion, Kahn's and Pepper's own forecast that not much is likely to change will probably not be overturned by the book's appeal for change.

HENRY S. ALBINSKI

Pennsylvania State University
University Park

LENORE MANDERSON. *Women, Politics, and Change: The Kaum Ibu UMNO, Malaysia, 1945-1972*. Pp. xiv, 294. New York: Clarendon Press, 1981. $35.95.

One of the neglected areas of scholarship in virtually all social science disciplines, especially sociology and anthropology, is the study of the role of women in politics and change. This unfortunate situation is, however, changing, with more scholars writing about the subject than before and with journals, such as *Signs*, a University of Chicago Press journal on women's studies, being published.

The book under review, *Women, Politics, and Change* . . . by Lenore Manderson, a lecturer in social anthropology at the University of New South Wales, is a pioneering and significant contribution to scholarship on women. Manderson's thesis is "that in Malaysia, despite major historical and political developments, the role of women in essence has not changed: women and men have interpreted the role of women in politics within the boundaries of the traditional interests and concerns of women."

This book is based on the author's Ph.D. dissertation submitted to the Australian National University in August 1977. Field work on this study was conducted in Malaysia from June to November 1974 and from October 1976 to January 1977. The author relied heavily on oral and written sources, published and unpublished, including newspapers and periodicals in Malay and English, and Malaysian government and United Malay National Organization (UMNO) documents and files. The author likewise utilized participant observation, questionnaires, and interviews.

Manderson, in this reviewer's judgment, has attained to a considerable degree her stated purpose in ten substantive and well-organized chapters. The book deals mainly with a description and critical evaluation of the growth of the major women's section of the major party in Malaysia. This women's group, known as the *Pergerakan Kaum Ibu* UMNO, has been the leading catalyst for women's rights in that country. The author documents in great detail the philosophy, organization, and activities of the Kaum Ibu from 1945—the year of formation—to 1972—the height of women's visibility in government. In all her discussions, Manderson tries to focus on the changes in women's traditional interests and roles, especially in the home and the community.

The book is significant for theory, method, and application in anthropology. Manderson demonstrates clearly the idea that the concepts tradition and modernization are never segmented but are a continuity. The author's combination of oral and written sources and the traditional anthropological techniques (participant observation, interview) are very instructive to readers. Her findings will be useful not only to Malaysian society and government but also to scholars and administrators of the Third World concerned with the plight of women in society. The book is well documented with charts, statistics, and bibliographical sources.

In sum, Manderson's book is a pioneering volume of great significance in women's scholarship. Both Manderson and the publisher deserve our gratitude and congratulations for this much-needed publication.

MARIO D. ZAMORA

College of William and Mary
Williamsburg
Virginia

PAUL OQUIST. *Violence, Conflict and Politics in Colombia.* Pp. xiv, 263. New York: Academic Press, 1980.

Paul Oquist's book is about *La Violencia*, a 20-year period of widespread civilian violence in the republic of Colombia that lasted from 1946 to 1966. His study describes the events leading up to this period of violent conflict, deals with its causes and consequences, and analyzes the various social processes that occurred during this momentous period in Colombia's history. The author argues that previous writings on la violencia are unsatisfactory and have provided only partical explanations for this complex phenomenon. Pointing to the lack of an integrated theory, the author offers instead what he calls a sociostructural explanation.

The main hypothesis is that la violencia was not a single process, but rather a whole series of different social conflicts that became intensified as a result of the partial collapse of the Colombian state. This state lost its efficiency and even its physical presence in many areas largely because of a series of intense sectarian rivalries between Colombia's two rival political parties, the Liberals and the Conservatives, both controlled by the country's oligarchy. The partial collapse of the state "conditioned an entire series of social contradictions into conflicts with a high potential for violence." These social contradictions, or conflicts of interests, included a partisan struggle for power between two socially heterogeneous parties; traditional rivalries between villages with "vendetta mentalities"; conflicts over control of local power; land tenure conflicts involving a three-way struggle between large landowners, colonists, and native groups; such phenomena as the forced appropriation of the lucrative coffee crop; and finally, coerced abandonment of agricultural plots due to the threat of violence. Only after two periods of a United Front government following a short-lived military coup did the widespread violence subside as the government slowly regained enough strength, with a little help from the United States, to either suppress or control various social conflicts.

Oquist shows that the greatest violence, especially intense class conflicts that became predominant in the latter part of la violencia, occurred in areas characterized by both the greatest social contradictions and a collapsed state. On the other hand, those areas with either a strong structure of social domination, especially areas of strong paternalistic control where liberals and conservatives worked out an implicit alliance, or where the state maintained its authority and physical presence, most urban areas, were immune to the violence.

To those who interpret la violencia as primarily a conflict between different fractions of the bourgeoisie, he shows that these authors have not been able to identify the groups and leaders that correspond to such specific interest groups as large, semifeudal landowners, industrialists, or "parasitic commercial interests." At the same time he also argues that writers who stress interclass struggles to the point of ignoring intra-elite contradictions have ignored the strong liberal or conservative partisan loyalties of many participants during this period. However, while justly criticizing scholars who have failed to relate the fierce partisan struggle to specific group interests, Oquist fails to specifically answer the difficult question of the relationship between factionalism and class conflict on the national level by stating that the ideological differences between the two leading parties were arbitrary or accidental.

Oquist also criticizes all previous researchers for treating la violencia as a "unitary phenomenon" to be understood by a single set of explanations. However, his alternative structural explanation is not immune to similar objections. He too emphasizes one single underlying factor, namely the "ossified survival" of the nineteenth century two-party political system, which did not allow for any sharing of power with the opposition. Since he does not explain why this pattern of political behavior continued well into the twentieth century in Colombia, he can be accused of harboring a type of "weight of tradition" or "cultural lag" thesis. His saving grace, however, is that he does spell out exactly what makes Colombia structurally different from other Latin American nations; namely, that class struggles involving the "popular sectors" coincided with intraclass disputes involving the traditional hierarchy which, in turn, coincided with the emergence of a politically active middle class.

The absence of any bibliographic references to the many works in political anthropology on local level politics indicates a lack of awareness of a literature that could well have added insights into his own analysis. Oquist's case study is sophisticated and logical, though not free from some unnecessary jargon more typical of sociology than history. Despite these minor omissions and several misgivings due to my own intellectual biases, I think Oquist's book is an impressive piece of work that will provide a real challenge for other researchers.

F. J. SCHRYER

University of Guelph
Guelph
Ontario

THOMAS Q. REEFE. *The Rainbow and the Kings: A History of the Luba Empire to 1891.* Pp. 306. Berkeley: University of California Press, 1981. $24.95.

The Luba-Lunda empires have never enjoyed the popular fame of those precolonial African states that emerged as modern political units, like the Swazi, the Sotho, and the Tswana, or those that fought large-scale colonial wars, like the Ashanti and the Zulu. Yet these great empires of the savanna were among the largest and most highly organized of precolonial states, the Luba Empire at its height stretching from the borders of Angola and Zambia to Lake Tanganyika. Moreover, like all the greatest African states, this was an autochthonous empire that owed nothing to international trade—which was indeed eventually to destroy it. The Luba Empire remained insulated from international trade until the mid-nineteenth century, enjoying a symbiotic relationship with its own regional trade, which it both fostered and fed upon. Great traditions of art, metalwork, music, and praise-poetry developed within the state, as well as extensive mechanisms for tribute bearing, lineage connection, and peripheral control. By the late nineteenth century these states provided the Victorians with powerful evidence of their oft-repeated assertion that peoples of the savanna were racially and culturally superior to those of the forest.

Thomas Q. Reefe's book reads like a familiar story that nevertheless bears repeating. He provides the most complete survey of the Luba myths of origin, and demonstrates well the extent to which each of the episodes operated as metaphors for both significant characteristics and the sanctions of the state. He makes some attempt to correlate the myth variations in various parts of the state, and illustrates well the power of the myth to engross peripheral lineages into it. He makes fresh attempts to disentangle the kinglists, well informed by David Henige's skepticism about the too-literal use of oral tradition in historical chronology. Because there are no written sources for Luba history until the nineteenth century, the eighteenth-century expansion and crises of the state are clear enough in outline, but sketchy in chronological precision. Reefe does what he can with the available traditions. Finally, he describes the irruption of Arab-Swahili ivory and slave traders, together with European explorers, hunters, and missionaries, from the mid-nineteenth century, providing a useful new survey of a now very familiar story.

This is very much old-style state history. Reefe seems to have made no attempt to collect popular traditions, family histories, or above all, economic information. Those anxious to derive some impression of life within the Luba Empire, of the socioeconomic cycle of village and community, and the extent to which the Empire really impinged upon it, will be disappointed. We learn little about the degree of economic specialization, the role of particular craft and trading groups, and, while there is a great deal on trade, the reader remains hazy about the articulation between the economic and political mechanisms of the state. In all this, Reefe was perhaps constrained by the particular concerns of the period of his field research in the early 1970s, but more seriously, there is nothing on the role of art and music in the state, and the author never pauses to provide a picture of how the Luba court actually worked, how the officials operated, and how relations with the periphery were maintained. Perhaps the title, *The Rainbow and the Kings,* is intended to signal Reefe's primary concern with myth, but the fact is that the second half of the book moves into a detailed survey of disruption that cries out for matching detail on the local manifestations of the Empire. The book is a valuable reworking and reordering of the myths and history of the Luba kingdom, in the light of modern historical skepticism and understanding of the role of myth, but it breaks little new ground in the more detailed understanding of the state.

JOHN M. MacKENZIE

University of Lancaster
Lancaster
England

ARYEH Y. YODFAT and YUVAL ARNON-OHANNA. *PLO Strategy and Tactics.* Pp. 225. New York: St. Martin's, 1981. $22.50.

Scholarly analysis of the Palestine Liberation Organization (PLO) has not kept pace with the organization's evolution from one or several Palestinian actors to the internationally recognized representative of the Palestinian people. *PLO Strategy and Tactics* redresses this neglect by providing a comprehensive, up-to-date survey of the PLO's aims and activities together with an examination of its labyrinthian structure.

In addition to reviewing well-known events, each of the book's three sections offers new insights. Chapter 1 dissects the ambiguous PLO reaction to Anwar Sadat's peace initiative, striking militarily against Palestinians, Egypt, and Israel while publicly expressing an apparent willingness to recognize Israel. Chapter 3 explains the paradox of the Palestinian National Covenant precluding PLO acceptance of any land transfer from Israel. Chapter 4 explores connections between the diverse ideologies of the various parts of the PLO and the geographic origin of their members by distinguishing between Palestinians from the coastal plain and from the mountains. The authors illuminate in Chapters 5 and 6 international influences, including Sino-Soviet relations and Soviet success and failure in the Arab world affecting Chinese and Soviet attitudes and policies toward the PLO. Detailed appendices of organizational charts and documents complete the book's substance. The work's richness fades, however, by treating relations between Western Europe and the PLO as an afterthought even as they have led to a virtual recognition of the PLO by the European Community.

Unfortunately, the substantive informational contributions are diluted by four interrelated problems: the book's argument is insufficiently articulated, it is not unbiased, the book's organization is unclear, and its command of English is modest. The central concern of the book seems to be the PLO's ideological commitment to destroy Israel, which Yodfat and Arnon-Ohanna suggest derives from a perception of the "Palestinian problem," a term they fail to define clearly. There are three components to the Palestinian problem. What is Palestine? Who are the Palestinians? Who represents the Palestinians? Only the last question is treated explicitly.

If ideology is the primary determinant of the PLO's tactics and strategy, as the authors seem to argue, then it should precede, not follow, a review of PLO activities. This organizational confusion is compounded by what reads like an awkward translation. These failures detract seriously from the book's value, and sadly they may be more attributable to a publisher's failure to edit and translate than to the authors' inability to present their case.

LILY GARDNER FELDMAN

Tufts University
Boston
Massachusetts

EUROPE

GARY B. COHEN. *The Politics of Ethnic Survival—Germans in Prague 1861-1914*. Pp. xvii, 344. Princeton, NJ: Princeton University Press, 1981. $27.50.

Cohen's book definitely fills a gap, documenting what happened within just 50 years. At the outset of this period, Prague was, on the surface, a German city, while five decades later the German ethnic group had almost lost its struggle for survival. A sociologizing historian, Cohen draws an analogy between the same struggle waged, with analogous results, by the Swedes in Finland and the Germans in Estonia and Latvia, proving that there was little the once domineering ethnic groups could do, surrounded by the high tide of the local population in the century of nationalism. It is fascinating to follow how this powerful upper-middle-class and middle-class minority divides, changes, develops new political structures, without really being able to challenge the nationalism of the majority, with which it shares some common interests.

Like the other two cases to which Cohen draws our attention, the Prague Germans were not a colonial elite, but people deeply rooted in the city and in the country which progressively excluded them. The weakness of Cohen's approach is that the fate of the Prague Germans in the researched period cannot be explained only on the ground of sociopolitical data. The phenomena is a strongly cultural one—the Prague German literature dominating this aspect—and this is how it will mainly be remembered, as it was exactly in this period when this cultural originality reached its peak.

From a sociopolitical point of view, Cohen's study whets the appetite for a continuation that would examine what role the German and German-Jewish ethnic minority played in the new capital of Czechoslovakia after 1918, what dilemmas it faced at the end of the 1930s, and how it confronted the fact of Prague again becoming for a short period a city governed by the Germans, this time under Hitler's flag.

A. J. LIEHM

University of Pennsylvania
Philadelphia

JAN AKE DELLENBRANT. *Soviet Regional Policy: A Quantitative Inquiry into the Social and Political Development of the Soviet Republics.* Pp. 192. Atlantic Highlands, NJ: Humanities Press, 1980. $30.00.

This book seeks to apply the western theory of social mobilization to a communist nation—the Soviet Union. Dellenbrant investigates three hypotheses in the process: (1) modernization has been on the increase; (2) geographical distribution reveals increased equality between regions; and (3) the more social mobilization, the more political recruitment. The author relies on statistical analysis as he proceeds through his data.

Dellenbrant generally confirms two of his three hypotheses; the one on equalization remains unconfirmed. He further concludes that all of the union republics show impressive socioeconomic development: urbanization, education, production, communications, and standard of living. However, differences in levels of development among the republics appear as great in 1973 as they did in 1956. As one might anticipate, the Central Asian republics continue to lag behind the RSFSR (Russia) and the western republics. Even in recruitment of new party members, the above differences continue.

Dellenbrant clearly demonstrates that the Soviet Union is modernizing significantly as supported by a large amount of quantitative data. He also proves that the "haves" (western republics) and the "have-nots" (Central Asian) remain in their respective positions in receiving benefits from the Soviet largesse. Thus, the communism of the Soviet Union is a consciously developmental process of political rule, but it is not a very equalizing type of rule.

RICHARD C. GRIPP

San Diego State University
California

BEATRICE FARNSWORTH. *Aleksandra Kollontai: Socialism, Feminism, and the Bolshevik Revolution.* Pp. ix, 432. Stanford, CA: Stanford University Press, 1980. $28.50.

The emergence of modern feminist movements in the West has generated an increased interest in the problems facing Russian and Soviet women and in the effect the October Socialist Revolution has exerted on the fate of the family institution in Soviet Russia.

Professor Farnsworth examines in her book the personal life and political activity of Aleksandra Kollontai, one of the leading personalities in the prerevolutionary Russian socialist women's movement, and a key figure in Soviet politics of the early post-revolutionary period who has been, at one time or another, a member of the Communist Party Central Committee, a commissar of public welfare, the head of the party's C.C. Women's Section, and the first woman ambassador.

Most of the book, nine chapters out of twelve, cover less than a decade in the life of Kollontai, and deal with the period up to the middle of the 1920s, when Kollontai was removed from real power and sent abroad on a diplomatic assignment. She was victimized for advocating radical and controversial policies related to problems of women, the family, marriage, and communal living, as well as for her participation in different splinter groups opposing the policies of Lenin. The personal and family life of Kollontai is presented against the background of the general political atmosphere of immediate post-revolutionary Russia, with particular emphasis on the development of the new Soviet laws and policies defining and regulating the place of women in the new socialist state. Much attention is devoted in the book to the work of different political and administrative bodies in which Kollontai participated, as well as to her relationship with other leading bolshevik women, such as N. Krupskaia,

I. Armand, S. Smidovich, E. Stasova, and others.

The Kollontai that emerges from the pages of the book is an impulsive, highly idealistic, spontaneous woman. She is, however, also controversial and ambivalent. The daughter of a tsarist general and aristocrat, she advocates the expulsion of nonproletarian elements from the party. She advocates freedom of speech and criticism within the party but she has no tolerance for those who oppose her demands for the introduction of vague, sometimes impractical, reforms in family living.

Beatrice Farnsworth appears to sympathize with the idealism of Kollontai and with the causes she has been fighting for. She seems to identify with her heroine, and she often takes issue with those who oppose and criticize Kollontai. Yet she fails to give a convincing explanation as to how it was possible for Kollontai to survive the Stalinist purges. It is evident that Kollontai compromised her conscience. For the few comforts and privileges she has been granted by the Stalinist regime, she sacrificed her idealism and her faith in socialism and women's equality by supporting Stalin's opportunistic foreign and internal policies and by agreeing to rewrite the history of the bolshevik revolution.

Despite Farnsworth's somewhat subjective approach to the treatment of her subject, the book under review is a valuable addition to western studies of the turbulent 1920s in Russia. It is well researched and documented, and only opening the archives in the Institute of Marixism-Leninism in Moscow, where Kollontai's manuscripts are stored, could perhaps shed new light on the subject under investigation and fill in the missing and unexplained links in the fascinating biography of Aleksandra Kollontai.

N. N. SHNEIDMAN

University of Toronto
Ontario

EMMANUEL LE ROY LADURIE. *Carnival in Romans.* Trans. Mary Feeney. Pp. xxiv, 426. New York: George Braziller, 1980. $8.95.

This book is the third magnificent creation of one of the world's finest historians. In *The Peasants of Languedoc* (1966), Ladurie taught us to perceive "the immense respiration of a social structure." With reference to the Province of Languedoc he showed us the truth of Malthus for the preindustrial order. He demonstrated clearly how food production dictated the population curve as well as the entire economic, social, and cultural life of the people of Languedoc from 1500 to 1700.

In *Montaillou: The Promised Land of Error* (1975), he used the records of an inquisition in early fourteenth-century southern France to examine the total way of life of a medieval village. Ladurie's examination ranges from the subtle and intimate matters of sex, marriage, incest, and priest sexuality as well as language, gestures, magic, superstitions, and folklores, to matters of social relations, economics, and crime. In effect, Montaillou becomes for Ladurie the microcosm of the traditional rural order.

Carnival in Romans also is a study of the world in microcosm. In the study of a horrible massacre that occurred during carnival time, 1580, in one small, southwestern French town (Romans, population 7500-8000), Ladurie seeks the nature of revolt in sixteenth-century rural France. Describing introductorily the meaning of the carnival in Romans, Ladurie writes in his preface, "Fifteen-eighty was the eye of the hurricane, a period of relative calm between two equally devastating phases, the first infused with Calvin's spirit, the second inspired by Loyola." As for the Dauphine revolt's popular leagues, which flourished just before and after the carnival in Romans, with a few specific exceptions "they were led neither by devout

Catholics nor by monks. They simply regrouped craftsmen, peasants, and bourgeois, each of whom defended its own profession or social interests, and was willing to fight for them if need be." In the most general terms, class warfare was the key to the struggle that occurred in Romans and the countryside.

Carnival was in fact the climax of a vast regional revolt. The majority confronted, at ever desperate levels, the problem of diminishing population, shrinking income, and increasing expenses and taxes. "It was," in Ladurie's words, "a rebellion against government and taxes." This tax rebellion—one of so many that filled the world of that time—set craftsmen in the village against the city government, and the bourgeois and peasants in the countryside against the nobles, outlaw noble armies, and ultimately the crown itself.

In his study Ladurie compares and contrasts types of revolt in preindustrial Europe. On the one hand, he finds that "the 1579-1580 episode in Romans was a nearly perfect example of class struggle." On the other hand, although the revolt in its middle-class and peasant grievances anticipates the French Revolution, it is not a modern revolution. Class alliances were not pure—the interests of the upper bourgeoisie in the city are not the same as their interests in the countryside; class reactions were not homogeneous—for example, not all types of craftsmen participated equally in the rebellion; the *Lumpenproletariat*—the thieves, the prostitutes, and the destitute—did not enter the revolt; and most importantly, the ideology of equality—equality of law and citizenship—did not exist.

In the microcosm of Romans, Ladurie also offers us a cross-section of sixteenth-century society. He makes us vividly aware of how much that world, in contrast to our own, was rural and organized around status and the smaller communities of religion, work, village, and region.

Ladurie concludes his work, "An isolated incident, the Carnival in Romans illuminates, reflects on the cultures and conflicts of an era. These include strictly urban struggles, municipal problems which set the craftsmen and the butcher trade in opposition to the patrician ruling group; traditional peasant agitation molded into an assault on a system of landholding that was becoming aggressive, capitalistic; the violent rejection of the government and taxes, both revealing of social conflict. There was also a place for the Catholic, medieval, Renaissance, and soon to be baroque folk traditions of festivity; the bourgeois, semilearned, and semiegalitarian ideologies drawing inspiration from classical authors. . . . The Carnival in Romans makes me think of the Grand Canyon. It shows, preserved in cross section, the social and intellectual strata and structures which made up a 'tres ancient regime.'"

Yet, in addition to offering us a social and mental stratigraphy of sixteenth-century France, Ladurie does something else that every historian should do. He tells a good story. A terrible story! He tells us how one representative of the patrician class, Judge Guerin, organized a real purge during Carnival—when the world was turned upside down and poor taunted rich and vice-versa. Ironically, tragically, what was pretended and feigned became brutally real in Romans Carnival, 1580. The leading representative of the craftsmen was killed outright. And with Romans secured for the patricia, Guerin successfully directed the forces of authority against the rebels in the countryside. Great numbers were killed. Carnival—the world of illusion and mask—turned cruelly real. Guerin, victor, built his fortunes out of his defeat of his enemy, craftsmen leader Paumier. In fact, the Guerin family crest was created by a crudely savage play on words: the crest became the uprooted apple tree, *le pom-*

mier (Paumier arrache). The God of Carnival could have been no more hideous that year. Few stories from the dark era of the St. Bartholomew's Massacre are more hideous than this one told by Ladurie's darkly magnificent *Carnival in Romans.*

JOSEPH AMATO

Southwest State University
Marshall
Minnesota

JILL STEPHENSON. *The Nazi Organization of Women.* Pp. 246. Totowa, NJ: Barnes & Noble Books, 1981. $22.50.

At first glance Nazi Germany would seem an unlikely topic for a monograph written from the women's study viewpoint. Nazi organization, society, and, most especially, Nazi ideology would seem almost "neolithic" to the modern scholar of women's studies. Stridently chauvinistic in theory as well as in practice, the Nazis were absolutely certain about women's place in society. It was in "Kirche, Kuchen, and Kinder," as "wives, mothers, and homemakers." However, as with most other aspects of Nazi Germany, social reality did not correspond with Nazi ideological myths. Women were indeed needed in Nazi political and administrative life, emphatically so during the brutal last years of the war. In their policy of *Gleichschaltung,* the Nazis attempted to coordinate all social, economic, and political associations. This meant that all groups in German society had to be oriented to the ideological and organizational models of Nazi mythology. Just as much as labor unions and churches, women's associations had to be coordinated.

The prototype of the Nazis' women's association, the *NS-Frauenschaft,* predated the Nazi seizure of power. This group is the central focus of Professor Stephenson's pioneering monograph. Professor Stephenson analyzes the history of this Nazi women's group from the Nazis' emergence in the 1920s as a minor extremist group to their demise in 1945. It is a remarkable study, rich in detail, tightly reasoned, and superbly organized.

The monograph's conclusions bring no surprises to either scholars of women's studies in general or the Nazi era in particular. As was the case with men in the Nazi era, only a small minority of women were Nazi fanatics. The German masses were in the main apathetic to the ideals of these zealots. In the main, women's associations were window dressings for the Nazis, with the exception of the war years. Women in Germany even more than in America underwent changes in economic roles due to the exingencies of the war effort. Far less than in the United States, this transformation was not because of ideological preference.

JOHN S. WOZNIAK

Fredonia
New York

THORPE, D. R. *The Uncrowned Prime Ministers.* Pp. xv, 263. London: Darkhorse Publishing, 1981. Distributed in the United States by Humanities Press, Atlantic Highlands, N.J. $20.75.

Austen Chamberlain, George Curzon, and R. A. Butler—the three subjects of D. R. Thorpe's novel study—each appeared destined, one almost writes inevitably destined, to rise to the position of leader of the government in Britain. None of them ever achieved that role. To be sure, Thorpe points out, bad luck played a significant part. Chamberlain and Butler lacked the driving opportunism—the word is not used pejoratively—that climbing to the top of the greasy pole requires. Curzon had his full measure of that quality, but he had the ill-fortune to be a Peer at a time when Labour was emerging as the official opposition. Since it was unrepresented in the House of Lords that fact meant to many that the prime minister must be in the Commons where he could answer the Labour leader with full authority.

But each case was different. Chamberlain had two opportunities, in November 1911 above all, when his reluctance to split the Conservative Party by an all-out contest with Walter Long led to Andrew Bonar Law's first round of leadership, and in October 1922 when his loyalty to the Lloyd George coalition again led to Bonar Law's leadership and subsequent brief prime ministership. Eventually, Chamberlain had a notable tenure as Stanley Baldwin's foreign secretary, but clearly he could have had the premiership—had he really wanted it. An unwillingness to compromise on principles or his conception of the conservative party's interest combined with a reluctance to fight for the top prize ensured that he would not.

Curzon, born with every advantage, viceroy of India at the age of 39, breathtakingly ambitious, assumed that he would be chosen to succeed a dying Bonar Law in May of 1923. Stanley Baldwin, his major rival, was not quite the unknown that some popular accounts make him out to have been. Curzon, waiting in sleepy Montacule House, in the country beyond the reach of a telephone, was insulated from the discussions that quite clearly suggested to George V that the prime minister must be a member of the House of Commons. The blow was a bitter one to Curzon; one is tempted to comment that it was not so bitter for the country.

Butler came nearer the premiership than either Chamberlain or Curzon, in January 1957 when Harold Macmilian succeeded Anthony Eden and in October 1963 when Lord Home took up the reins from Macmillan. In 1957, Butler wanted the leadership, but he was a waverer in the Suez crisis and got the worst of both worlds. Probably simple physical weariness was a factor in his failure, although Harold Macmillan's ringing success as minister of housing had put his claim in the forefront of consideration. In 1963, the situation was different. Butler was already a one-time loser and he simply did not convey the aura of confidence to make him appear an electoral asset. Somehow, despite his great intellectual gifts he never learned to fight for his own advantage.

No very satisfactory generalizations come out of this study. About the best Thorpe can suggest is that the most important assets for a successful assault on the top post are patience, luck, opportunism, and the absence of enemies. Above all, the absence of enemies. The principle of negative choice, which was strong in the Conservative party, dictated the failures of Chamberlain, Curzon, and Butler.

HENRY WINKLER

University of Cincinnati
Ohio

VALENTIN TURCHIN. *The Inertia of Fear and the Scientific Worldview.* Pp. xviii, 300. New York: Columbia University Press, 1981. $19.95.

This is a book of many parts, some excllent, others less so. It is divided into three main sections, entitled "totalitarianism," "socialism," and "totalitarianism or socialism?" But within these three are some 80 distinct subsections. In treating so many topics in fewer than 300 pages Turchin has created for himself a formidable task. Even with superb organization and logical topical arrangement—qualities which, unfortunately, the book does not possess—doing justice to the multitude of subjects considered would be very difficult. As it is, the many short essays—some are snippets of only one or two pages—give the book the lurching, stop-and-go quality of a slow local train. The reader, doomed to travel the route Turchin has laid out, may well abandon the trip in frustration before the end of the line. This would be a shame, for there is much to be gained by the persevering reader.

Valentin Turchin was a leading Soviet physicist until his dissident activities led to his emigration to the United States in 1977. His aim in this book is to sketch his ideas concerning a twentieth-century socialism based on a modern scientific world view. This scientific socialism is very different from its Marxist namesake. As a backdrop to this new socialism, Turchin first makes an analysis of totalitarianism. On this subject the author is at his best, perhaps because of his first-hand experience with the machinery of totalitarianism during the 1970s. His treatment of the subject is not a sustained, rigorous analysis, but it does contain a number of useful and suggestive insights, and his discussion of totalitarianism as a dynamic, developmental process—according to Turchin, Soviet totalitarianism is now in the third or "steady state" phase—could provide the basis for making the concept a more useful analytical tool.

Turchin describes socialism as "the religion of the future global civilization." What is this religion to be based on? A scientific world view of the twentieth century which is fundamentally different from its nineteenth-century counterpart. This new scientific world view is relativistic rather than absolutist. It carries over into attitudes toward society as well. It rejects "immutable laws" and a single "correctly" structured society. As Turchin puts it, "In all its aspects, modern science is striving to make us evolutionists, and gradualists in politics."

The two main themes of the book, then, concern the stages of totalitarianism and the development of a new non-Marxist scientific socialism. That these matters are returned to again and again suggests not only that the author considers them important but also that the book could have used substantial editing to make it less repetitive. As it stands, the book is a brilliant but disorganized analysis whose major asset may be the numerous intellectual gems scattered through the text. The review will conclude by quoting three of these:

> Everyone must solve in his own way the dilemma that the totalitarian society poses before anyone in a creative profession: conscience or work. Most of the people who are called 'decent' sacrifice their work in part and their conscience in part [P. 14].

> [By the late 1960s] the Great Fear of the Stalin era no longer existed, but the *inertia* of fear was still at work. The founders of the new system had not labored in vain: terror had left its mark. It lurked in the nooks and crannies of consciousness. It mutilated souls. It altered notions of ethical values—of good and evil. [P. 19].

> Marxism is deficient not because it is a form of religion (that is one of its virtues), but because it does not want to admit openly that it is a religion, and because it is based on a stage in scientific thought that has been superseded [P. 132].

DONALD D. BARRY

Lehigh University
Bethlehem
Pennsylvania

LAWRENCE L. WHETTEN. *Germany East and West: Conflicts, Collaboration, and Confrontation.* Pp. 215. New York: New York University Press, 1980.

Whetten's academic and governmental background, including 20 years of residence in Europe, uniquely qualify him for this study, sponsored by the Council of Foreign Relations. Although the writing is at times turgid—highlighted by an 18-line sentence on page 30—the book represents one of the best analyses of the relations between the German Social Democrats and the communists in the East and between the Federal Republic and the German Democratic Republic, and their relationships with the major powers.

The most important and ambitious chapter deals with the evolution in the conceptualization and conduct of Soviet foreign policy as it relates to Germany and U.S.-Soviet relations. The author notes that by 1985 the United States will have a land-based ICBM force of no more than 650 older generation Minutemen III. If the Soviets continue to modernize existing ICBM systems and those under development, they could enjoy a six-to-one advantage in useful payload and possibly a numerical advantage in reentry vehicles. Whetten observes that the B-1 was cancelled without a reciprocal Soviet concession or the provision of an adequate alternative: "Under these circumstances, there is likely to be adverse effects on American threat perceptions, arms-control negotiations, and domestic pressures within the United States to correct the anticipated imbalances."

"After the age of innocence passed for the Carter Administration," he says, "political cinfidence no longer rested on the notion of self-regulation, but reverted to the sounder concept of reciprocity and interrelating agreements on negotiable issues." The highest Soviet foreign policy priority still is "to manipulate the relationship [with the United States] for the advancement of the 'historic forces.'" Whetten refers to the western advantages of a stronger economic base and political freedoms, which he believes provide the West with "crucial leverage" in its relations with the Soviet bloc. But while he had previously referred to growing Soviet conventional and nuclear military capabilities, he omits mention of these in his summation. It is hard to see what leverage the West has, confronted by superior Soviet power in every sector.

In his conclusion, Whetten states that one unforeseen complication of *Ostpolitik* has been that "it has diversified the social structures of the GDR, making them potentially both more fragile and brittle." This diversification suggests that "new forms of political pluralism may be emerging in the GDR." This observation, together with Whetten's tendency to see substance and success in Ostpolitik generally, are open to question.

The left-wing of the SPD, and now former Chancellor Brandt's endorsement of the Nordic Neutral Zone (as outlined by the USSR) continue to accommodate GDR and Soviet objectives, to the detriment of the FGR and the United States. The swing to the CDU, notably in West Berlin, and the developments in Poland—Whetten is quite optimistic about the prospects of the Polish government—suggest that conclusions about the success of Ostpolitik and detente are premature.

ANTHONY T. BOUSCAREN
Le Moyne College
Syracuse
New York

UNITED STATES

ALEINE AUSTIN. *Matthew Lyon: "New Man" of the Democratic Revolution, 1749-1822.* Pp. xii, 192. University Park: Pennsylvania State University Press, 1981. $16.50.

Historians of the American Revolution have concurrently studied the effect of this break from British control on social, economic, and political relations within and between the former British colonies. Was the American Revolution an internal revolution as well? And if it was to a conservative degree, what factors contributed to the forging of a more democratic ideology and politics? Aleine Austin's brief biographical study of Matthew Lyon, a "'new man' of the democratic revolution," addresses these questions. She concludes that Lyon's "emergence as a political leader signifies the entrance of a new breed into American political life after the Revolution."

Based on limited available primary sources, Austin surveys the economic and political career of this recent immigrant (1764) and indentured servant. Austin describes Lyon's rise to successful entrepreneur and manufacturer during the revolutionary and postrevolutionary eras, political leader in Vermont and the Jeffersonian Republican party, and trenchant critic of the Alien and Sedition acts (being the only U.S. congressman indicted and convicted under the Act). Austin then recounts Lyon's decision to move to Kentucky in 1801, subsequent business activities, reelection to Congress (1803-1810), and eventual failures in business and politics.

Lyon emerges from this study as a complex, but contradictory personality —democratic only in the political and social spheres, challenging the aristocratic and deferential politics of the Federalists and of postcolonial society and politics. Lyon's business career highlights the conservative dimension of postrevolutionary America. Lyon both benefited from and consciously sought government assistance in the success of his business ventures, no apparent qualms about conflict of interest, and was committed to a system ensuring only equality of opportunity and not equality in principle.

Both because of the limited availability of primary sources and Austin's failure to explore in depth and with sophistication Lyon's political and economic philosophy, this study has limited value to the student of the impact of the American Revolution. It supplements, to a degree, other monographic and general studies; for that it is a welcome and helpful contribution.

ATHAN THEOHARIS

Marquette University
Milwaukee
Wisconsin

PHILIP L. DUBOIS. *From Ballot to Bench.* Pp. xi, 318. Austin: The University of Texas Press, 1980. $22.50.

Philip Dubois's book is a timely, important, data-rich analysis of a judicial catch-22: by what best means can state judges reach the bench and be both accountable to the public and yet politically independent? Several dilemmas are present. First, judicial races are generally regarded as low saliency contests by voters and thus voter turnout is lower than for other statewide races. Second, judges are prohibited by the code of judicial conduct from entering the fray of electoral politics by campaigning for office in the manner of other politicians. Third, voters know little about the qualifications of candidates in judicial elections with the result that ballots are often marked without any meaningful information to support that choice. Fourth, in those instances where there is voter interest, it is often because of the unpopularity of the judge's past decisions rather than the incumbent's judicial qualifications.

The debate over the best selection process has taken several paths. Until the mid-1800s, judges were chosen by the legislature or by the governor with confirmation by the legislature. Then elections became popular, first partisan and later nonpartisan. In 1937, the American Bar Association's proposal of a "merit plan" took root. Under the merit plan process a nonpartisan judicial nominating commission selects three names for each judicial vacancy. The governor appoints one to the vacancy who later appears on a merit retention noncompetitive ballot for a public vote. Rarely is a judge turned out of office. The promise of this plan, often called the Missouri Plan, is that judges will be of higher caliber, will be more independent, and will be more accountable to the public than judges elected in partisan or nonpartisan elections. As Dubois demonstrates however, there is scant evidence to support these suppositions.

Dubois, a political scientist, uses the claims of the Missouri Plan as a yardstick to determine whether or not the other selection procedures fall short. His analysis covers all statewide elections from 1948-1974 for justices of state courts of last resort in the 25 nonsouthern states that utilize partisan, nonpartisan, or merit retention systems. Dubois's effort is the first to systematically analyze judicial election data within a longitudinal comparative framework for different selection systems. Additionally, he analyzes partisan voting on eight state supreme courts. He may have taken on too much as well. The fine points of the study can get murky when one sorts though local, informal, and professional norms, the political cultures, and the varying degrees of political party influence in the states as they influence the selection system. However, this is a minor criticism.

Dubois does not set out to fashion an argument for a new judicial selection procedure but his findings certainly illustrate the need for one. He effectively debunks the claims of the merit plan proponents, demonstrates that accountability is best realized in the partisan ballot and that politics permeates all methods, but finds none of the selection systems promotes both accountability and judicial independence. This is a scholarly, well-documented work that will be invaluable to those involved in judicial voting behavior, public law and judicial selection systems.

JOHN H. CULVER
California Polytechnic
State University
San Luis Obispo

DON E. FEHRENBACHER. *Slavery, Law, and Politics: The Dred Scott Case in Historical Perspective.* Pp. viii, 326. New York: Oxford University Press, 1981. $16.95.

This volume is an abridgment for nonhistorians and students of Fehrenbacher's 1978 Pulitzer Prize-winning study, *The Dred Scott Case: Its Significance in American Law and Politics.* It covers the same ground as the original, omitting half the text and the lengthy, annotated footnotes. The *Dred Scott* decision (1857) ranks high among the critical events leading up the Civil War but until Fehrenbacher, it had not been put in the full legal and political context it deserves. In *Dred Scott* the Supreme Court for the first time struck down a major federal law. Yet the case had modest beginnings. Scott, a Missouri slave who had lived with his master for several years in Illinois and the Minnesota Territory, initiated a petition for freedom in 1846 on the grounds that his residence on free soil emancipated him. This was a fairly common suit in Missouri and usually ended in freedom. But when postponed by technicalities and appeals, it got caught up in the hardening sectional attitudes of the 1850s toward slavery in the West and the verdict truned against Scott.

The issue of slavery in the territories had long been a part of American politics. The Missouri Compromise of 1820 had offered what seemed like a permanent solution by prohibiting western slavery north of 36° 30′ while leaving the rest undecided. But the question was reopened during the Mexican war when the Wilmot Proviso threatened to outlaw slavery south of the line as well. When the Kansas-Nebraska Act of 1854 repealed the Missouri Compromise and permitted all territories to have slavery if they wanted it, northerners feared the institution would spread to free northern lands. The more Congress fumbled with the question, the more people began to desire a judicial solution that might be more permanent. Thus it was no surprise that when *Dred Scott* finally reached the Supreme Court, Chief Justice Taney used the occasion to make a broad statement on the slavery question that went far beyond the narrow boundaries of the case. Taking a partisan, proslavery position that was backed by the court's southern majority, Taney declared that Negroes were not citizens and had no right to sue for freedom in federal courts. The Missouri Compromise, he said, was unconstitutional because it deprived slaveholders of the right to take their property into all federal territories. Needless to say, instead of solving the slavery question, this decision merely aggravated the problem. Its effect, though, was short-lived since the Twelfth, Fourteenth, and Fifteenth Amendments to the Constitution virtually nullified *Dred Scott.*

Throughout this rather complex narrative, Fehrenbacher remains both lucid and eloquent. He never loses sight of his main objectives despite the meticulous research that even this abridged version reveals. Only when discussing Taney himself, whom Fehrenbacher depicts as an abolitionist-hating southern extremist, does his evenhanded approach break down. This obvious bias aside, Fehrenbacher builds his argument with great care from the legal antecedents of the early republic through the case's rather small impact on post-Civil War law. In the final analysis, Taney's decision displayed an "extraordinary cumulation of error, inconsistency, and misrepresentation, dispensed with . . . pontifical self-assurance." Taney was the radical innovator; by contrast, the two dissenting northern judges followed established precedents in upholding the Missouri Compromise and declaring Scott free. Many of the murky questions associated with *Dred Scott* have been cleared up by this book. It is unfortunate that Fehrenbacher could not find enough evidence to discover the motives of those involved in it, although he does refute the long-held notion that *Dred Scott* was deliberately contrived by abolitionists as a test case.

In all, this is an important, absorbing work. Like in many recent legal studies, law is placed thoroughly within the political and social framework of the period. Indeed, the case itself occupies less than half the text. While scholars may regret the lack of documentation beyond a brief bibliography and students may encounter trouble because of the failure to define many important legal terms, this shorter edition of Fehrenbacher's work should appear to a broad readership.

DOUGLAS E. BOWERS
Agricultural History Branch
U.S. Department of Agriculture

RONALD L. FEINMAN. *Twilight of Progressivism: The Western Republican Senators and the New Deal.* Pp. xiv, 262. Baltimore and London: Johns Hopkins University Press, 1981. $18.50.

This book examines the relation between 12 western progressive Republican senators and the policies of Franklin Roosevelt. Feinman deals primarily with domestic concerns, although he examines as well progressive isolationist attitudes as World War II approached.

He emphasizes that the progressives, never a homogenous block, never voted unanimously to support or defeat major legislation, although they were closer perhaps in foreign policy than in any other area.

The progressives generally disagreed with Hoover's attempted solutions to the Depression, but were reluctant to favor Roosevelt publicly for election. When he won office, however, they supported enthusiastically his public works projects. Despite such support they refused any cabinet or other government position. Fiercely independent and highly principled, they would compromise neither principles nor independence. This attitude, Feinman argues, rendered them less influential than they might otherwise have been had they worked formally as a group.

Gradually the progressives grew estranged from Roosevelt for many reasons. They thought the president was at least partially responsible for the tragic death of Senator Bronson Cutting. They opposed vehemently Roosevelt's attempt to pack the Supreme Court. And as Roosevelt himself grew more concerned about inflation than depression and began to cut government spending for public works from 1938 on, he naturally alienated those progressives who believed public works essential for a sound economy and employment for the "common" man.

Bitter disagreement over foreign policy increased their alienation. Save for George Norris of Nebraska, they opposed every step by which Roosevelt pushed Congress and the nation from the neutrality of 1935 to open support for Britain by 1940.

The book moves forward well and amasses a great deal of evidence to support its conclusions. Perhaps its greatest weakness is that it seldom shows, and perhaps cannot show conclusively, how much influence the progressives had on Roosevelt. Policies both favored the president would have probably pursued anyway, and those the progressives disapproved of, such as the attempt to pack the Supreme Court, he pushed regardless of their opposition. The reader knows how Roosevelt stood with the progressives, but is not so sure of how they stood with him.

Although Feinman is alive to their shortcomings, he admires the progressives' honesty and integrity. He points out that, after Vietnam and Watergate, Americans can certainly appreciate progressive concern that the presidency was taking too much power unto itself at the expense of Congress.

FRANKLIN B. WICKWIRE

University of Massachusetts
Amherst

LEWIS L. GOULD. *The Presidency of William McKinley.* Pp. xi, 294. Lawrence, KS: Regents Press, 1981. $15.00.

This volume admirably fulfills the purpose of the American Presidency Series which the editors describe as "presenting historians and the general reading public with interesting, scholarly assessments of the various presidential administrations." Of all the presidents, McKinley has been one of the most controversial. Conservatives have generally seen him as a man of character and principle who used the tools at hand—patronage, press, and prejudice—to accomplish worthwhile goals, while liberals have regarded him as the last of a series of colorless, spineless post-Civil War presidents, a mere tool in the hands of political boss and manipulator Mark Hanna. In this latest scholarly reassessment Gould takes a stand somewhere between the extremes but essentially tilts in favor of McKinley. His conclusion is that McKinley was "a political leader who confirmed the Republicans as the nation's majority party; he was the architect of important departures in foreign policy; and he was a significant contributor to the evolution of the modern presidency."

Although elected for two terms, McKinley had served only four years and a few weeks when an assassin's bullet struck him down. Any estimate of his place in history must be based mainly on his record in war and diplomacy. There is irony in this situation because the election of 1896 was fought primarily not on the basis of foreign but domestic policies. Not yet recovered from one of the worst depressions in its history the nation's main concern was financial: the gold standard versus bimetallism. Oddly enough, once McKinley was in office the money question was solved more or less providentially. It was foreign policy questions, the revolt in Cuba and Spain's brutal attempts to put it down, that required attention. McKinley is often portrayed as following a policy of drift and at last going to war with Spain because of propaganda and jingoism. Gould maintains, on the contrary, that "McKinley sought to persuade Spain to relinquish Cuba peacefully and then turned to war when it became apparent that Madrid would never acquiesce. His diplomacy 1897-98 was tenacious, coherent, and courageous." When war came McKinley used his powers as commander-in-chief to the full to control and direct the efforts of the military to achieve the goals established by civilian authority. As every textbook in American history makes clear, the war department was not ready for so vast an effort and there were weaknesses in leadership, organization, and particularly, support. But McKinley can hardly be blamed for these inadequacies which were the results of years of neglect and he moved as quickly as he could to correct them.

Following the military and naval victories there was the question of the peace treaty with Spain. In the process of winning the war the United States had picked up the Philippines. The questions now were whether the United States should turn them back to Spain, turn them over to some European power, allow them their independence, keep one or two strategically important islands, or keep all of them. Gould suggests that the oft-repeated story about McKinley receiving devine guidance on this matter after several nights of prayer may be a bit fanciful. McKinley's final instructions to his peace commissioners to take all the islands "were the logical culmination, indeed the inevitable result of the policy that he had pursued since the tentative news of Dewey's victory."

HARRY L. COLES

Ohio State University
Columbus

LEON HURWITZ. *The State as Defendant: Governmental Accountability and the Redress of Individual Grievances.* Pp. xv, 211. Westport CT: Greenwood Press, 1981. $27.50.

In the chaotic growth of modern society the individual is being coerced, conformed, and threatened in new and unique ways by social and economic changes very often fostered by his increasing impersonal and remote governmental structures.

Professor Leon Hurwitz of Cleveland State University considers the western nations' attempts to come to grips with these tangled relations of its people to oft-times insensitive and impenetrable bureaucracies, whose edges are beginning to curl from the smoulder of disenchantment. The book begins with a historical overview of governmental accountability that states Hurwitz's theme that:

> The ability of a private citizen to complain against his or her government, and have a reasonable expectation that the complaint will be heard and acted upon in an impartial manner, is a relatively new development in the Western historical and political fabric.

In this first chapter he moves perceptively through the thoughts of the pre-Christian Greeks, touching on the views of Confucian China, Hindu civilization; the turbulent periods of Hobbes and Locke; and effortlessly transports us to the bitter conflict between former President Nixon and the press culminating with a discussion of what Hurwitz calls the "west's abnormality," indicating that:

> the *West's abnormality* is only of recent vintage, because for most of their history, even the Western democracies refused to permit the state to be placed in the uncomfortable position of defendant. Much of the European experience (and by extension, the American experience) leading to the contemporary avenues of redress was basically a process of overcoming the doctrines of rex gratia dei and sovereign immunity.

There then follows a series of chapters on various means that western nations have attempted to deal with the problem through varied systems of political and legal redress. The procedures described in chapters 2 through 4 relate to society's more institutionalized avenues of redress available to the individual vis-à-vis the state.

In chapter 5, the author views parliamentary political activity which he finds ebbs and flows according to the political realities of the day, and which is attuned to the contemporary atmosphere, such as President Carter's linkage of human rights to American foreign policy.

He then moves gracefully in chapters 6 and 7 to the public supranational institutions, such as the European Convention on Human Rights, indicating that some societies have progressed one step beyond domestic avenues into the area of collective internation guarantees of the individual right to expect humane treatment from one's government. If, after all domestic avenues have been exhausted, the individual still believes his rights have been violated by governmental action, such a person can then "appeal" to a "higher authority," for example, a supranational institution or a private transnational agency, such as Amnesty International.

In his concluding, none-too-optimistic chapter Hurwitz shares his view that although the institutions and processes described in the book are not daily household concerns with widespread media coverage, and although few individuals are directly affected, they have nonetheless had some impact.

While much more could be said about the multifarious and diversified ideas expounded in this complex book, which has an appeal to the historian, the sociologist, the political scientist, and the lawyer, perhaps the most important role of this book is that the author clearly intends it to serve as a catalyst to whet the appetite of the reader and to provoke further examination and exploration as to what measure of justice and sensitivity can be brought to the relationship between the citizen and his rulers.

JUDGE GERALD L. SBARBORO
Circuit Court
Chicago

DOUGLAS KINNARD. *The Secretary of Defense.* Pp. 252. Lexington, KY: University Press of Kentucky, 1981. $19.50.

This book's principal claim to originality is its comparative analysis of six secretaries of defense who had the greatest impact on the development of the national defense establishment. Three themes, according to Kinnard, emerge from this analysis: the interdependence of the defense budget, domestic politics, and strategic policy; the dependence of the secretary's role on his president's interest and style in managing national security affairs; and the declining influence of the senior military. The case studies of individual secretaries are essentially synoptic overviews of the administrations that these secretaries served with emphasis on defense politics.

Kinnard assigns considerable importance to James Forrestal's lack of sufficient authority to lead the defense establishment as a key factor shaping his tenure. Without that authority he was perennially unable to extract agreement from the Joint Chiefs on a force structure to implement "containment" that did not cost more than Harry Truman's political requirements allowed. Charles Wilson and Neil McElroy enjoyed much greater statutory authority than Forrestal, but they never utilized the full potential of that authority because their president, Dwight Eisenhower, was in large measure his own secretary of defense. Kinnard suggests that their lack of government experience and ignorance of military affairs may have been positive qualifications so far as Eisenhower was concerned.

The first defense secretary to fully utilize the position's authority was Robert McNamara, who in Kinnard's opinion achieved the highest degree of centralized civilian control over the military of any secretary. However, his main instrument of control—the Systems Analysis Office—created an adversarial relationship with the Joint Chiefs and turned defense-oriented senators against him. When he dissented from Lyndon Johnson's policies on the Vietnam war, he found himself politically isolated.

Melvin Laird skillfully avoided isolation, even though excluded from important policy areas by Richard Nixon's centralization of foreign and national security decision making in the White House through Kissinger's National Security Council staff. Laird, unlike McNamara, had a natural political base in Congress and the political instincts to mobilize the Joint Chiefs behind his programs. By emphasizing a team approach to management, downplaying systems analysis to a supporting role, and trading a promise to rebuild in the post-Vietnam area for military support of withdrawal, he preserved dominance over the defense establishment and a strong position within the administration.

James Schlesinger followed Laird at a most difficult time. Withdrawal from Vietnam, congressional reserve about military expenditures, Watergate, and Kissinger's invincible position within the administration presented formidable obstacles to anyone who wished to press a security policy at variance with détente. Although "probably the most qualified person ever to have assumed the office," Schlesinger's broad government experience and status as an eminent strategist were insufficient to keep him in office when his public statements made Gerald Ford appear "soft on defense" heading into the battle for renomination against Ronald Reagan.

The case studies are executed with confidence and clarity, but conceptual underdevelopment and unexamined assumptions occasionally marr the overall effect. For example, Kinnard makes general statements about the "success" of each secretary without indicating the basis for such a judgment. McNamara is said to have been the most successful at establishing "control" over the military, but his means of control were, in the long run, damaging to morale and disruptive of his own ability to lead the defense establishment. Kinnard's admiration for technocratic skills reappears in his judgment of Schlesinger as "most qualified," but his study of Laird provides ample evidence that if preservation of the military's willing obedience and ability to extract congressional consent while serving the president loyally are the ultimate standards of success, then political savvy is the primary qualification. Kinnard is sensitive to these issues and makes intelligent observations about them but never deals with them in a systematic fashion. As a contribution to social science, the book also is open to criticism for failure to integrate its findings with existing theory, particularly in organizational behavior and bureaucratic politics. But readers will find it very useful as a concise introduction to the history of one of our most important public offices.

WILLIAM S. TURLEY
Southern Illinois University
Carbondale

ARTHUR S. LINK et al., eds. *The Papers of Woodrow Wilson*, vols. 34-36. Vol. 34, pp. xv, 567; vol. 35, pp. xxii, 563; vol. 36, pp. xix, 684. Princeton, NJ: Princeton University Press, 1980-1981. $30.00 each.

These volumes make their stately way toward the true Armageddon of the 1910s: America's intervention in World War I. The arguments respecting that era have long been raked over. Yet Wilson's full role in its affects estimates of present crises as well as past.

Volumes 34 and 35 show an odd imbalance between vital American drift into an antagonistic posture toward Germany, and Wilson's personal life. Literally scores of pages are devoted to letters expressing Wilson's love of Edith Bolling Galt which are a clear repeat of his far earlier letters to his first wife, Ellen Wilson, during their courtship and after. They are different in tone from the passionate letters Wilson directed to Mary Allen Hulbert while married. An apparent, though as it proved, unreal fear that the Hulbert letters might be made public creates a crisis in Wilson's mind in which he admits "platonic" love for Hulbert—"a folly long ago loathed and repented of" which he has tried to "expiate by disinterested service and honorable, self-forgetful, devoted love," that is, to Mrs. Galt. Mrs. Galt emotionally promises to stand by him, and volume 35 sees them married.

Mexican revolution and Haitian chaos form part of a pattern that needs to be read through the haze and complexities of present-day Third World and imperialist controversies. Bryan, pushed out as secretary of state, and Theodore Roosevelt, hot for an armed America, are both despised by Wilson and his associates. Mrs. Galt is violent in her hatred of Roosevelt, and there is certainly brashness in his scorn of Wilson's "elocution substituting for action," and Roosevelt's belief that no one owes allegiance to a president unless he shows "loyalty" to the country. But Bryan, though he seems fatuous to Colonel House for wanting for America peace at any price, is in retrospect part of a peace movement that deserved much more regard than either House or Wilson gave it.

Wilson declares that "the people of this country count on me to keep them out of the war." But he and House and Secretary of State Lansing are plainly on England's side. They do not want Germany to win, and, misled by Earl Grey and other English spokesmen, no more than hope for a compassionate Allied peace. But there are pitfalls in action that create pitfalls in thinking. Wilson's attempts to force Great Britain to let cotton—used in munitions—on to the continent are in part due to pressure from southern cotton growers. Also bluntly economic is Secretary of the

Treasury William McAdoo's urging of credit to Great Britain for the purchase of war materials: "To maintain our prosperity, we must finance it."

Preparedness budgets vie in Wilson's mind with responses to the central powers' efforts to fight the British boycott of goods and arms to the continent. Wilson's "freedom of the seas" slogan does not include free trade with Germany. It would "greatly prolong the war." This can only mean that Wilson wants an early German defeat. Yet he negotiates so cautiously on German submarine sinkings as to draw the praise of the pacifist Oswald Garrison Villard. The nuances of policy, however, are less real than self-deceiving. It is typical of the *Papers'* tendency that to American Ambassador Page in London, the German government's willingness to "come down" from defense of a submarine sinking is no evidence of humanity or willingness to compromise, but of German military weakness, itself a doubtful estimate.

The actual horrors of war at sea and on land continue to elude these *Papers*, except in some emotional passages in Ambassador Page's reports from London. There is poignancy in many of the 1915-1916 exchanges as they seem to sustain American nonintervention and promise peace for America—a peace we know is not in waiting.

What is lost in this era is an older progressivism of peace and domestic concerns that gave a sense of unity to ethnic and labor and other American elements. Newton D. Baker, a Cleveland Progressive, becomes secretary of war. With Brand Whitlock in Belgium and Frederic C. Howe as commissioner of immigration for the Port of New York, Baker is one of the very few seasoned Progressives still visible. The Progressives will lose credibility for their part in bringing America into the European war. It helps with perspective a bit to follow Wilson's battle in these volumes to put Louis D. Brandeis on the Supreme Court, in the face of rock-hard malice and patently reactionary lies.

It is tragic that American willingness to help build a League of Nations, dangled temptingly by Britain's Earl Grey, involves Wilson's dreams of future peace more than it does those of the larger public. This means that he and House will be free to operate with fewer outer checks that inner checks. House's confidentiality with British leaders, unbridled, is dismaying, unless one agrees that England had to win the war for future peace to be assured.

Volume 36 features Wilson coming "out from the seclusion of Washington" to tour the country and put his eloquence to the cause of preparedness. His tour and rhetoric are well received, despite the caveats voiced by the antimilitarists. The entire campaign reads strangely like the reverse of his postwar tour and campaign for the League of Nations.

Wilson's preparedness addresses protest that his sole goal is peace. But a telegram from House in Paris criticizes the German Ambassador Bernstorff's proposed apology for German action at sea because it mentions freedom of the seas: "It will irritate the Allies and give Germany hope where there is none." Meanwhile, another campaign is in the offing: the presidential election in November. It will provide a modern opportunity to examine the role of the electorate as well as of the president.

LOUIS FILLER

The Belfry
Ovid
Michigan

LAURENCE E. LYNN, Jr. and DAVID deF. WHITMAN. *The President as Policymaker: Jimmy Carter and Welfare Reform.* Pp. xiii, 351. Philadelphia, PA: Temple University Press, 1981. $19.95. Paperbound, $9.95.

Laurence Lynn's and David Whitman's objective was to explain how U.S. presidents can mold policy making so that their programs have the greatest chance of success. To this end they examined welfare reform under Presidents Roosevelt, Eisenhower, Johnson, Nixon, and Carter with heavy emphasis on Carter. Lynn and Whitman found that all except Carter formulated welfare programs that were enacted by Congress in something near their original form and which in some sense worked administratively. In January 1977, Carter announced that Housing, Education, and Welfare Secretary Joseph Califano would finish a comprehensive welfare reform plan in three months which would then be presented to Congress. The plan that was ultimately sent to Congress, two years later, was neither comprehensive nor did it receive congressional approval. Carter's failure could hardly have been more complete.

To understand this result, contrasts between Carter and successful welfare reform presidents were drawn. The other presidents were able to fit their welfare policies into their presidential master plans and were able to make these conceptions clear to others; avoided becoming enmeshed in technical detail not important to their central aspirations; used people close to them to maintain original policy directions; kept themselves informed of policy-making progress and interceded when events went awry; controlled conflict within their administrations; and recognized the deeply political nature of welfare reform—especially in terms of Congress—and acted accordingly. Carter did none of these things. Little attention was devoted to the reasons for his dismal performance, but Lynn and Whitman speculated that the most important were, not surprisingly, his personality and inexperience in Washington.

This volume harkens back to a major point made by Richard Neustadt in *Presidential Power.* When a president is trying to induce subordinates to act against their will or merely to do something novel it is not enough for him to simply issue orders (especially ones as vague as Carter's) and then sit back waiting for them to be fulfilled. His subordinates will find ways to bend the president's words to their interests, and when there are many subordinates, all with different and often conflicting interests, the nearly inevitable result is paralysis and confusion.

This is an excellent case study of occurrences in a complex policy area, and it has all the virtues and drawbacks that one might expect in such a work. It may be too much for someone with a general interest in policy formulation but without a desire to delve into the intricacies of welfare reform; it will be a rare reader who stays with every twist and turn of the long descriptive chapters on welfare reform in the Carter administration. But it is this same length and detail, as clearly presented as the subject matter permits, which makes Lynn's and Whitman's generalizations convincing.

CARL GRAFTON

Auburn University
Montgomery
Alabama

RICHARD NEELY. *How Courts Govern America.* Pp. xvii, 233. New Haven, CT: Yale University Press, 1981. $15.00.

This book is not likely to replace Cardozo's *Nature of the Judicial Process,* nor was it intended to do so. Richard Neely, the author, serves as Chief Justice of the West Virginia Supreme Court, a court to which he was first elected at age 31. This made him at that moment the youngest judge of a court of last resort in the English-speaking world. It did not necessarily make him a judicial philosopher, however, or even a very keen student of the American governmental and political system.

Now apparently reflecting upon a decade of experience, Chief Judge Neely offers his highly popularized, frequently irreverent, and remarkably oversimplified view of the political role the courts play in American "democracy." His views of the other branches of government and of American politics in general rarely rise above the level of caricature. They do, however, seem to fit his own characterization of his approach: "cheerful cynicism." Indeed, if the American governmental-political system (minus the courts) were to conform to Neely's interpretation, one doubts that even the most idealized court system would be able to save "democracy" from its own excesses, trivialities, and corruption.

It has to be said in all fairness, that Neely is not at all pretentious about his book nor does he hide his own anti-intellectualism. His preface frankly acknowledges a willingness "to draw a few generalized conclusions" about the evolution of the Anglo-American legal systems. In his first chapter one is warned that he will show why court systems must perform political functions by dwelling on the "dangers" of other institutions rather than on their "strengths." This is possible because the strengths of the other institutions, we are told, "are adequately handled in eighth-grade civics books." Neely is perfectly candid in telling the reader that "the intellectual, theoretical courses at Yale Law School [from which he graduated after Dartmouth], seemed nonsense to me—all form and no function." Further, he continues: "It is a sad fact that I earned a C- from the great Alexander Bickel in Constitutional Law, because I could never understand what was going on in his course." So much for judicial self-restraint.

Judge Neely is a judicial activist who sees the courts as a bulwark of our "democracy." One wishes he would slow down enough to go back and read Number 78 of the *Federalist* papers, that quaint old essay.

JOHN C. DONOVAN

Bowdoin College
Brunswick
Maine

DAVID M. O'BRIEN. *Privacy, Law, and Policy*. Pp. xiv, 262. New York: Praeger, 1979. $21.95.

DAVID M. O'BRIEN. *The Public's Right to Know: The Supreme Court and the First Amendment*. Pp. x, 205. New York: Praeger, 1981. $21.95.

We think of the Free World as that part of the planet in which a man's house is his castle, a haven from all official intrusions. Those who disagree with us will fight to the death for our right to give voice to our disagreement. Within the limits of the law of libel, our newspapers are free to report what their reporters see and what their editors think. Realities may fall short of these ideals, but the contrast with the totalitarian world gives meaning to the value of freedom. We still retain more than enough freedom to make clear the distinction between free and unfree, but many forces combine to prevent the growth of freedom.

Here is a pair of treatises that explores the great strains on freedom in America. The men who framed our Constitution assigned a primacy to liberty of the citizen and were remarkably prescient in providing for it. Nevertheless, to keep that Constitution in good working order has required a Supreme Court with special talents for adjusting the tensions between the principles laid down in that constitutional consensus of 1791 with the requirements of national defense, the advance of technology to heights undreamed of in the eighteenth century, and the sensitivities of elected officials and their supporting casts of bureacrats. O'Brien sweeps through the history of constitutional law as to the right of privacy and the right to know. His command of case law is exhaustive. As a good political scientist, he has not been content with comparing the niceties of reasoning from one justice to another; he has roamed through social science in search of principles and ideas. His sense of proportion keeps him modest; he has no new doctrines to lay down, but it is improbable that any of the important arguments on these matters have escaped him.

Privacy is a word that cannot be found in the Constitution, but the right to it is readily inferred. Rights to freedom of religious belief, to freedom from unreasonable search and seizure, and the right to refuse to incriminate oneself all are grounded on a fundamental right of privacy. It may not be in the Constitution in the literal sense that uninstructed "strict constructionists" would like, but life, liberty, and the pursuit of happiness cannot mean what they say unless the right of privacy is to be preserved. Until 1965, the Supreme Court had no special difficulty in finding enough privacy rights in the First, Fourth, and Fifth Amendments to strike down threats to this freedom. But in 1965, faced with the need for a theory that would prevent the government from meddling in contraceptive practices in the bedroom, the Supreme Court decided that in addition to the Bill of Rights, the implicit right of privacy might as well be made explicit. The decision in *Griswold* vs. *Connecticut* (381 U.S. 479) was a landmark in stopping for good and all the state's interference in the marketing of condoms and diaphragms; it was also a landmark in establishing a constitutional right of privacy that is independent of the Bill of Rights. The reasoning adopted by the Court and expressed in Justice Douglas's majority opinion was uncharacteristically metaphysical, with unlawyer-like references to a constitutional "penumbra" from which there "emanated" certain rights. It remained for a less sophisticated Congress to conclude in the Privacy Act of 1974 that "the right of privacy is a personal and fundamental right protected by the Constitution of the United States." Short work was made of the Court's agonies, though what entitled the Congress to make such a determination is not made clear. It was a prelude to an important statute that limited the processes whereby federal agencies may acquire, store, and disseminate information about citizens. That built a fence around the American cottage, which is certainly no castle. Constant vigilance will keep it in repair.

To create a constitutional doctrine that establishes and protects the privacy of the citizen is a laborious and as yet uncompleted task. The definition of terms is perplexing; it is notoriously difficult to assign a meaning to the word privacy that is suited to use in a statute. O'Brien is especially useful in his review of the numerous attempts at a rigorous definition and describes with precision the flaws that have been found in each.

Is it an exaggeration to suppose that more importance is now attached to the right of privacy than was the case in simpler days? Judgments in such matters are hard to make, but it seems to me that in this era of American history we are more than ever sensitive to the intrusion of Orwellian Big Brothers and to the insidious technology that can be put at their command. Even though scoundrels may abuse the rights that the Supreme Court has discovered in the archaic language of the Constitution, even though the forces of law and order may be frustrated by new constructions made in our fundamental law to meet requirements never foreseen in the *Federalist* papers, it seems that it is better to have too much liberty than too little. As Madison put the matter, "That liberty is often carried to excess, that it has sometimes degenerated into licentiousness, is seen and lamented, but the remedy has not yet been discovered."

He was writing about the freedom of the press, and that is the topic of O'Brien's more recent book. Licentiousness is still rife on the newstands, and a formula for distinguishing it from liberty still eludes the courts and the political philosophers. Unlike privacy, freedom of the press is expressly provided for in the First Amendment: it is not to be abridged. Unfortunately, the meaning of abridgment is open to some dispute. Although the Supreme Court is not disposed to prevent a publisher from printing what he knows, it sees no reason to allow his reporters untrammeled access to information about the conduct of the courts and other governmental institutions. The tension between the government's need for secrecy and the citizen's right to know what his elected officials are doing is slowly pulling the Constitution toward the convenience of the courts and the bureaucracy. The causes for this shift are the legitimate interest of national security and the privacy of the citizen accused in court but not yet found guilty. Much more thought must be given to the formulation of a policy that will protect liberty and prevent licentiousness. An irresponsible press is intolerable, but even worse is a press that cannot tell citizens what they need to know. The condition of *Pravda* is rightly derided by the Free World, but the way to that condition is slippery and quickly traversed.

Professor O'Brien is a young and energetic scholar who has given us a full account of the state of our rights. These volumes are invaluable sources for lawyers and judges concerned with the preservation of the Constitution from the self-styled strict constructionists. They will be rewarding for citizens concerned with what and how judges and lawyers think about these issues of such surpassing importance.

JOHN P. CONRAD
Sam Houston State University
Huntsville
Texas

GEORGE C. OSBORN. *Woodrow Wilson in British Opinion and Thought.* Pp. 539. Gainesville, FL: Alachua County Printing & Publishing, 1980.

The effect that American foreign policy had on England during the years of the Woodrow Wilson administration is a subject worthy of careful analysis though it is a subject that has been given some attention by numerous Wilson scholars. *Woodrow Wilson in British Opinion and Thought* is essentially what its title indicates, a study of Wilson and his policies as perceived by certain British intellectuals, diplomats, and in particular, the English press. The bibliography of George C. Osborn's book is considerable including various manuscript collections, memoirs, and much of the secondary literature on Wilson. For the most part, however, Osborn's study is a long narrative depicting the manner in which prominent individuals such as James Bryce or editorial writers and columnists for British newspapers and journals viewed Wilson's leadership during and immediately following World War I. This is all very interesting and there are some important ideas and perceptions that are included in the Osborn discussion. But in providing any coherent analysis of what British thought represented, what importance Wilson and his ideas had on British governmental policies or on American and English relations, this study has little to add to what we have already come to know.

It is not that Osborn does not at times discuss these issues or that some of the numerous figures he quotes do not imply certain critically important perceptions concerning Wilson and American diplomacy. But what is missing is a clear context to evaluate the "opinion and thought" the author presents. Too much of the book is simply a series of quotations, personal reflections, and attitudes, derived from disparate sources that seem to have little significance other than as a gauge to judge Wilson's popularity or lack of in England at any given time. Whether certain journals or newspapers, intellectuals or politicians, expressed opinions that had any importance other than to themselves is never made clear. By apparently including almost everything written or said about Wilson in England, Osborn ends up by not giving us much of any basic substance.

The book does have merit as a compendium of public and private responses of certain British writers and leaders on the Wilson administration. It does include many interesting commentaries on how British thought reacted to the shifting policies of the Wilson years from the beginning of World War I through the "rejection of Wilsonian idealism." But for an interpretive analysis of these and other events, one must still turn to others for insight.

JOHN B. KIRBY
Denison University
Granville
Ohio

TERRY SANFORD. *A Danger of Democracy: The Presidential Nominating Process.* Pp. 184. Boulder, CO: Westview Press, 1981. $12.95.

This October the president of CBS announced that CBS would not cover the 1984 presidential conventions gavel-to-gavel. Only major developments would be covered live; the rest would merely be summarized. His argument was the conventions now take a back seat in importance to the primaries. "All of us," he said, referring to recent conventions, "have witnessed the embarrassment of anchormen struggling in a desperate effort to create broadcasts out of nonevents."

CBS and Terry Sanford, one-time presidential candiate, former governor of North Carolina, and now president of Duke University, share the same view of the presidential nominating process in which the primaries are where the action is and the convention has all the flair, excitement, and significance of a rubber stamp. But Sanford—despite his easy prose and open style—is, in fact, quite deeply troubled about the way in which we select our most important political leader. His altogether logical underlying assumption: a faulty selection process will inevitably mean a much-weaker-than-necessary chief executive.

The early part of this slim volume is history, tales—with a hint of nostalgia—of presidential selections from our distant and more recent past. But Sanford's heart is in the present. And in the future. He rails at what passes for systematized selection today so that he might alert us to repair that "system" in time for tomorrow. The trouble, he suggests, grows out of good intentions: more democracy. But "the danger of democracy is that we will use its name in vain, and in its name so unstructure our political institutions that nothing can be decided, or decided wisely.... We must not forget that the democratic voice ... is often best expressed through representative government."

Sanford's claim is that party efforts to gain more democratic participation have had the effect of diminishing their own influence almost to the point of self-destruction. But they are, he insists, an imperative. "For two centuries the American political parties have afforded a consensus-building apparatus.... The function of a political party is to iron out differences, to reach acceptable compromises and adjustments, and to unify."

The problem, then, is twofold: how to restore to the party a good deal of its institutional clout, and how to nominate presidential candidates sanely and sensibly. Not surprisingly, given Sanford's historical analysis, the solutions, at least in part, are one and the same. He would have us follow three critical steps—all of which deserve to enter the realm of considered debate. First, "elect representative delegates who are free to think for themselves as guided by the generalized and communicated desires of those who elected them. Second, elect the delegates in time for them to become educated about the presidential candidates and give them an opportunity to listen to their constituents at length. Third, hold presidential primaries that guide and instruct but do not bind and distort."

Presidential scholars will be familiar with the main themes of this book. Moreover, academics have reached virtual consensus on items such as the decline of the party, and how lamentable that is; the chaos of the current primary system, and how lamentable that is. Sanford's book, though, has two special strengths: its accessibility to those who are not so familiar with the ground it covers, and the sense of urgency it conveys about a defect in our political machinery.

BARBARA KELLERMAN
Fairleigh Dickinson University
Rutherford
New Jersey

JORDAN A. SCHWARZ. *The Speculator: Bernard M. Baruch in Washington, 1917-1965*. Pp. xvii, 679. Chapel Hill: University of North Carolina Press, 1981. $27.50.

Bernard M. Baruch, the "park bench statesman," has enjoyed a reputation unique in American history. Though never elected to any public office, he presumably exerted a significant influence on national policy for nearly half a century. He is said to have been an unofficial adviser to every president from Woodrow Wilson to Lyndon B. Johnson. In particular, he is remembered as chairman of the War Industries Board during World War I and as the American representative on the United Nations Atomic Energy Commission immediately after World War II.

Five volumes flattering Baruch, including two volumes of memoirs, have appeared previously. One biographer described him, in 1946, as a "100%-smart man who stood on call, ready to help" the "95%-smart men" in office, and who did a lot of "ghostwriting for them." Now, at last, Jordan A. Schwarz has provided a thorough and objective study of the man who "transcended a career as a successful speculator in Wall Street finances to become a speculator in Washington politics."

Quoting though not endorsing John Kenneth Galbraith's opinion that Baruch was "magnificently fraudulent," Schwarz does concede this much: "The public image of Baruch was essentially Baruch's own creation." Not especially apt with the pen, Baruch turns out to have been no ghostwriter at all; instead, he depended on others to do his writing for him. His chief publicist, Herbert Bayard Swope, credited him with the "Baruch plan" for the international çontrol of atomic energy, though the plan was not really Baruch's. "Baruch knew that he had been chosen to present the American plan because he was insurance against domestic right-wing hostility" in the view of the man who chose him, Harry S. Truman. Like Truman, other presidents also neutralized Baruch by listening to him or pretending to do so.

In this debunking but by no means denigrating book, Schwarz puts Baruch's ideas and actions into the context of their time, and a rich context it is as he develops it. It includes much of the thinking about war finances and market stabilization from World War I to the Vietnam intervention. Schwarz modestly disclaims definitiveness, since he has not exhaustively treated his subject's Wall Street operations. Still, he reveals more about Baruch, even about his private life and especially about what his Jewishness meant to him, than any previous biographer has done. In preparing the work he has consulted, among many other sources, more than 80 manuscript collections in addition to the Baruch Papers. Always in command of his material, he presents it in clean and sturdy prose. This is highly recommended reading for anyone interested in Baruch, his times, and his contemporaries, or the persisting problems of economic mobilization and price control.

RICHARD N. CURRENT
University of North Carolina
Greensboro

MARTIN SHAPIRO. *Courts: A Comparative and Political Analysis.* Pp. ix, 245. Chicago: University of Chicago Press, 1981. $20.00.

Professor Shapiro begins his 245-page comparative probe of the behavior of courts as political actors with the observation that "this book has two purposes and so ought to have two prefaces." The volume also qualifies for two reviews.

Professor Shapiro accomplishes with felicity a transference to the textual medium of the provocative, challenging, and occasionally goading style of the distinguished teacher. The brevity of text, incisiveness of inquiry, and breadth of references and citations serve admirably to spur discussion and research by students and faculty in courses focusing on the judicial process and comparative legal systems. Like an intellectual compactor, Shapiro compresses into virtually every statement powerful insights, assumptions, and wisdom. Typical is this summary of empirical reality, logic, and social and political choice bearing on courts as law makers: "In addition to the simple fact and logical necessity of judicial law making, it is clear that many societies, including even those that seek to separate judicial from administrative and legislative office, quite deliberately vest major law making functions in courts."

Shapiro develops his own alternative to the traditional prototype of the judiciary as an independent judge applying preexisting legal norms in the aftermath of adversary proceedings so as to reach a definitive decision in which one of the parties is adjudged legally right and the other found wrong. His analytical structure builds upon the intermix of law making, conflict resolution, social control, and union of judging and administration performed regularly in most courts. The examples he considers from the courts of England, the civil law system, Imperial China, and Islam enhance the functional and empirical comparativeness of his propositions. This succinct volume is an inspiring teaching instrument.

The second review focuses not on the book as educator but on how Professor Shapiro proves his case. In this respect, the volume's brevity and breadth become its detractors. More is claimed than can be definitively proven or probed with such economy of prose and pages. The author's device of choosing "those comparative and historical materials that seemed best suited to falsify the propositions I have advanced" is at best meretricious. I say meretricious not because his choices of materials do not serve some of his purposes, but rather, because they divert the reader from inquiry into the nuances of how courts perform their political roles to preoccupation with whether those roles are properly depicted. What starts as a superb probe of the subtleties and variations in the political functions and modus operandi of the judiciary succumbs to an academic game of "mirror, mirror on the wall, whose judicial prototype is the fairest of them all?"

VICTOR G. ROSENBLUM
Northwestern University
Chicago
Illinois

JAMES L. SUNDQUIST. *The Decline and Resurgence of Congress.* Pp. xi, 500. Washington, DC: Brookings Institution, 1981. $32.95. Paperbound, $15.95.

This book offers a thorough review and intelligent appraisal of congressional-executive relations in the twentieth century. The central problem of defining the respective roles the Congress and president are to play in national government has been the focus of many works, but Sundquist's study is especially valuable because it is written from a congressional perspective that examines recent efforts by Congress to reassert itself in the context of long-term historical trends.

For most of the past 50 years, prevailing opinion supported the presidential leadership model as providing the formula for the harmonious and effective working together of the two branches. This model assigned responsibility for representing the national view to the president and gave the local view to Congress. The president would control the general shape and direction of public policy while Congress would refine presidential proposals to better serve specific constituent interests. As long as Congress could support the president's basic policy goals, this division of labor worked reasonable well.

The weakness of the presidential leadership model becomes apparent, however, when the presidency and Congress are controlled by different parties. The model survived the Eisenhower era but collapsed under Nixon when "Congress found itself dependent for leadership on a presidency it had created for that purpose but could no longer follow." Congress' efforts to free itself from presidential dependence led to "the greatest spurt of congressional reforms since the Revolution of 1910 transformed the House."

The longest section of *Decline and Resurgence* analyzes what has happened since Congress resolved to sever its dependence on the president and to take independent action in major policy areas. Sundquist finds that despite changes that have improved congressional effectiveness in some areas, the basic constraints that caused Congress to delegate responsibility for national leadership to the president originally are still present. "The capacity to produce a comprehensive and integrated program," he argues, "remains missing in Congress."

In the final chapter entitled "The Unending Conflict," Sundquist reviews a series of reforms ranging from four-year House terms to the introduction of a parliamentary system that have been proposed to bring more unity to national government. Sundquist finds none of the institutional reforms practical—either because they stand no chance of being adopted or, in the case of more modest proposals such as those for the creation of legislative councils, because they would soon be subverted by political pressures. "The only recourse left for those who worry about the disunity of government," he declares, "is exhortation, the offering of gratuitous advice to presidents and congressmen and to the voters who elect them."

Among the exhortations Sundquist believes should be made to presidents is to plan their programs in genuine collaboration with party leaders in Congress. Congressmen are urged to concentrate on improving their capacity to do what they do best in the areas of oversight and representation rather than trying to develop their own comprehensive programs. Sundquist concludes by exhorting voters to curb their penchant for ticket splitting and to work to strengthen "the web that gives to the government its semblance of unity—the political party.

JAMES D. FAIRBANKS
University of Houston
Downtown College
Texas

KENNETH W. THOMPSON. *The Presidency and the Public Philosophy.* Pp. 219. Baton Rouge: University of Louisiana, 1981. $15.95.

This book represents the culmination of a lifetime devoted to understanding the complex relationship between statecraft and political philosophy. To say that the work reflects maturity and scholarship is an understatement. Professor Thompson has brought to his task a vast wealth of information and anecdote. He applies them with verve and dispatch in an effort to bring order and comprehension to the tangled skein of tortuous interlacing that has made up the connection between individual actions and the social good. He is an expert in unraveling the roles played over time by various groups as they have searched for their "just share" of economic and social benefits. It is due to his insightful perusal of the gamut of group demand over the span of American history that the reader is given a panoramic view of how private interest has affected the public philosophy. We stand indebted for the prescience and the precision with which he has dissected the American scene.

This work will stand as a monument not only to the author, but also to that small intellectual praetorian guard that has stood its ground against the Philistine horde bent on gouging the commons and making mammon its god. Had it not been for these all too precious few dedicated to the proposition that without vision the people perish, America would long since have gone down the primrose path to utter chaos, which is the logical end of those who live only for material wealth and have no criteria to judge the spending thereof except to say that what pleases them at the moment is the only matter of importance. Professor Thompson has fought constantly the Lilliputian minds that have long wielded too great an influence in the public forum.

Several matters need a bit of tidying up. The title is somewhat overwhelming: *The President and the Public Philosophy* connotes a concept of the presidency that the author never clearly sets forth. One tends to lose the president in the maze of philosophic comment about the American public culture. Here and there reference is made to the role played by a president in handling the conflicting pressures that drive the American state, but a steady theme regarding how the presidency has been effective in that handling is elusive. Further, there is little effort to show how the changing concept of the presidency has affected and has been affected by the changing social attitudes. One wishes more had been said about the individual presidents in their reactions to the prevailing public morality that obtained when they were in office. This is a pity because Thompson more than most of us has had close contact with the relationship between the state and the society. He knows his political history and the place of the presidency in that history. Unfortunately, this knowledge does not surface often enough.

Some loose ends obtain: the use of the term "critical mass" is beggared a bit. It is stated that "as American history makes clear, no social group has ever become a political force before constituting itself a critical mass in the society." Unless it is understood what a critical mass is—one of numbers or of force—the phrase tends to become uncritical. At one point, the indication is that the median age in the late 1970s in the United States was about 25. Actually, in 1979 it was 30. This is an important difference. Also one minor item: in the discussion of the role of youth in the society, it is stated that those in college in the early 1970s had "forged their own anchors in a sea of turbulent change." Thompson does not say whether they *dropped* the anchors. Apparently, they did not!

It was a distinct pleasure and benefit to have had the opportunity to review this work. It is one of the too few gems that have found their way into print in these parlous times.

PAUL DOLAN

University of Delaware
Newark

EUGENE VICTOR WOLFENSTEIN. *Malcolm X and the Black Revolution.* Pp. xi, 422. Berkeley, CA: University of California Press, 1981. $16.95.

Mr. Wolfenstein, who is a professor of political science at the University of California, Los Angeles, and research clinical associate, Southern California Psychoanalytic Institute, attempts to explain Malcolm X's life and philosophy through the use of Freudian group psychology and Marxist analysis. The data on Malcolm X come from previously published work. The methodology rests on a rather sweeping Marxist view of general historical trends with respect to the status of Blacks in society.

While not an empirical study of Malcolm X, the book is an important one for students of psychohistory. The bibliography and footnotes are excellent for introducing students to the method, and provide a sweeping review of the pertinent Marxist and Freudian literature.

MIRIAM ERSHKOWITZ

Temple University
Philadelphia
Pennsylvania

SOCIOLOGY

NICHOLAS ABERCROMBIE, STEPHEN HILL, and BRYAN S. TURNER. *The Dominant Ideology Thesis.* Pp. x, 212. London: George Allen Unwin, 1980. $28.50.

This is a serious book that deserves to be taken seriously. For the non-Marxist, Abercrombie, Hill, and Turner sometimes take their ideas too seriously, their arguments twist too torturously, and their attempts "to save the theory" of leftist orthodoxy appear too transparent. Yet anyone interested in exploring the relations between ideas and history, ideology and economics, will find much to think about in these pages.

The basic theme of the book is a critique and reinterpretation of the dominant ideology thesis formulated first by Marx and Engels in the *German Ideology:* "The class which has the means of material production at its disposal has control at the same time over the means of mental production, so that thereby, generally speaking, the ideas of those who lack the means of mental production are subject to it." Every word in a passage like this is important and worthy of careful scrutiny. Moreover, the theoretical implications of the passage are considerable. For example, many Marxists have concluded that it helps explain the contemporary political acquiescence of subordinate classes. In addition, modern sociological theory accepts at least some of the premises of the passage when it proposes ideas about a common culture and a shared value system throughout all societies.

Abercrombie, Hill, and Turner mount an elaborate attack against both the premises and conclusions of the dominant ideology thesis. First, they suggest the thesis rests on a misreading of Marx and Engels. Second, they demonstrate the thesis involves a variety of unresolved theoretical problems, such as a failure to explain the means by which ideologies and common cultures are passed along. Third, and most provocatively, they present a historical picture of English feudalism and early and late capitalism in order to prove the ever-present heterogeneity of coexisting belief systems and the absence of coopted lower classes in thrall to the dominant ideology of the period.

Instead, returning to orthodoxy, Abercrombie, Hill, and Turner declare that the importance of ideology has been vastly overrated and Marx was right when he claimed the primacy of the "dull compulsion of economic relations." It is here that non-Marxists may demur. How can the ideological ingredients of modern nationalism and scientific technology be dismissed so facilely? In addition, who can deny that the orthodox Marxism, so faithfully set forth by Abercrombie, Hill, and Turner, might itself be declared a vagrant ideology in search of a future ruling class? Finally, why are they so intent on rescuing a Marxist theory that falsely predicts a revolutionary, not a politically passive working class in late capitalist societies?

Despite these questions, this book contains many stimulating passages about the sociology of common culture, commodity fetishism, the coercive quality of everyday life, and the work of Weber, Durkheim, and assorted twentieth-century Marxists.

RICHARD M. HUNT

Harvard University
Boston
Massachusetts

MICHAEL W. AGOPIAN. *Parental Child-Stealing.* Pp. xix, 147. Lexington, MA: Lexington Books, 1981. $16.95.

ANSON D. SHUPE, Jr. and DAVID G. BROMLEY. *The New Vigilantes: Deprogrammers, Anti-Cultists, and the New Religions.* Pp. 267. Beverly Hills: Sage, 1981. $20.00. Paperbound, $9.95.

Each of these books focuses on a different kind of deviance and on a different aspect of deviance. Agopian is concerned with the "nature and patterns of parental child-stealing" while Shupe and Bromley attend to "the process of constructing and applying deviant labels." Neither book makes a worthwhile contribution to our understanding of deviance.

Agopian's book seems to have been researched and written too hurriedly. The resulting problems include: a chapter on family violence that is at best marginally relevant to the rest of the book; an absence of information to help the reader fit the findings on child stealing into a more general deviance framework; failure to help the reader appreciate the severity of punishments accorded parents found guilty of child stealing by providing comparable data for other offenses; an inventory of reasons for child stealing supported by statements from offenders with no indication of even which reason is most frequent; the provision of figures on the racial distribution of offenders but no figures on the distribution of the named racial groups in the relevant California population; and questionable recommendations for deterring child stealing that pay no attention to the deterrence literature.

Even with all the problems listed the book may be of some value to those interested in the problem of parental child stealing because of a scarcity of research on the topic. The chapter on "The Law and Parental Child-Stealing" may be of especial value.

The New Vigilantes is interesting, brings together much useful information, and is written in an easily readable style. Persons attentive to the news media may find familiar many statements about the Unification Church and other "new religions" (or "cults"), about deprogrammers such as Ted Patrick, and about the Jonestown, Guyana tragedy. But Shupe's and Bromley's organization of the data produces greater understanding of the conflict between the cults and the anti-cult movement (ACM) than media accounts. There is also substance in the discussion of the history of the ACM and of the sociocultural conditions that generated and gave continuity to it. And the account of strategies used by deprogrammers to escape legal sanction for their kidnapping of adults is instructive of the vagaries of the law.

Unfortunately, some of the most important questions raised are not satisfactorily answered. For example, the brainwashing charges against the cults could have been better evaluated by considering conversion and membership-maintenance strategies in the light of the scientific literature on brainwashing. Instead, Shupe and Bromley suggest that brainwashing was not occurring because some people left the cults without having been deprogrammed. Also, Shupe and Bromley explain deprogramming as an "interactive product" of a set of factors that they list; but this conclusion is mere speculation uninformed even by reference to research evidence on the relationship between the listed variables and abandonment of group membership.

More importantly, Shupe and Bromley seem to believe that they have specified the "process of constructing and applying deviant labels." But they fail to consider how the ACM's efforts to discredit the cults fit into a general labeling framework and whether their empirical findings are consistent with other findings. Indeed, not even a summary statement of the process for their single case is presented. Further, it is doubtful that the labeling process can be determined by examining an unsuccessful attempt to label. After all, the ACM failed in its efforts to raise funds, attract members, and mobilize public officials at any level. Shupe's and Bromley's conclusion then that "the impact of the ACM campaign was devastatingly effective" only increases the number of exaggerated or inadequately supported claims in the book.

ROY L. AUSTIN

Pennsyvania State University
University Park

ARNOLD BIRENBAUM. *Health Care and Society.* Pp. 261. Totowa, NJ: Allanheld Osmun, 1981. $28.50.

This book draws upon much of the recent research literature relating to the social and economic aspects of medical care. In the title of the book, the term health care is used, but most of the services available in America remove or limit disease and do not maintain health or prevent disease. Therefore these types of medicine are better described by the term medical care. The text provides a good summary of the conclusions based on studies of various types of medical services, including the people receiving and giving them and the institutions in which they are given. The growth of medical care through the expansion of professional and ancillary jobs by the employment of technology has resulted in a greater economic investment by society with some effects that are subject to criticism. New techniques of curing have also resulted in new methods of malpractice and billing practices that are not always consistent. For instance, the cost of medical care is not always reduced when physician assistants or nurse practitioners serve the patient instead of the physician. Various instances of medical malfeasance described here give rise to Birenbaum's observation that the poor patients are getting form without substance in their medical care, which is paid for with public funds by Medicaid.

The technology that has made some outstanding medical achievements possible, has, in other instances, not attained the health goals achieved in other countries where little or no technology is available or applied; for example, childbirth in Great Britain, where 96 percent of all babies are delivered by midwives, is safer. The use of technological aids by physicians also raises the issue of the physicians' monopolistic control in which they both own and use technology for profit, such as in the use of dialysis machines to treat kidney disease.

Other topics of special interest discussed include unions for physicians and other medical professionals, strikes, hospital administration and organization, national health insurance, community care of the mentally ill, convalescents, the elderly, and the women's movement in medicine. None of these issues are discussed in depth, but enough information is given to get the reader started and to delve into the references provided at the end of each chapter. The book is a good introductory text to the complexities of modern American medicine.

AUDREY B. DAVIS

Smithsonian Institution
Washington, D.C.

KENNETH BOCK. *Human Nature and History: A Response to Sociobiology.* Pp. x, 241. New York: Columbia University Press, 1980. $18.95.

Kenneth Bock, a sociologist from Berkeley, has written an able defense of the "human sciences" against the criticism of ethologists and sociobiologists. The book opens with a short history of ideas about human nature demonstrating that from the Greeks to the present, humanists have recognized that man is a part of the animal kingdom. Darwinian evolutionary theory, genetics, and now sociobiology have, perhaps, sharpened our views of human nature so that we know a little more about it than, say, Thomas Hobbes. But the theory of evolution, which has been revolutionary for the biologist, has not been of much use for the students of culture and society. Sociobiology is just the latest in a rather standard, recurring, simple-minded approach to human problems. Sociobiology is another attempt to understand social and cultural experience by looking, not at that experience itself, but by looking at something outside that experience. But sociobiology has made no progress in explaining cultural differences and developments by any theory of natural selection.

Humanists continue to try to understand cultural phenomena by looking at their histories. Why some societies thought that kings were divine and then ceased to believe that, why some groups are monotheistic and others are polytheistic, how men came to build gothic cathedrals and invent polyphonic music are questions that cannot be answered by the geneticist but which may be partially answered by historians. Human cultural evolution and human organic evolution are not very closely related. The biologists themselves tell us that human organic evolution is slow and that we are not very different from our ancestors of a million years ago. But almost all human cultural development has taken place within the last 10,000 years. Man's biological nature did not change between 1981 B.C. and 1981 A.D., but his social and cultural institutions went through a myriad of metamorphoses.

Bock's book is well written and judicious. He leans over backward to be fair to sociobiology, but concludes that there is nothing especially new or promising in it. Bock's own points are not original but this is a useful, brisk, and convincing summary of the usual arguments.

RICHARD SCHLATTER

Rutgers University
New Brunswick
New Jersey

RUTH BORDIN. *Woman and Temperance: The Quest for Power and Liberty, 1873-1900.* Pp. xviii, 221. Philadelphia, PA: Temple University Press, 1981. $17.50.

This study describes the birth and development of the Woman's Christian Temperance Union (WCTU) movement from 1873 to 1900. Its importance lies in the fact that, in its heyday, the WCTU motivated many middle- and upper-class American women to move out of the home and, for the first time, engage in community affairs. Bordin calls this the first mass movement of American women.

The story of the WCTU is an almost classic example of the sociologists' theory of a social movement. In the first place, it had a stirring cause—to remove the blight on society caused by alcohol—the evil effect of which was clearly visible in the pubs and streets of the day. In the second place, it began at a time when middle- and upper-class women were seeking a way to fill in their new leisure time. For the trend to limit families and the influx of many Irish women—immigrants with few skills, but able to take over much of the domestic work formerly allotted to the wife—had liberated them from many household tasks.

Abolishing alcohol, too, was a message that many of the women could understand, for their own lives had been touched, or destroyed, by heavy drinking. It also was an "evil" that was being loudly denounced by the church and in the media. And, even the women who had not suffered personally from the effects of alcohol could respond to the leader's widely held theme that women were the guardians of the morals of society, and, as such, were the ones who should tackle this corrupting influence.

Probably the great opposition to the movement in the early days and the actions of the women in shutting down saloons and so on were exciting adventures to those just liberated from the shelter of domestic life.

Finally, the early movement had a charismatic leader—Frances Willard—a remarkable woman, far ahead of her times in terms of ideas, inspiration, and courage. She became president of the WCTU in 1879 and held that position until she died in 1898. She insisted on broadening the WCTU's role so that it gradually became the most powerful organized force for women. However, by the mid-1890s, other women's organizations had grown up, such as the General Federation of Women's Clubs, which began to compete with and challenge the WCTU's position. But, even if the WCTU's importance declined, and it had fewer members, it had played the important role of being the catalyst that introduced middle- and upper-class women to a wider world of action and interest. It had enabled them to gain experience, and helped them to realize their potential skills and power. An informative appendix describes studies that have been made of WCTU leaders.

Sociologists, as well as historians, will welcome this careful but fascinating account of a social movement that was so effective in training women for new community roles.

AILEEN D. ROSS

McGill University
Montreal
Quebec

RICHARD CRITCHFIELD. *Villages.* Pp. x, 388. New York: Anchor Press/Doubleday, 1981, $17.95.

Critchfield is a journalist whose work has often appeared in the *Christian Science Monitor*—indeed, articles about 11 of the 17 villages discussed were published in that source. As the jacket itself informs us, this collection of vignettes is "in the tradition of the traveler-storyteller-amateur anthropologist" and has no pretensions to scholarly standing. Starting out as a war correspondent Critchfield found his interests shifting to the problems of village people—especially those in the Third World, people with whom he found himself much in sympathy possibly because of his own background and upbringing in a semirural midwestern American setting.

The book is divided into two main sections: "People" and "Ideas." There are 32 pages of black-and-white photographs which, aside from identifying some of the individuals who appear in the pages, add little information. There is a brief postscript subtitled "Village Characteristics"—consisting of such categories as "individual," "family," "sex and love," "the agricultural moral code," "religion"—which, in paragraphs of a hundred or so words, gives "what might be called" characteristics of "a universal village culture"—as those have been discussed by Oscar Lewis, Robert Redfield, and in Critchfield's own previous writings. Finally, there is a section of "notes" that briefly reviews sources from which Critchfield drew and that would be of interest to the reader. They range from Cocteau's *Orphee Noire* and Woody Allen to Breasted's *A History of Egypt* (1905) and Clifford Geertz's *Agricultural Involution: The Processes of Ecological Change in Indonesia* (1963).

Critchfield has read widely in the anthropological literature and clearly draws heavily on the methodology and insights of that discipline. He is honest, however, in pointing out that, "a journalist is not an anthropologist, just as a story is not a study. . . . A reporter writes his impressions." Still, "to understand people well enough to write about them, you need to live with them, share some of the struggle and the idleness, the losses and the gains, and in time come to identify with them. In anthropology you also have this 'participant-observer' method." Herein are the flaws and the virtues of the book: it is impressionistic and, by scholarly standards, unsystematic in its reporting; the language is colorful rather than precise; and the worldwide coverage—for example, Brazil, Morocco, Sudan, Nepal, Vietnam, Iran, Indonesia—inevitably leaves one with the feeling of having visited "21 cities in 14 days." The author is clearly biased in favor of villages over urban milieus. But—and this is true even when one is cringing because of the breathless journalistic style which, too often, marks the pages—it is fascinating, and draws one into the lives of real people, national strains, and world dynamics. Undergraduate students, to whom I read selected passages, were delighted with it and several said it impelled them to "wade through the heavier stuff in the library." For anyone interested in rural people it is well worth the reading.

M. ESTELLIE SMITH

State University of New York
Oswego

FRED R. DALLMAYR. *Beyond Dogma and Despair: Toward a Critical Phenomenology of Politics*. Pp. ix, 358. Notre Dame, IN: University of Notre Dame Press, 1981. $19.95.

When a philosopher tries to resolve the long-standing misunderstanding between science and the humanities, the effort merits sympathetic attention, but also a little scepticism. Dallmayr's collection of 11 previously published articles on this theme is laudably cohesive, suitably literate and scholarly, and amazingly temperate in assessing the numerous writers who populate the drama of reconciliation that constitutes his tentative solution to a genuine intellectual dilemma. Essentially, Dallmayr tries to combine (1) aspects of that melange that use the labels of existentialism, phenomenology, and hermeneutics and (2) selected portions of Marxism and of the "critical" theory of the Frankfurt School.

Part 1 reviews the basic problem of empirical social science (not merely political science) by contrasting its "images of man" with those of the philosophical anthropology of Plessner and Gehlen—both of whom are difficult to classify. Part 2 is a masterly critical review of existential phenomenology (including the works of Husserl, Schutz, Winch, and Apel). However, the chapter relating Hobbes and existentialism contains a very strained and unsatisfying comparison. Likewise, the chapter on Enzo Paci's rather shaky combination of phenomenology and Marxism—which is supposed to be a tribute to Paci—in effect demonstrates both Paci's defects and the intellectual difficulties of similar symbioses by O'Neill, Gouldner, and Gurvitch. Part 3, on Marxism and critical theory, deals primarily with Lukacs and Habermas, plus a sympathetic analysis of Apel's attempt to combine scientific and hermeneutic orientations with a psychoanalytic model. It ends with a rather vague and unsatisfying compromise in which Dallmayr fastens on dialectic tension, the role of incongruity in human experience, and the belated recognition of the necessity of dealing with "intersubjective discourse." A host of sociologists have long recognized this, under the concept of "meaningful social action."

However, despite my appreciation of its scholarship and tone, this work reflects the wisespread but, in my opinion, erroneous notion that the salvation of the social sciences lies in philosophy—despite the fact that the former emerged because of the demonstrably inherent limitations of the latter. The crucial problems of man in society, in its environment, cannot be treated responsibly by the alternative dogmatisms of narrow positivism or abstract, verbal humanism devoid of method. We would do well, I believe, to ponder the message of Walter Kaufmann's *Critique of Religion and Philosophy*. And though I recognize the tentative nature of Dallmayr's "critical phenomenology," I must regretfully conclude that, on the basis of this work, there is only "faith" that there is something "Beyond Dogma and Despair."

ALVIN BOSKOFF

Emory University
Atlanta
Georgia

BARBARA LESLIE EPSTEIN. *The Politics of Domesticity: Women, Evangelism, and Temperance in Nineteenth-Century America*. Pp. 188. Middletown, CT: Wesleyan University Press, 1981. $17.95.

In *The Politics of Domesticity*, Barbara Epstein highlights four periods of intense religious activity to document the emergence of women's consciousness of their difference from and antagonism to men. Three conceptual themes order her analysis—sexual differences, sexual antagonisms, and feminism. Concomitant with this development was a reorganization of relations between men and women, especially among the white, Protestant, middle classes of the Northeast and Midwest. Within this group the conflict between men and women shaped female culture, a conflict often denied by women but rooted in the structure of their relations with men and exacerbated by a society that devalued women.

During the Great Awakening, 1740-44, there were few substantive differences between male and female conversion experiences. Epstein, however, employs gender categorization to provide revealing and suggestive insights into these accounts. Can these descriptive differences, however, be ascribed to the inferiority of women within Puritan thought? More debatable is Epstein's assertion that there was little public discussion of the family or the role of women in colonial New England. Simply, the family was the foundation of Puritan thinking. Epstein's documentation here is weak; there is much absent.

In the Second Great Awakening, 1797-1840, conversion experiences became sharply dissimilar, indicating growing conflict between the sexes. Changes, including the destruction of the home economy, the decline of the church as a factor in shaping values, and the growing importance of education, brought a new degree of dependence upon men and a change in relations between the sexes. Women expressed their dissatisfaction indirectly through their religious experiences.

The Temperance Movement, particularly the Women's Crusade of 1873-75 and later the Women's Christian Temperance Union (WCTU) in the last two decades of the nineteenth century, provided women with a medium to transform their hostility from religious to secular channels; women's culture was being politicized. The saloon became a symbol of the exclusion of women and children from men's lives. The WCTU was able to fuse the values and attitudes of female evangelism and the Women's Crusade. According to Epstein the moral stance propounded by the WCTU was shaped by their perception of female interests and by their antagonism to the dominant masculine culture. The WCTU, however, fell short of genuine feminism and was often contradictory.

The chief merit of this volume is also its basic flaw. How much of female behavior and relations can be understood as conflict, as hostility toward men and their dominant masculine culture? Epstein correctly contends that an understanding of female culture is essential, but unfortunately her female culture constitutes too narrow a base for sweeping generalizations about women in the nineteenth century. Epstein also would have benefited from a systematic utilization of culture as a conceptual tool. This monograph, however, will prove valuable in provoking further research and analysis concerning female culture in the nineteenth century.

RICHARD S. SLIWOSKI

Merrimack Valley College
Manchester
New Hampshire

JAMES S. HANS. *The Play of the World.* Pp. xiii, 210. Amherst: University of Massachusetts Press, 1981. $15.00. Paperbound, $7.95.

There are two elements that make up a play: desire and production. G. Deleuze and F. Guattari felt that all values connected with play turned to the unconscious. Hans points out that no differentiation between the valuable and nonvaluable items could be then drawn. More appreciated by Hans is the work of Girard. Girard connected play with mimetic violence which is said to antidate western civilization. Considering production, Hans conceives of the production, consumption, and *enregistrement* as one process by which risk as well as freedom increases. A dichotomy between production and play is inadequate. Play is said to be the root of all productive activities and this is especially illustrated in the chapter called "The Aesthetic." The importance of the latter concept is stressed by F. Schiller. Hans considers the aesthetic as fundamental and not peripheral. It validates "not only our everyday world but also all of the fields of action."

Turning to the capitalist as well as Marxist societies, Hans considers both doomed. He feels that geopolitics is important but the present world appears to him as transgeopolitical. The capitalist system, founded on an individual identity, pushed centralizing tendencies so far as to lead to a continually decentralizing world. The most interesting point in my judgment, is Hans's emphasis on the integrative role of the ethical.

Emphasis on the quantitative measurement is challenged. The Tayloristic model of an organization that is similar to a machine is discarded. What matters is to develop a playful model of life. Referring to Nietzsche one should revise or reevaluate current values. In regard to space and time Hans wishes us to drop thinking of the two dimensions as homogeneous and continuous. Though we have been doing it for the last 2500 years, Einstein has helped us to conceive multiple and nonhomogeneous spaces and times. We have not merely reevaluation of the idea of progress measured additively but, also of the belief that our rational cognition permanently keeps increasing. Neither must there be any progress nor rationality, but a change within different temporal frames of reference as well as other understandings of reality such as playing.

This is an innovative book. My criticism is, however, that the author, a professor of English, seems uninformed of similar criticism of positivistic epistemology, if I may use the term. The literature quoted is certainly not a completely satisfactory index; it appears that G. H. Mead, P. A. Sorokin, and H. Bergson, as well as several others could have been referenced. It is also worth observing that while validity of the earlier epistemological self-confidence has been challenged in several fields, and rightly so, computer technology has also challenged the above epistemological skeptics by simultaneously increasing our ability to quantitatively analyze and eventually discover some new relations.

JIRI KOLAJA

West Virginia University
Morgantown

ALFRED KADUSHIN and JUDITH A. MARTIN. *Child Abuse: An International Event.* Pp. x, 304. New York: Columbia University Press, 1981. $25.00.

This study of child abuse in the family context is based on 830 well-documented abuse cases. It is an excellent scholarly compendium with restrictive use of the term "abuse." Kadushin and Martin were primarily concerned with the "abused child," not violence directed toward children. Readers must first divest themselves of the preconceived parochial position regarding violence toward children as if often headlined in newspapers, such as: "Boyfriend kills infant because it would not stop crying." Also excluded for purposes of this study was sexual abuse inasmuch as this was perceived as a different diagnostic category.

An excellent recap of the history of child abuse in the United States is highlighted in chapter 1 entitled, "Physical Child Abuse: An Overview." A rediscovery of child abuse with a medical orientation is reported to have happened in 1962, which led to the development of legislation both on a national and state level. A federal child abuse prevention and treatment act was passed in 1974; and in 1978, expanded to more encompassing, enabling legislation under Title XX funds for protective services. By 1977, 8 percent of $2.5 billion federal Title XX funds were allocated to protective services.

It was especially noted that no significance was found to the previously accepted assumption that abusing parents were themselves abused as children. Also, after allowing for such justifiable explanations of discrepancies in reporting, lower social economic groups are disproportionately represented so as to indicate it is not a "classless" phenomenon. As the title of the book foretells, child abuse—an interactional event—is a two-part or bipolar event. This particular work has special merit in that it highlights the fact of bidirectionality. It sensitizes the precept of child behavior as an antecedent to parent's behavior, not solely as a consequence of parents' behavior.

One of the studies that was used to support the bidirectional sensitivity was that by Yarrow in 1963, who found that the foster mother behaved quite differently with different children. Each child evoked different kinds of behavior from the foster mother in response to the unique individual differences the child brought to the relationship. This Supports the hypothesis of child rearing over the years that each child is different, despite parents, at a later date, stating they treated/responded to each of their children the same.

This study makes an implied case for two-parent families, despite contemporary journalism, for as stated in chapter 5, "a disproportionate percentage of abusers are the young, single female heads of families with limited education and low level employment skills, caring for three children on a very limited income." It could be assumed that respite time can be more easily secured with two parents sharing responsibilities as well as more money to counteract their noneffective remonstrations by providing minivacations or personal time out.

Although Kadushin and Martin are careful to say that although record, review, and interview data suggest that child abuse interactions began as a consequence of some noxious or aversive behavior on the part of the child, that is not to say that other considerations are unimportant. They credit other factors listing latent inactive potentials for abuse as developmental, situational, and ideological. These factors are also operative when such behavior is generated during the abusive incident.

Other studies have alluded to such points before, but they are usually not handled as systematically nor are they so well documented. This work, in addition, disclaims to a large measure the past assumptions that the parent is the total enunciator of the event. Kadushin and Martin bring forth important new insights which, although alluded to in past studies, usually never surfaced in a true academically verifiable manner through statistical documentation and primary interview data. As such, Alfred Kadushin and Judith A. Martin, with the assistance of James McGloin et. al. have done the field a very great service to bring to our attention, in a documented, organized presentation the previous suspicion that parents somehow are often the victims, even when they appear to be the victimizers. Because of this new scholarly look into a rediscovered social problem of apparently increasingly recorded magnitude due, in part, to its ambiguous boundaries, this book is highly recommended reading for the serious student and most certainly for the active practitioner in the field of child abuse.

KENNETH G. SUMMERSETT
Newberry Regional Mental Health Center
Newberry
Michigan

MORRIS J. MacGREGOR, Jr. *Integration of the Armed Forces, 1940-1965.* Pp. xx, 647. Washington, DC: Center of Military History, United States Army, 1981. $17.00.

Black participation in the American armed forces has become so commonplace that it is almost possible to forget how tenaciously and successfully U.S. military leaders opposed it. But, as Morris J. MacGregor, Jr.'s *Integration of the Armed Forces* reminds us, at the outset of World War II the American military establishment was characterized by a policy that ranged from rigid segregation in the Army and Navy to total exclusion of nonwhites from the Marine Corps. The quest for racial purity touched everything from blood banks to cemeteries. Not until 1954 was the last racially segregated unit in the American armed forces disbanded, and then only after a hard-fought victory over the fears and prejudices of U.S. military officials. So distraught did America's top brass become at the supposed social consequences of dropping the color bar that, in 1950, the chair of a special presidential commission asked Omar Bradley, in exasperation: "General, are you running an Army or a dance?"

This monograph is the first volume in a new Defense Studies Series produced by the historical offices of the U.S. Armed Forces. Like most official histories, it is detailed, comprehensive, and somewhat lacking in drama and innovation. Thanks to his employment as an Army historian, MacGregor enjoyed extraordinary access to Pentagon documents. This enabled him both to penetrate the usual curtain of secrecy surrounding military matters and—as he notes delicately—to unearth some of the "special files" developed by "officials overly anxious to shield their agency's record." In general, he appears to have made good use of them, producing a judiciously written, scholarly account.

The most original (and questionable) contention of the book is that, even more important than the usual factors adduced to explain integration of the armed forces—the growing pressures of the civil rights movement and the combination of executive orders and federal legislation—"was the services realization that segregation was an inefficient way to use . . . manpower." But by focusing upon the alleged imperatives of efficiency (or at least recognition thereof), MacGregor may be underestimating the influence of racial phobias. Admittedly, military officers produced many official memos couched in terms of effective manpower planning. But was this really in the back of their minds when they excluded blacks from officer training programs, created all-white honor guards, or fretted about racial mixing at social events? When, for that matter, were racial segregation and discrimination ever efficient and what retarded recognition of their inefficiency for centuries? The complete history of the rise and fall of racist institutions may necessitate supplementing the skills of the administrative historian with the insights of the social psychologist.

LAWRENCE S. WITTNER

State University of New York
Albany

DEBORAH DASH MOORE. *At Home in America: Second Generation New York Jews.* New York: Columbia University Press, 1981. Pp. xiii, 303. $15.95.

The children of immigrants have long been viewed as peculiarly susceptible to the tensions of marginality. Raised by parents who were embarrassingly foreign, they supposedly sought to destroy all vestiges of Old World culture in their lives. In reality, however, the process was far more complex, as revealed in the fine new book *At Home in America*, by Deborah Dash Moore—one of the only full-length analyses of the transitional second generation.

Moore has chosen to focus specifically on one of the most concentrated immigrant groups in American history: New York Jews. While certain aspects of their Old World heritage—respect for education, experience in nonagricultural occupations, familiarity with minority status—fit in nicely with their New World lives, other aspects were alien, and therefore were modified by their native-born children. The blending of traditional and nontraditional ways resulted in a unique ethnicity, Moore explains, giving new meaning to the word "Jew."

Beginning with a look at this group's distinctive residential patterns, she examines the way in which several intersecting aspects of Jewish life contributed to a sense of ethnicity among members of the second generation. She shows how Jews of like income and ideological orientation tended to cluster together, reinforcing specific shared traits as well as Jewishness in general; how the local public schools, at first a locus for contact with the gentile world because so many teachers were non-Jews, later became an arena in which Jewish culture was set forth as a legitimate aspect of American culture; how the synagogue and philanthropy, two underpinnings of Judaism, were transformed to meet the conditions of a decentralized, urban, middle-class community; and how Jews announced their arrival and their permanence in America through the establishment of Yeshiva College and active participation in New York politics. Moore delved into numerous obscure institutional records in preparing this valuable synthesis, and old photographs enhance her text.

At Home in America is not without flaws, however. Too often, the author quotes others instead of using her own words and ideas. Topics such as work and women's roles could have been more thoroughly examined. Moore also writes as if all her readers were familiar with the city of New York and Jewish culture. She seems blithely unaware that the various neighborhoods she refers to are difficult for the non-New Yorker to keep straight, and she uses some Yiddish and Hebrew terms without defining them. Moore's tendency toward thick and occasionally repetitious writing also detracts somewhat from her book. But these criticisms aside, *At Home in America* is a stimuating case study of a fascinating story: the way in which the children of immigrants bridged the gap between Europe and America, and developed a meaningful new identity in a new land.

LAURA L. BECKER

Clemson University
South Carolina

PETER F. NARDULLI and JEFFREY M. STONECASH. *Politics, Professionalism, and Urban Services: The Police.* Pp. xv, 207. Cambridge, MA: Oelgeschlager, Gunn & Hain, 1981. $22.50.

Nardulli and Stonecash view local police departments as public service agencies. Rejecting the usual bureaucracy-organizational approach, with varying degrees of effectiveness, they discuss the demand for police services, the police response to this demand, and political influences upon the police service delivery system.

The present work is a distant echo of Lasswell's *Politics: Who Gets What, When, How* (1936)—so distant that his name does not appear in the Index. The "who" in Lasswell's analysis are politicians—and their associated Machines; for Nardulli and Stonecash the "who" are populations—blacks, working-class whites, students at the University of Illinois, the commercial-industrial land users, and the well-to-do white residents of the country club district.

While there is an interesting "reassessment" of the literature that hints at more than the authors eventually deliver, and a superficial political and social discussion of Champaign, the heart of the book is a reanalysis of administrative data supplemented by some interviews of members of the Champaign department that are not systematically reviewed. The statistical technique that is used throughout is multiple regression analysis.

Among other things, Nardulli and Stonecash conclude that calls for police services go down as the socioeconomic level of the area goes up—among whites—and that in the largely black north end area there is a marked hesitancy to call the police. While the first police response to an assault report seems to be based on rational-professional criteria, subsequent police activity with respect to the same report seems to be strongly influenced by the racial attitudes of the officers concerned and the race of the suspect. However, when it comes to attacks on property, police service is largely governed by the availability of resources at the time and judgments about the urgency of the report; nonetheless, police dispatch more cars when responding to a call from the black north end. In the case of automobile accidents, the attitudes of the individual officers about ticketing vehicles is the critical element—this has especial relevance to students, since most of the automobile cases occur in Campustown.

As long as Nardulli and Stonecash stay with straightforward analyses of relatively simple variables such as demographic characteristics, time of response, number of cars dispatched, number of tickets given, and alcohol use in evidence, their discussion of the statistical analysis is acceptable. However, their measures of the attitudes of the officers and administrators involved in the service delivery system are weak, as Nardulli and Stonecash themselves point out. These attitudes presumably are intervening variables in the series of service delivery decisions. It would have been desirable if Nardulli and Stonecash had done a comprehensive set of interviews with both police and the citizenry to complement their available administrative data. Finally, the effort to generalize from the police to "urban service delivery processes" falls flat largely because they merely allude to other areas of the total publicly financed service delivery system rather than exploring in greater detail the implications of service delivery analysis as it might be revealed in the existing literature.

LEONARD BLUMBERG

Temple University
Philadelphia
Pennsylvania

MILTON SILVERMAN, PHILIP R. LEE, and MIA LYDECKER. *Pills and the Public Purse.* Pp. xvi, 231. Berkeley: University of California Press, 1981. $15.95.

Believing that expansion of national health insurance plans in the United States—mostly Medicare and Medicaid—is inevitable and will include coverage of prescription drug costs, Silverman, Lee, and Lydecker urge that the key policy options be fully considered now, before legislation is placed before Congress, probably during this decade. The main argument for drug insurance is that, despite the revolutionary new drugs that have been discovered by the industry and the greater awareness and skill of physicians and clinical phamacists, *"many patients cannot afford to pay for the drugs they need."* Such patients are, for the most part, the elderly, whose Medicaid and Medicare coverage is inadequate for their individual situations, and persons of any age who are victims of chronic or disabling illnesses that can be alleviated by drug treatment.

Nearly all the key issues and policy options involve, to a greater or lesser degree, many other classes of patients and many services going beyond merely prescribing and administering medication both out of the hospital as well as to inpatients.

Silverman, Lee, and Lydecker present their recommendations in 13 policy areas that embrace all important considerations save one, namely economics. Adopting as their goal the most beneficial drug program, they specifically eschew economic considerations and in fact give short shrift to a couple of relatively simple and pragmatic approaches to allocate resources in proportion to both actual need and the availability of public subsidies.

Because economic considerations are so consistently ignored, the evaluation of the myriad issues and the selection of options to be recommended has a sort of "other-worldly" patina. An economist's touch would perhaps have resulted in a better organization of the quantitative information on cost, numbers of prescriptions, types and numbers of patients, and distribution of costs between drugs and professional services or among classes of patients. It is very difficult—where not actually impossible—for the interested reader to judge the scale and proportions of many of the important issues demanding a decision.

Having been completed only a short time before the 1980 presidential election, the book is somewhat anachronistic, the more so because it is so obviously a holdover from The Great Society. Dr. Lee was assistant secretary for health and scientific affairs in the former Department of Health, Education, and Welfare under President Johnson; Dr. Silverman was his special assistant, and Ms. Lydecker a research associate of Dr. Silverman; all are now associated with the University of California at San Francisco, of which Dr. Lee was chancellor from 1969 to 1972.

The long and thorough familiarity of Silverman, Lee, and Lydecker with their subject tends to outweigh their penchant for grand government schemes. They succeeded pretty well in treating all these issues thoroughly and evenhandedly, even at the expense of a certain amount of repetition and a number of inconsistencies. Much of the repetition appears due to the fact that the present book is an update of the earlier *Pills, Profits, and Politics,* (Silverman and Lee, 1974), amalgamated with the *Proceedings of the National Conference on Drug Coverage Under National Health Insurance* (Silverman and Lydecker, eds., 1978).

The book is well indexed and will undoubtedly be valuable when the current "less government is more" philosophy and the financial health of the Social Security System permit the Congress to contemplate action on a drug insurance program.

WALTER V. CROPPER

Philadelphia
Pennsylvania

ECONOMICS

LEONARD A. CARLSON. *Indians, Bureaucrats, and Land: The Dawes Act and the Decline of Indian Farming.* Pp. xii, 219. Westport, CT: Greenwood Press, 1981. $29.95.

Leonard Carlson has written a book that should appeal to a wide group of scholars. In examining the effects of the Dawes Act on American Indian farming activity, Carlson provides a historical account of federal land and Indian policy and the subsequent reduction of the size of Indian reservations. From the Act's passage in 1887 to its repeal in 1934, federal Indian policy was aimed at converting Indians into so-called civilized farmers. The Dawes Act empowered the Indian Bureau to divide Indian reservations into acre allotments, assign an allotment to each family, and open remaining lands to white settlers. The last suggests that the Indian Bureau was "captured" by land interest groups. Carlson also argues that the failure of the allotment program to actually promote Indian farming is consistent with economic theory and has important implications about the application of property rights to a group that is allegedly unprepared for the consequence of market exchange.

Carlson offers two models of bureaucratic behavior to explain the checkered path the allotment process followed. The first contends that the federal government acted as an ideal guardian of Indian property. Not surprisingly, the guardian model does not withstand inspection. Second is the "capture model," based on the view that regulatory agencies come to reflect the interest of the regulated group. Carlson presents a twist on the standard capture model. The Indians did not capture the Indian Bureau but, rather, land hungry whites were the captors. Using empirical tests Carlson claims that reservations with the more valuable lands were allotted first, irrespective of whether the Indians were prepared for agriculture—a result that supports the capture hypothesis. Allotment of the better lands first is consistent with a modified version of the guardianship model, and Carlson is not altogether convincing here. Attempting to explain Indian Bureau behavior is a difficult task. Carlson may have done better had he replaced the capture metaphor with a more neutral analysis of supply and demand for the Bureau's services.

Chapter 4 offers the theoretical foundations for Carlson's contention that allotment would contribute to a decline in Indian farming. Underlying the predictions from the model is the premise that most reservations had developed quasi property rights before the Dawes Act was passed. Carlson's evidence on customary use rights is informative and generally convincing. Prior to allotment, customary use areas could not be sold to whites, but after passage of the Dawes Act and subsequent revisions policy changed. The model predicts that Indians would choose to sell some of their land to whites.

Evidence supports prediction of decreased farming activity, but Carlson seems annoyed by another implication from the model. The model indicates that the ability to sell land to whites increased the welfare—or utility—of Indians. Carlson's attempts to deal with that issue is the weakest part of the book. His suggestion that the property rights paradigm may not have been applicable to the American Indian is unconvincing but it is, nevertheless, worth thinking about and may be Carlson's strongest contribution. Carlson has taken a difficult topic. The reader should think about what is missing in the analysis without losing respect for the complexity of the issues.

RONALD N. JOHNSON

Montana State University
Bozeman

ROBERT M. COLLINS. *The Business Response to Keynes, 1929-1964.* Pp. xii, 293. New York: Columbia University Press, 1981. $24.00.

There have been a number of good studies of the evolution of American economic policy since the New Deal. The chief contribution this book makes is to look at the process from the standpoint of business-government relations. Collins tells the story of how business—or really how the U.S. Chamber of Commerce, the National Association of Manufacturers, and the Committee for

Economic Development (CED)—adapted itself to the Keynesian revolution and thus helped shape policy. It was not true, Collins argues, that "the New Economics was somehow imposed on a reluctant business community by anti-business liberals"; business was more active and more flexible than that, and by embracing the most conservative variant of Keynesianism, it was able to counteract the more radical versions of the doctrine and help assure that policy would develop in an acceptable manner. Thus *The Business Response to Keynes*, unlike so many works in this genre, is not a mere compendium of business attitudes. Instead, Collins focuses on how business influenced policy, and his analysis is subtle, well balanced, and firmly rooted in an impressive array of sources. On the whole he is careful not to claim too much: he sees influence as being exercised in a pervasive but rather indirect fashion. The CED, for example, developed concepts "which shaped the parameters of the debate over federal fiscal policy"; it served "as a combination training, recruiting and legitimizing agency."

This approach is quite persuasive, but occasionally Collins overreaches himself. He claims, for example, that the Chamber of Commerce, in helping draft the Employment Act of 1946, "stymied the thrust of an incipient reform movement rooted in left-wing Keynesianism." But the watering down of the original Full Employment Bill was in no way due to muscle flexing on the part of business; as his own evidence shows, it was essentially a result of the relatively conservative temper of the House of Representatives. The Chamber merely supplied technical assistance to the moderately conservative Congressman who cast the pivotal vote in this affair.

The one basic problem with the book also derives from Collins's tendency to push his argument too far. This book is mainly about business-state relations; to a certain degree, it is also about the internal politics of business organizations. It is not a study of the evolution of economic doctrine. But this simple fact does not prevent Collins from claiming that the "power of businessmen" in large part accounts for the "domestication" of Keynesian theory—that is, for the shift from the socially radical "stagnationist" approach to the more conservative interpretation of Keynes that became entrenched in American economic thought after World War II. Keynesianism certainly did move to the right during the 1940s, but the idea that the activities of organized business were in a major way responsible for the shift is simply not supported in the text. My own view, moreover, is that the claim itself is mistaken: stagnationism as a serious economic theory, as distinct from a set of social and political preferences, was dead—indeed, abandoned by its chief creator—long before the business groups discussed here made any important contribution to the debate on economic policy. The basic issue here—the degree to which social forces shape economic doctrine—is important, and it really should have been treated with the care and sophistication that mark the main part of Collins's argument. But taken as a whole, this is an intelligent and valuable book, one that sheds a good deal of light on an important aspect of contemporary American history.

MARC TRACHTENBERG

University of Pennsylvania
Philadelphia

RUDOLF HILFERDING. *Finance Capital: A Study of the Latest Phase of Capitalist Development.* Tom Bottome, ed. Pp. ix, 466. Boston: Routledge & Kegan Paul, 1981. $60.00.

Marxist prose is heavy going, and the content of this difficult and abstruce book is certainly no exception to the rule. Nonetheless, the appearance of the first English translation of this Marxist classic following its initial 1910 publication is certainly a double occasion of congratulation for which editor, translator, and publisher are to be duly commended.

Whether heretical, heterodox, or merely revisionist, Hilferding remains a critically important figure within the Marxist dispensation, and one who, in Schumpeter's words "without renouncing communion with the old defenders of the faith . . . did much to overhaul the system." Regarded initially as an organic extension of *Capital*, within historical retrospective Hilferding's work comes through as much more than that, a contribution that has borne the test of time especially well. This is especially apparent in the theses asserting that capitalism might actually grow in stability through concentration and denying that, since "latest" does not necessarily mean "last," the breakdown of capitalism from purely economic causes is inevitable.

Perhaps the nuclear core of the book is Hilferding's almost physiological dissection—he was initially trained in medicine—of the banking securities mechanism. Beginning with an exposition of money and credit in the production-exchange-distribution process, Hilferding easily moves to a Marxist analysis of the mobilization of monied capital and the phenomenon that Veblen calls the displacement of the captain of industry by the captain of solvency. From this premise follows a perception of the construction of competition as an ineluctable consequence of the mechanism itself, and the ultimate eventuation of crises and the pathology of imperalism, the latter becoming Hilferding's virtual cachet.

The content of this sequence parallels much of Veblen and Berle-Means in earlier times and anticipates much of the work of Professors Hyman Minsky and David Bazelon in our own. Nonetheless and notwithstanding dazzling flashes of insight, financial perceptions from the perspective of 1910 come through as both ponderous and almost unbearably quaint. While the forevision of capitalism's inner logic culminating in imperialism abroad and hypercartellism at home may well afford an instance of observation changing the phenomena, the Hilferding forevision may well afford an explanation of the comparatively benign phenomenon of the conglomerate-raising proclivity of the giant corporation.

There is, as noted, a second occasion of commendation in the appearance of this book, for its publication at this time affords some measure of justice through historical remembrance and recognition of Hilferding, who died under unexplained and uninvestigated circumstances at the hands of the Gestapo just 40 years ago.

GERALD T. DUNNE

St. Louis University
Missouri

JOSEPH P. KALT. *The Economics and Politics of Oil Price Regulation: Federal Policy in the Post-Embargo Era.* Pp. xx, 327. Cambridge, MA: MIT Press, 1981. $35.00.

From 1971 to 1981, through its regulation of the domestic petroleum industry, the U.S. government presided over one of the greatest transfers of wealth in history. Billions of dollars that would otherwise have gone to domestic oil producers went instead to oil refiners or consumers, largely as a result of legislation designed to prevent American oil companies from charging world prices equal to those charged by the Organization of Petroleum Exporting Countries (OPEC).

Such action by the U.S. government was, of course, politically inevitable. No administration or Congress could have permitted American oil companies to reap the full benefits that OPEC pricing would have given them, without losing its mandate at the next election. Nevertheless, the controls imposed inevitably had some harmful consequences in terms of reduced domestic oil production and increased dependence on OPEC —with political consequences—and the cost of a bureaucracy to administer the program.

Joseph Kalt, an assistant professor of economics at Harvard, has made a sustained effort to use the tools of economic analysis to determine how great the economic costs of the controls were. He examines both the crude oil control program, with its complex divisions of oil into "old," "new," and many other categories, all at different prices, and the entitlements program, which was designed to ensure that refiners should not be penalized in relation to their competitors if they had less access to the cheaper crudes. While precise quantification is impossible, Kalt concludes that crude oil producers' losses exceeded by $1-5 billion a year the combined gains of refiners and consumers, totaling $14-44 billion annually. This "deadweight loss" is accounted for by the larger than optimal levels of consumption in the control years, and the less than optimal levels of oil production.

Although President Reagan decontrolled oil prices early this year ahead of schedule, the study remains a valuable monograph on the costs of regulation, even though the overall conclusion—that controls have economic costs and that policy is determined by political interests and ideologies—was never in doubt. The chapter on Senate voting on energy issues was presumably needed to justify the word politics in the book's title; it does not mesh with the rest of the book and could be omitted.

WALTER E. ASHLEY

Pace University
New York

ERVIN LASZLO and JOEL KURTZMAN, eds. *Western Europe and the New International Economic Order, Representative Samples of European Perspectives.* Pp. xxi, 129. New York, NY: Pergamon Press, 1980. $15.00.

Four of the major objectives of the United Nation's New International Economic Order (NIEO) are (1) the relocation of industries from the industrialized countries to the developing countries; (2) international control of the ocean floor rather than control by the coastal states, and possible use of the income from undersea mining to provide aid to the less developed countries; (3) an integrated program of control over the prices of 18 raw materials produced primarily in the less developed countries that would sharply raise raw material prices; and (4) larger financial aid to the less developed countries. The difficult problem of lining up Western European support for this program is the topic of this book. There are seven chapters written by scholars from different countries.

The chapter by Helge Hveem of the International Peace Research Institute in Oslo, about a third of the book, concerns support in the Scandinavian countries for the New International Economic Order. Athough the Scandinavian countries have been among the new order's leading advocates in international organizations, Hveem finds that these countries have been hesitant in carrying out all of the program's objectives, and he concludes that public support for NIEO is mixed and declining.

Most of the authors of the other chapters of the book view the Western European countries as undergoing not only a deep economic crisis, but also serious deterioration in human relations and destruction of the environment. They are critical of institutions in the Western European countries such as the nation-state, profit-maximizing business enterprises, multinational corporations, and the market system; and they deplore the emphasis on productivity, "the destruction of the social community by industrialization," mass consumerism, the dominance of self-interest, and the results of "technological innovation at any cost." This faulting of the Western European countries is highly exaggerated, particularly in comparison with conditions in most of the less developed countries. The authors envision the creation of a society with "worldwide solidarity of autonomous peoples," international organizations to fight famine and share the raw materials of the world equitably, the restoration of civic responsibility, manufacturing enterprises free of pollution, small economic and political units, and international peace.

The book was prepared primarily for the use of the United Nations Institute for Training and Research and the Centro de Estudios Economicos y Sociales del Tercer Mundo in Mexico. For students in the United States, reading this provocative book could be a useful introduction to the point of some persons in the United Nations.

COLIN D. CAMPBELL

Dartmouth College
Hanover
New Hampshire

JOSEPH A. PECHMAN, ed. *Setting National Priorities: The 1982 Budget.* Pp. xii, 275. Washington, DC: Brookings Institution, 1981. $19.95. Paperbound, $7.95.

This study is the latest in the many competent, accurate, and objective works on public policy that have emanated from the most famous and most established think-tank in Washington. Since it deals with important changes in the composition and direction of federal expenditures, this study is particularly interesting and useful. Much of it is by necessity dry, but the book is understandable for the uninitiated layman, and relatively brief given the complex nature of the federal budget. Like previous volumes, it provides the interested reader an overview and the necessary details of that most important political question, who gets the money? To no one's surprise, this study indicates that there have been some recent changes in the answer to that question.

Brookings' mandate includes a "position of neutrality" on public issues, so interpretations and statements of budgetary alternatives are couched in restrained and cautionary language. The authors do state in the excellent "Introduction and Summary" that "the fiscal policy objectives of the Reagan administration will be difficult to achieve." They admit that the success of Reaganomics is based on a network of assumptions, and that if inflation does not abate, the economy does not grow, supply-side economics does not increase federal revenues, there is—nicely understated—"considerable danger that inflation will not be moderated and that the growth objectives of the program will not be achieved." The reader has to exercise his imagination to envision the political and social consequences of that, although that vision is, no doubt, a suppressed nightmare for Republican politicians with future ambitions.

This volume, then, does well what Brookings has always done. Indeed, in the last chapter, "A Change in Direction," A. James Reichley deals more directly with the politics of the budget, and even with something of the roots of the Reagan coalition. He sees Reagan espousing at just the right time a Madisonian restraint on federal power at home, combined with a restored Hamiltonian activist foreign policy. He correctly sees the administration's problem at home as one promoting economic growth without seeming cold-blooded or unwilling to face stubborn facts, and broad as one promoting American national interests without seeming chauvinistic or war-mongering. He even discusses the "moral issue," the desire for the "restoration" of traditional values, and speculates as to whether we are seeing a "Reagan Revolution" in both economic and social policy at the federal level.

What this current volume has in clarity and neutrality it lacks in boldness. That is the style of the organization, to be sure, but this reviewer for one would like to see much budgetary analysis that delves further. One gleans from this work that the Reagan domestic program may be one of the greatest political gambles of our history, and if it does not work, Laffer curves and Kemp-Roth one day may be regarded as insanities. If it does, then there may be an era of Republican ascendancy. But if the inner cities are torched, school systems go bankrupt, and millions are unemployed by the fall of 1984, not even the pristine logic of Milton Friedman will be able to halt another political shift. In any case, such political speculation deserves the attention of those who study budgets, since after all, budgets are political documents with political consequences. There are many other questions. Budgets are rational manifestations of political forces, which are partially irrational. What irrational forces helped to shape this particular budget? Is a budget based on high principle, or unspoken emotions, such as hatred and contempt of the poor, revenge against the effete, and a desire for imperial domination? Power over who gets the money is reflected in a budget, but both the roots and the consequences of that power invite political analysis as to the whys and wherefores of budget making. Thus the Brookings volume does well what that valuable institution is used to doing, but the political scientist who wants to explore the political dynamics of budgeting must look elsewhere.

JAMES E. COMBS

Valparaiso University
Valparaiso
Indiana

BERNARD H. SIEGAN. *Economic Liberties and the Constitution.* Pp. 383. Chicago and London: University of Chicago Press, 1981. $19.50.

Siegan has written a provocative, tough-minded book, which challenges the conventional wisdom in jurisprudence of those who want a social service state. His arguments are lean and strong, and they are founded on thorough scholarship. Starkly put, Siegan espouses classic liberalism's philosophy of individual liberty with a few accommodations to the interdependencies of contemporary life. Concepts of enduring primacy for Siegan are property rights, obligations and rights of contract, and limited government.

In the book's first two sections (of four), Siegan approvingly expounds how the federal judiciary established and used the prerogative of judicial review to protect individual liberty and property rights. An early judicial error in that development was to interpret the ex post facto clauses as limited to criminal, not civil (economic) matters. For Siegan a less confined interpretation would have barred the demise of economic due process. The socioeconomic wisdom of the Supreme Court reached the high watermark for Siegan in the *Allgeyer, Lochner, Adair* and *Coppage* decisions (1897 to 1915), which served as precedents for economic due process until Roosevelt transformed the Court in the 1930s. "By 1939 it was clear that a party aggrieved by economic legislation had to find constitutional relief outside any notion of a substantive liberty of contract."

From there Siegan seeks to persuade his readers that economic liberty ought to be held at least as high the rights to free expression. Thus governmental regulation of economic interests should be viewed with the same alarm as governmental censorship of information. He argues that there are sound grounds for the Court to strike down restraints on economic activity because (1) the Constitution warrants it, (2) the judiciary lacks authority to eliminate those constitutional protections, (3) regulatory legislation has been demonstrably harmful to economic efficiency, (4) legislatures lack competence for socioeconomic regulation, and (5) judicial withdrawal from socioeconomic review is not coherent or principled.

Persuasive or not, Siegan is a good legal scholar. His contemporary ideological kin are Milton Friedman, Friedrich Hayek, Robert McCloskey, and Richard A. Posner. Trust in the economic marketplace and fear of the political arena mark his views of public processes. His analysis is most shallow when he characterizes the infirmities of legislative processes. For him the legislature's curse is its continual compromising, which "severely retards the effectiveness of the political process. Assuming the Perfect Plan is introduced in the legislature, it is likely to be quite imperfect by the time it clears public hearings, committee, and floor votes. Sometimes the situation can be compared to surgery conducted by a team composed of Christian scientists, exorcists, and surgeons."

Siegan's line of legal reasoning may attract the Reagan administration. Opportunities to make appointments to the

Burger Court could advance that reasoning into operational strategies. The book merits reading, and its readers in places of power bear watching.

JACK R. VAN DER SILK

Sangamon State University
Springfield
Illinois

MARTIN B. ZIMMERMAN. *The U.S. Coal Industry: The Economics of Policy Choice.* Pp. xv, 205. Cambridge, MA: MIT Press, 1981. $25.00.

BRUCE A. ACKERMAN and WILLIAM T. HASSLER. *Clean Coal/Dirty Air, or How the Clean Air Act Became a Multibillion-Dollar Bail-Out for High-Sulfur Coal Producers and What Should Be Done About It.* Pp. x, 193. New Haven, CT: Yale University Press, 1981. $20.00. Paperbound, $5.95.

Those who have tried to achieve a coherent energy policy for the United States have been beset by the same problems that have always plagued public policy on any important issue in this pluralistic nation. There are simply too many conflicting interests to be served, and too many politically significant groups that will be affected by a decision. Particularly on an environmental issue, trade-offs have been necessary in order to render decisions. In the American political process, based as it is on fragmented decision making in response to first one group pressure and then another, such trade-offs and other interactions generally arise more as unintended consequences than as explicit considerations. The book at the head of this review attempts to provide a basis for more coherent decision making in regard to coal policy; the second is a thoroughly documented study of the fragmented decision making on the same subject that took place in the late 1970s.

The coal problem has a history of presenting a number of difficult choices. In the first place there has been a continuing conflict between environmental goals and the goal of substituting coal for important fuel. Then there have been problems arising out of the different types of coal and the different techniques used in mining. The large incremental supply of low sulfur (thus, comparatively nonpolluting) coal is found in the western United States, principally Montana and Wyoming. That coal, however, is produced by strip mining, which at best is environmentally destructive and under the climatic conditions of the West may well lead to catastrophic and irreversible effects. The eastern coals found where deep mining techniques are appropriate are polluting because of their high sulfur content, most of which can be removed by scrubbing techniques such as flue gas desulfurization. So costly are such methods, however, that they place eastern coal at a competitive disadvantage, thus probably thwarting the goal of substituting fuels and also leading to conflict in the political arena between eastern and western coal operators. Additionally, scrubbing creates a new problem of sludge disposal.

Even though Zimmerman knows about pluralistic politics, his book is nevertheless based on the belief that the difficulty in choosing among alternatives in the energy area arises out of the fact that we have a poor understanding of costs and benefits, and his aim is to provide some of the information needed to make more rational choices. Using econometric modeling techniques, he takes certain goals as given and then asks: What will it cost to reach that goal? For example, what would a moratorium on strip-mining leases in the West do to the cost of coal and electricity by 1990? What does sulfur regulation at various levels do to costs? Armed with such knowledge, policymakers can better decide whether the goal is worth the cost, or so runs the reasoning. One interesting conclusion, which seemed persuasive to me and should certainly be taken into account by policymakers, is that no matter what one does with coal, the effect on industrial oil consumption—therefore oil imports—is very small. The desire for oil independence should not be allowed to play any part in debates about, say, sulfur regulations or restrictions on strip mining. The real choices, as the book makes clear, are difficult enough without being confused by extraneous issues.

As Zimmerman offers us the data for making rational choices among alternatives, a major point of Ackerman and Hassler is that the American political process is such that the data will surely not be considered the final word and that all important decisions will be made in terms of interest group power. Essentially an analysis of the Environmental Protection Agency's (EPA) 1979 order requiring universal scrubbing of all types of coal, the book traces that decision to a "bizarre coalition" of environmentalists and producers of high sulfur coal.

The first four chapters show how spokesmen for a great many different interests, including President Carter and his secretary of energy, came to view the scrubber as a solution to their political problems. For Secretary Schlesinger it seemed the quickest way to calm environmental anxieties about the increased coal burning he considered essential for the comprehensive energy policy the President had charged him to develop. For eastern coal, universal scrubbing meant that the cleaner western coal would not gain a price advantage; for environmentalists, forcing the western coal to become even cleaner promised to provide an additional protection for ambient air quality in the pristine areas of the West. The EPA's study of the legislative history of the Clean Air Act and its amendments brought forth only a legally incoherent hodgepodge and finally resulted in an agency decision that could not be justified in terms of any cost-benefit calculations. There is, in fact, no doubt that the full-scrubbing requirement, by not permitting standards to be met by substituting cleaner burning coal, leaves some of the nation's most populous areas with a poorer air quality than they would have had if matters had simply been left as they were. The process that allowed such an outcome suggests a redefinition of our understanding of agency politics in a pluralistic political culture. Ackerman's and Hassler's effort to explain the EPA's decision in terms of a Congressional effort to overcome the well-known limitations of the paradigmatic New Deal-type agency is insightful and persuasive at nearly every point.

Essentially, the whole matter is said to be a problem of confusing legislative and expert agency roles. Where the New Deal erred in permitting too much expert discretion in establishing its agencies, framers of the Clean Air Act erred in overspecificity as to technical details. Ackerman's and Hassler's suggestions for reform fit quite neatly with Zimmerman's thesis. "Instead of speaking vaguely of the 'public health'," they say, "the task is to define clear and operational goals through the democratic process and then challenge the experts to meet these goals in a fair and efficient fashion by a specified date." The experts, presumably, would be armed with the econometric projections supplied by Zimmerman and would thus be able to pursue the goals in Pareto-optimal terms. One does not have to adopt a conspiratorial view of history in order to observe that it is not simply agencies that are subject to "capture" by organized interests. On the contrary, the process of goal setting itself, if it is done by legislative enactment, is probably even more subject to the pressures of pluralistic politics than the agencies they create. But to acknowledge that there is no solution should not lead one to disparage halfway measures that promise relief. Surely we could more easily assign responsibility if the clear division called for by Ackerman and Hassler between setting ends—by Congress—and determining means—by agency experts—were to be adopted. In such a world we would at least have the satisfaction of pointing the finger of guilt at the party responsible for ignoring Zimmerman's cost-benefit calculations.

GEORGE H. DANIELS

Michigan Technological University
Houghton

OTHER BOOKS

ALTBACH, PHILIP G., ed. *Student Politics: Perspectives for the Eighties.* Pp. iv, 272. Metuchen, NJ: Scarecrow Press, 1981. $14.50.

ALDCROFT, DEREK H. *From Versailles to Wall Street, 1919-1929.* Pp. xii, 372. Berkeley, CA: University of California Press, 1981. Paperbound, $8.95.

AOKI, MICHIKO Y. and MARGARET B. DARDESS, eds. *As The Japanese See It: Past and Present.* Pp. ix, 315. Honolulu: University Press of Hawaii, 1981. $17.50. Paperbound, $7.95.

BARRY, DONALD D. and CAROL BARNER-BARRY. *Contemporary Soviet Politics: An Introduction.* Pp. xi, 420. Englewood Cliffs, NJ: Prentice-Hall, 1982. Paperbound, $12.95.

BERTRAM, CHRISTOPH, ed. *The Future of Strategic Deterrence.* Pp. 108. Hamden, CT: Shoe String Press, 1981. $19.50.

BEST, JOEL and DAVID F. LUCKENBILL. *Organizing Deviance.* Pp. xii, 288. Englewood Cliffs, NJ: Prentice-Hall, 1982. Paperbound, $12.95.

BLALOCK, HUBERT M., Jr. *Race and Ethnic Relations.* Pp. x, 133. Englewood Cliffs, NJ: Prentice-Hall, 1982. $11.95. Paperbound, $7.95.

BLOOMFIELD, LINCOLN P. *The Foreign Policy Process: A Modern Primer.* Pp. xv, 237. Englewood Cliffs, NJ: Prentice-Hall, 1982. $9.95.

BOBANGO, GERALD. *Religion and Politics: Bishop Valerian Trifa and His Times.* Pp. ix, 294. New York: Columbia University Press, 1981. $20.00.

BOLLENS, JOHN C. and HENRY J. SCHMANDT. *The Metropolis: Its People, Politics, and Economic Life.* Pp. vii, 461. New York: Harper & Row, 1981. No price.

BORKENAU, FRANZ. *End and Beginning: On the Generations of Cultures and the Origins of the West.* Pp. ix, 493. New York: Columbia University Press, 1981. $24.95.

BROWN, LESTER R. *Building A Sustainable Society.* Pp. xiii, 433. Washington, DC: Worldwatch Institute, 1981. $9.95.

BRUNEAU, THOMAS C. and PHILIPPE FAUCHER, eds. *Authoritarian Capitalism: Brazil's Contemporary Economic and Political Development.* Pp. xvi, 272. Boulder, CO: Westview Press, 1981. $26.00. Paperbound, $12.50.

BUZAN, BARRY and R. J. BARRY JONES, eds. *Change and the Study of International Relations: The Evaded Dimension.* Pp. xii, 241. New York: St. Martin's, 1981. $25.00.

CARLTON, DAVID and CARLO SCHAERF, eds. *Contemporary Terror: Studies in Sub-State Violence.* Pp. xvi, 231. New York: St. Martin's, 1981. $25.00.

CASSON, MARK. *Unemployment: A Disequilibrium Approach.* Pp. xv, 263. Somerset, NJ: John Wiley, 1981. $29.95.

CHANDRSAEKHAR, S. *"A Dirty Filthy Book."* Pp. xi, 217. Berkeley, CA: University of California Press, 1981. $16.95.

CHEN, STEPHEN. *Missouri in the Federal System.* Pp. viii, 226. Lanham, MD: University Press of America, 1981. $21.00. Paperbound, $11.00.

COCKERHAM, WILLIAM C. *Medical Sociology.* 2nd ed. Pp. x, 356. Englewood Cliffs, NJ: Prentice-Hall, 1982. $20.95.

COOPER, JOSEPH and G. CALVIN MACKENZIE, eds. *The House at Work.* Pp. viii, 368. Austin: University of Texas Press, 1981. $27.50.

COULOUMBIS, THEODORE A. and JAMES H. WOLFE. *Introduction to International Relations: Power and Justice.* Pp. xvi, 411. Englewood Cliffs, NJ: Prentice-Hall, 1982. $18.95.

CREIGHTON, JAMES L. *The Public Involvement Manual.* Pp. 344. Cambridge, MA: Abt Books, 1981. $19.50.

CRICK, BERNARD, ed. *Unemployment.* Pp. 151. New York: Methuen, 1981. Paperbound, $5.95.

CRITTENDEN, JOHN A. *Parties and Elections in the United States.* Pp. xvi, 364. Englewood Cliffs, NJ: Prentice-Hall, 1982. $17.95.

CURTIS, MICHAEL, ed. *Religion and Politics in the Middle East.* Pp. x, 406. Boulder, CO: Westview Press, 1981. $25.25.

CUSHMAN, ROBERT F. *Leading Constitutional Decisions.* 16th ed. Pp. xvi, 399. Englewood Cliffs, NJ: Prentice-Hall, 1982. Paperbound, $13.95.

DAVID, RICHARD, ed. *Hakluyt's Voyages.* Pp. 640. Boston, MA: Houghton Mifflin, 1981. $27.50.

DE NEUFVILLE, JUDITH INNES, ed. *The Land Use Policy Debate in the United States.* Pp. xiii, 269. New York: Plenum Press, 1981. $29.50.

DEBRAY, REGIS. *Teachers, Writers, Celebrities: The Intellectuals of Modern France.* Pp. 251. New York: Schocken Books, 1981. $19.95. Paperbound, $9.95.

D'ONOFRIO-FLORES, PAMELA M. and SHEILA M. PFAFLIN, eds. *Scientific-Technological Change and the Role of Women in Development.* Pp. xv, 206. Boulder, CO: Westview Press, 1982. $25.00.

DONALDSON, THOMAS. *Corporations and Morality.* Pp. ix, 214. Englewood Cliffs, NJ: Prentice-Hall, 1982. Paperbound, $11.95.

DORR, STEVEN R. *Scholar's Guide to Washington D.C. for Middle Eastern Studies.* Pp. 540. Washington, DC: Smithsonian Institution Press, 1981. $27.50. Paperbound. $12.50.

DOUGLAS, WILLIAM O. *The Court Years, 1939-1975.* Pp. 434. New York: Random House, 1981. Paperbound, $5.95.

DUBOIS, ELLEN CAROL, ed. *Elizabeth Cady Stanton-Susan B. Anthony: Correspondence, Writings, Speeches.* Pp. 272. New York: Schocken Books, 1981. $17.95. Paperbound, $6.95.

ERICKSON, MARILYN T. *Child Psychopathology.* 2nd ed. Pp. xii, 346. Englewood Cliffs, NJ: Prentice-Hall, 1982. $20.95.

ESPY, RICHARD. *The Politics of the Olympic Games: With an Epilogue, 1976-1980.* Pp. xii, 238. Berkeley: University of California Press, 1981. $12.95. Paperbound, $6.95.

EURICH, ALVIN C. *Major Transitions in the Human Life Cycle.* Pp. xi, 528. Lexington, MA: D.C. Heath, 1981. $23.95.

FAULKNER, ROBERT K. *Richard Hooker and the Politics of a Christian England.* Pp. x, 190. Berkeley: University of California Press, 1981. $22.50.

FENDER, JOHN. *Understanding Keynes: An Analysis of "The General Theory."* Pp. ix, 160. Somerset, NJ: John Wiley, 1981. $29.95.

FERNANDES, FLORESTAN. *Reflections on the Brazilian Counter-Revolution.* Pp. xii, 187. Armonk, NY: M. E. Sharpe, 1981. $25.00.

FERRIS, ELIZABETH G. and JENNIE K. LINCOLN, eds. *Latin American Foreign Policies: Global and Regional Dimensions.* Pp. xvii, 300. Boulder, CO: Westview Press, 1981. $26.50. Paperbound, $14.00.

FEUCHTWANGER, E. J. and PETER NAILOR, eds. *The Soviet Union and the Third World.* Pp. vi, 229. New York: St. Martin's, 1981. $25.00.

FLETCHER, ANTHONY. *The Outbreak of the English Civil War.* Pp. xxx, 446. New York: New York University Press, 1981. $39.50.

FONER, PHILIP S., ed. *Fellow Workers and Friends: I.W.W. Free-Speech Fights as Told by Participants.* Pp. viii, 242. Westport, CT: Greenwood Press, 1981. $29.95.

FRANKEL, B. GAIL and PAUL C. WHITEHEAD. *Drinking and Damage: Theoretical Advances and Implications for Prevention.* Pp. xvii, 99. New Brunswick, NJ: Rutgers Center of Alcohol Studies, 1981. $12.50.

GAMBLE, ANDREW. *An Introduction to Modern Social and Political Thought.* Pp. 264. New York: St. Martin's, 1981. $25.00.

GEORGE, T.J.S. *Revolt in Mindanao: The Rise of Islam in Philippine Politics.* Pp. vii, 294. New York: Oxford University Press, 1980. $21.00.

GITLIN, TODD. *The Whole World is Watching: Mass Media in the Making and Unmaking of the New Left.* Pp.

xiii, 327. Berkeley: University of California Press, 1981. $14.95. Paperbound, $6.95.

GITTLER, JOSEPH B. *Jewish Life in the United States: Perspectives from the Social Sciences.* Pp. xi, 324. New York: New York University Press, 1981. $20.00.

GOTTLIEB, DAVID. *Babes in Arms: Youth in the Army.* Pp. 173. Beverly Hills: Sage, 1981. $22.50.

GRAU, JOSEPH J., ed. *Criminal and Civil Investigation Handbook.* Pp. 1094. New York: McGraw-Hill, 1982. $47.50.

GRISULEVICH, I. R. and S. Y. KOZLOV, eds. *Ethnocultural Processes and National Problems in the Modern World.* Pp. 383. Moscow: Progress Publishers, 1981. $8.00.

GROW, MICHAEL. *The Good Neighbor Policy and Authoritarianism in Paraguay: United States Economic Expansion and Great-Power Rivalry in Latin America During World War II.* Pp. xi, 163. Lawrence: Regents Press of Kansas, 1981. $20.00.

HALSEY, A. H. *Change in British Society.* Pp. vii, 198. New York: Oxford University Press, 1981. $6.95.

HANCOCK, BETSY LEDBETTER. *School Social Work.* Pp. viii, 262. Englewood Cliffs, NJ: Prentice-Hall, 1982. $19.95.

HANDEL, WARREN. *Ethnomethodology: How People Make Sense.* Pp. xii, 170. Englewood Cliffs, NJ: Prentice-Hall, 1982. $9.95.

HECLO, HUGH and LESTER M. SALAMON, eds. *The Illusion of Presidential Government.* Pp. xiv, 359. Boulder, CO: Westview Press, 1981. $32.50. Paperbound, $11.50.

HELLER, FRANCIS H., ed. *Economics and the Truman Administration.* Pp. xviii, 193. Lawrence: Regents Press of Kansas, 1981. $17.50.

HENKIN, LOUIS, ed. *The International Bill of Rights: The Covenant on Civil and Political Rights.* Pp. x, 523. New York: Columbia University Press, 1981. $35.00.

HERGENHAHN, B. R. *An Introduction to Theories of Learning.* Pp. x, 454. Englewood Cliffs, NJ: Prentice-Hall, 1982. $20.95.

HSU, FRANCIS L. K. *Americans and Chinese: Passage to Differences.* 3rd ed. Pp. xxviii, 534. Honolulu: University Press of Hawaii, 1981. $22.50. Paperbound, $9.95.

JACOBS, JANE. *The Question of Separatism: Quebec and the Struggle over Sovereignty.* Pp. 134. New York: Vintage Books, 1981. Paperbound, $3.95.

KESSLER, FRANK. *The Dilemmas of Presidential Leadership: Of Caretakers and Kings.* Pp. xii, 404. Englewood Cliffs, NJ: Prentice-Hall, 1982. Paperbound, $11.95.

KINDERSLEY, RICHARD, ed. *In Search of Eurocommunism.* Pp. xi, 218. New York: St. Martin's, 1981. $22.50.

KINNARD, DOUGLAS. *The Secretary of Defense.* Pp. 252. Lexington: University Press of Kentucky, 1981. $19.50.

KLEIN, GEORGE and MILAN J. REBAN, eds. *The Politics of Ethnicity in Eastern Europe.* Pp. 279. New York: Columbia University Press, 1981. $20.00.

LAFFERTY, WILLIAM M. *Participation and Democracy in Norway: The "Distant Democracy" Revisited.* Pp. 193. Oslo, Norway: Universitersforlaget, 1981. Paperbound, $15.00.

LAIDLER, DAVID. *Introduction to Microeconomics.* 2nd ed. Somerset, NJ: John Wiley, 1981. Paperbound, $18.50.

LASZLO, ERVIN and DONALD KEYS, eds. *Disarmament: The Human Factor.* Pp. x, 164. Oxford, England: Pergamon Press, 1981. No price.

LERNER, WARREN. *A History of Socialism and Communism in Modern Times: Theorists, Activists, and Humanists.* Pp. xiii, 253. Paperbound, $13.95.

LIPSET, SEYMOUR MARTIN, ed. *Party Coalitions in the 1980s.* Pp. xvi, 480. San Francisco, CA: Institute for

Contemporary Studies, 1981. $19.95. Paperbound, $8.95.

LOSS, RICHARD, ed. *Corwin on the Constitution.* Vol. 1. Pp. 392. Ithaca, NY: Cornell University Press, 1981. $32.50.

LOVENDUSKI, JONI and JILL HILLS, eds. *The Politics of the Second Electorate: Women and Public Participation.* Pp. xviii, 332. Boston: Routledge & Kegan Paul, 1981. Paperbound, $15.95.

LOWE, JAMES TRAPIER. *Geopolitics and War: Mackinder's Philosophy of Power.* Pp. xvii, 715. Lanham, MD: University Press of America, 1981. $28.50. Paperbound, $19.75.

LUZIN, NIKOLAI. *Nuclear Strategy and Common Sense.* Pp. 350. Moscow: Progress Publishers, 1981. $4.00.

MARKS, ELAINE, ed. *New French Feminisms: An Anthology.* Pp. xiii, 279. New York: Schocken Books, 1981. $8.95.

MARTIN, GEORGE T., Jr. and MAYER N. ZALD, eds. *Social Welfare in Society.* Pp. xi, 600. New York: Columbia University Press, 1981. $30.00. Paperbound, $15.00.

MARTIN, LAWRENCE, ed. *Strategic Thought in the Nuclear Age.* Pp. ix, 233. Baltimore, MD: Johns Hopkins University Press, 1981. $18.50. Paperbound, $6.95.

MARTIN, RICHARD C. *Islam.* Pp. xiii, 178. Englewood Cliffs, NJ: Prentice-Hall, 1982. Paperbound, $7.95.

McCARTHY, THOMAS. *The Critical Theory of Jurgen Habermas.* Pp. xiii, 484. Cambridge, MA: MIT Press, 1981. Paperbound, $12.50.

McCONVILLE, SEAN. *The History of English Prison Administration, 1750-1877.* Vol. 1. Pp. xvii, 534. Boston: Routledge & Kegan Paul, 1981. $75.00.

McDONALD, HAMISH. *Suharto's Indonesia.* Pp. 277. Honolulu: University Press of Hawaii, 1981. Paperbound, $5.95.

McLYNN, F. J. *France and the Jacobite Rising of 1745.* Pp. 277. New York: Columbia University Press, 1981. $26.50.

MILLAR, JAMES R. *The ABCs of Soviet Socialism: The Soviet Economic Experiment, 1917-80.* Pp. xvi, 215. Champaign: University of Illinois Press, 1981. $17.50. Paperbound, $6.50.

MILLER, SALLY M., ed. *Flawed Liberation: Socialism and Feminism.* Pp. xxiii, 214. Westport, CT: Greenwood Press, 1981. $27.50.

MUIR, RICHARD and RONAN PADDISON. *Politics, Geography and Behaviour.* Pp. 240. New York: Methuen, 1981. $25.50. Paperbound, $12.95.

NAFF, THOMAS, ed. *The Middle East Challenge, 1980-1985.* Pp. xii, 179. Carbondale: Southern Illinois University Press, 1981. Paperbound, $12.95.

OAKESHOTT, MICHAEL. *Rationalism in Politics and Other Essays.* Pp. 344. New York: Methuen, 1981. Paperbound, $9.95.

OFFICE OF TECHNOLOGY ASSESSMENT. *MX Missile Basing.* Pp. 335. Washington, DC: Office of Technology Assessment, U.S. Congress, 1981. Paperbound, $8.00.

PALUMBO, MICHAEL and WILLIAM O. SHANAHAN, eds. *Nationalism: Essays in Honor of Louis L. Snyder.* Pp. x, 218. Westport, CT: Greenwood Press, 1981. $27.50.

PANFILOV, A. *Broadcasting Pirates.* Pp. 200. Moscow: Progress Publishers, 1981. Paperbound, $4.80.

PAUL, JEFFREY. *Reading Nozick: Essays on Anarchy, State, and Utopia.* Pp. xi, 418. Totowa, NJ: Rowman & Littlefield, 1981. $27.50. Paperbound, $12.95.

PEARCE, DAVID W., ed. *The Dictionary of Modern Economics.* Pp. 473. Cambridge, MA: MIT Press, 1981. $30.00.

PESKIN, HENRY M., PAUL R. PORTNEY, and ALLEN V. KNEESE, eds. *Environmental Regulation and the U.S. Economy.* Pp. vii, 163. Baltimore, MD: Johns Hopkins University Press, 1981. No price.

RASTYANNIKOV, V. G. *Agrarian Evolution in a Multiform Structure*

Society: Experience of Independent India. Pp. x, 373. Boston: Routledge & Kegan Paul, 1981. $29.95.

RAUCH, LEO. *The Political Animal: Studies in Political Philosophy from Machiavelli to Marx.* Pp. xiv, 250. Amherst: University of Massachusetts Press, 1981. $22.50.

REDENIUS, CHARLES M. *The American Ideal of Equality: From Jefferson's Declaration to the Burger Court.* Pp. 166. Port Washington, NY: Kennikat Press, 1981. $17.50.

RENDEL, MARGHERITA, ed. *Women, Power and Political Systems.* Pp. 262. New York: St. Martin's, 1981. $25.00.

RICHSTAD, JIM and MICHAEL H. ANDERSON, eds. *Crisis in International News: Policies and Prospects.* Pp. x, 473. New York: Columbia University Press, 1981. $28.50. Paperbound, $12.50.

RIPLEY, RANDALL B. and GRACE A. FRANKLIN. *Bureaucracy and Policy Implementation.* Pp. xii, 226. Homewood, IL: Dorsey Press, 1981. $8.95.

ROSSUM, RALPH A. and GARY McDOWELL, eds. *The American Founding: Politics, Statesmanship, and the Constitution.* Pp. 190. Port Washington, NY: Kennikat Press, 1981. $17.50.

RUSSETT, BRUCE and HARVEY STARR. *World Politics: The Menu for Choice.* Pp. xii, 596. San Francisco, CA: W. H. Freeman, 1981. $16.95.

SAICH, TONY. *China: Politics and Government.* Pp. xiii, 265. New York: St. Martin's, 1981. $22.50.

SAVITZ, LEONARD D. and NORMAN JOHNSTON, *Contemporary Criminology.* Pp. viii, 379. Somerset, NJ: John Wiley, 1981. Paperbound, $12.95.

SAYE, ALBERT B., JOHN F. ALLUMS, and MERRITT B. POUND. *Principles of American Government.* Pp. ix, 372. Englewood Cliffs, NJ: Prentice-Hall, 1982. Paperbound, $13.95.

SCHAPSMEIER, EDWARD L. and FREDERICK H. *Political Parties and Civic Action Groups.* Pp. xxvi, 554. Westport, CT: Greenwood Press, 1981. $49.50.

SCHLUCHTER, WOLFGANG. *The Rise of Western Rationalism: Max Weber's Developmental History.* Pp. xxvii, 178. Berkeley: University of California Press, 1981. $20.00.

SHENAYEV, V. N., D. Y. MELNIKOV, and L. MAIER, eds. *Western Europe Today.* Pp. 478. Moscow: Progress Publishers, 1980. $11.00.

SLAUGHTER, JANE and ROBERT KERN, eds. *European Women on the Left: Socialism, Feminism, and the Problems Faced by Political Women, 1880 to the Present.* Pp. vi, 245. Westport, CT: Greenwood Press, 1981. $27.50.

SNODGRASS, ANTHONY. *Archaic Greece: The Age of Experiment.* Pp. 236. Berkeley: University of California Press, 1981. Paperbound, $7.95.

SNYDER, LOUIS L., ed. *Hitler's Third Reich: A Documentary History.* Pp. xviii, 619. Chicago: Nelson-Hall, 1981. $33.95. Paperbound, $16.95.

STACK, JOHN F. Jr., ed. *Ethnic Identities in a Transnational World.* Pp. xv, 226. Westport, CT: Greenwood Press, 1981. $27.50.

STAUS, MURRAY A., RICHARD J. GELLES, and SUZANNE K. STEINMETZ. *Behind Closed Doors: Violence in the American Family.* Pp. viii, 301. New York: Doubleday, 1981. $5.95.

STEGENGA, JAMES A. and W. ANDREW AXLINE. *The Global Community: A Brief Introduction to International Relations.* 2nd ed. Pp. x, 190. New York: Harper & Row, 1981. No price.

STORING, HERBERT J. *What the Anti-Federalists Were For: The Political Thought of the Opponents of the Constitution.* Pp. vii, 111. Chicago: University of Chicago Press, 1981. Paperbound, $4.95.

STRANGE, SUSAN and ROGER TOOZE, eds. *The International Politics of Surplus Capacity: Competition for Market Shares in World Recession.* Pp. viii, 229. Winchester, MA: Allen & Unwin, 1981. $28.50.

SUBTELNY, OREST. *The Mazepists.* Pp. 280. New York: Columbia University Press, 1981. $20.00.

SUGDEN, ROBERT. *The Political Economy of Public Choice: An Introduction to Welfare Economics.* Pp. xiii, 217. Somerset, NJ: John Wiley, 1981. $32.50.

SZAJKOWSKI, BOGDAN, ed. *Documents in Communist Affairs, 1980.* Pp. xxxv, 387. Hillside, NJ: Enslow, 1981. $47.50.

TURKLE, SHERRY. *Psychoanalytic Politics: Freud's French Revolution.* Pp. x, 278. Cambridge, MA: MIT Press, 1981. Paperbound, $7.95.

TURNER, JONATHAN H. *The Structure of Sociological Theory.* Pp. xv, 488. Homewood, IL: Dorsey Press, 1981. $19.95.

TRISKA, JAN F. and CHARLES GATI, eds. *Blue-Collar Workers in Eastern Europe.* Pp. xvi, 302. Winchester, MA: Allen & Unwin, 1981. $37.50. Paperbound, $12.95.

VON MISES, LUDWIG. *Epistemological Problems of Economics.* Pp. xxxi, 239. New York: Columbia University Press, 1981. $20.00. Paperbound, $7.00.

WARREN, DONALD I. *Helping Networks: How People Cope with Problems in the Urban Community.* Pp. xii, 248. Notre Dame, IN: University of Notre Dame Press, 1981. Paperbound, $10.95.

WEST, CHARLES K. *The Social and Psychological Distortion of Information.* Pp. xi, 147. Chicago: Nelson-Hall, 1981. $17.95. Paperbound, $8.95.

WESTERN, JOHN. *Outcast Cape Town.* Pp. xvi, 372. Minneapolis: University of Minnesota Press, 1981. $22.50.

WICKMAN, PETER and TIMOTHY DAILEY. *White-Collar and Economic Crime.* Pp. xviii, 285. Lexington Books, 1981. $22.50.

WILLIAMS, PAUL, ed. *The International Bill of Human Rights.* Pp. 160. Glen Ellen, CA: Entwhistle Books, 1981. Paperbound, $3.25.

WILSON, WOODROW. *Congressional Government: A Study in American Politics.* Pp. 249. Baltimore: Johns Hopkins University Press, 1981. $5.95.

WOODWORTH, JAMES R. and W. ROBERT GUMP. *Camelot: A Role Playing Simulation for Political Decision Making.* Pp. xiv, 137. Homewood, IL: Dorsey Press, 1981. Paperbound, $8.95.

WRIGHT, JAMES D. and PETER H. ROSSI, eds. *Social Science and Natural Hazards.* Pp. 213. Cambridge, MA: Abt Books, 1981. $20.00.

YATES, P. LAMARTINE. *Mexico's Agricultural Dilemma.* Pp. xv, 291. Tucson: University of Arizona Press, 1981. $19.95. Paperbound, $8.95.

INDEX

ERRATUM

In the September 1980, vol. 451, issue of THE ANNALS, proper crediting and footnoting were inadvertently omitted in Mary Jo Huth's article, "New Hope for the Revival of America's Central Cities." The following extract from pages 124-25 should have been credited to Laurence A. Alexander, "Recycling Downtown," *Nation's Cities*, 12: 18-19 (Dec. 1974):

. . . Almost all downtowns demonstrate survival potential. Some downtowns are still on the declind; some have reached the bottoming-out point; and still others have already moved onto the upward-swing process; only when it is completed can fresh regrowth begin—a regrowth which does not merely replicate the old, but which is new both in terms of activities and in terms of physical form. Some characteristics which epitomize the evolution of our nation's downtowns, however, are as follow: (1) downtowns are developing as more compact and higher areas. Cities that never had a building higher than three or four stories are breaking through to six- or eight-story buildings, and some big city downtowns feature 100-story super highrises; (2) there is more creative and successful multiple use of urban space dictated by economic considerations and the physical need for compactness; (3) some exciting downtown parks, plazas, and activity centers have been developed; and (4) there is more pedestrian emphasis, more housing, more attention to urban design and graphics, a careful blending of intensity and openness, and in general, a more exciting look than in the past, reflecting the more vigorous dynamics of the new downtown. The combination of these traits has resulted in many central business district's becoming far more useful, desirable, and viable than most people thought possible only a few years ago. Moreover, the timing is right for downtown revitalization in terms of the strong current interest in strengthening bus systems and other forms of mass transit whose efficient and profitable operation is dependent upon busy downtown destinations.

Now available. . . an important reference book for every institutional and personal library. . .

THE ANNALS

of The American Academy *of* Political *and* Social Science

Ninetieth Anniversary Index

1976-1980
Volumes 423-452

CUMULATIVE INDEX TO SUBJECTS, CONTRIBUTORS, TITLES, NAMES, BOOKS REVIEWED, AND BOOK REVIEWERS

$20 softcover **$32 hardcover**

20% discount to members of The Academy
Rates to members: $16 softcover, $25.60 hardcover

Most previous indexes to The Annals are available, in short supply. Write to Sage Publications for information.

Please send orders, including *all member orders,* to:

SAGE PUBLICATIONS, INC.
275 South Beverly Drive
Beverly Hills, Calif. 90212 USA

Institutions and individual nonmembers in India and South Asia, write to:
SAGE PUBLICATIONS INDIA Pvt. Ltd.
P.O. Box 3605
New Delhi 110 024
INDIA

Institutions and individual nonmembers in the UK, Europe, the Middle East and Africa, write to:
SAGE PUBLICATIONS LTD
28 Banner Street
London EC1Y 8QE
ENGLAND

A Contemporary Critique of Historical Materialism

Anthony Giddens

Gidden's latest book takes on the two great schools of sociological theory about the development of societies—functionalism and historical materialism—and finds them wanting. At the center of the book is a critique of historical materialism as a theory of power, as an account of history, and as a political theory. "[Giddens is] the foremost interpreter of modern social theory writing in English." —*Times Literary Supplement*
$24.50 hardcover, $10.95 paperback

Authoritarian Socialism in America

Edward Bellamy and the Nationalist Movement

Arthur Lipow

A lucid, penetrating inquiry into a major authoritarian current within the history of American socialism. "An important book. It brings a new perspective on aspects of the socialist movement that sheds light on some of the reasons for its failure. . . . should be required reading for all those interested in the history and sociology of American radicalism." —Seymour Martin Lipset $28.50

Competitive Comrades

Career Incentives and Student Strategies in China

Susan L. Shirk

"Shirk's account of the secondary educational system as it was in the early 1960s, and is again now, is both a fascinating description of the impact of competition on student life and attitudes, and an elegant analysis of the dynamics of change in post-revolutionary societies." —Andrew J. Nathan "A fascinating and remarkably subtle analysis of the world's first nationwide experiment in what she aptly calls virtu-ocracy." —Ronald Dore $24.00

New in paperback—

Political Women in Japan

The Search for a Place in Political Life

Susan J. Pharr

Tracing developments that led to the grant of suffrage to women in Japan during the Allied occupation, Pharr analyzes the process by which young Japanese women today overcome numerous constraints to become involved in politics. She examines both the satisfactions of political volunteerism and the psychological and social costs associated with it. $6.95

New in paperback—

Breaking and Entering

Policewomen on Patrol

Susan Ehrlich Martin

"An exceptionally insightful view of women working in a man's world." —Choice
$7.95

University of California Press

Berkeley 94720

Announcing a new work in four volumes

Theoretical Logic in Sociology

by Jeffrey C. Alexander

"Promises to be the most significant contribution not only to the history of sociological theory, but also the substantive study of key theoretical problems in sociology, to be published in the current decade. . . . The man reads and writes with enormous sophistication, lucidity, and theoretical penetration." —Lewis A. Coser

Volume 1. Positivism, Presuppositions, and Current Controversies

In this introductory volume Alexander argues against the positivist persuasion in contemporary sociology and for the independence of a nonempirical "theoretical logic." Rejecting a purely subjectivist approach to science, he develops a model that can help resolve the controversies surrounding the postpositivist writings of historians and philosophers of science. Yet even most contemporary theoretical debate, Alexander believes, falsely simplifies the nature of sociological reasoning and ignores the most basic theoretical concerns. Criticizing social theories that presuppose dichotomous choices, he lays out the elements of a more synthetic, multidimensional position. This volume outlines a new and powerful framework for the understanding of general sociological ideas, an undertaking that will be completed in four volumes.

$25.00 at bookstores

University of California Press

Berkeley 94720

COLUMBIA REGARDS AMERICA & THE WORLD

AMERICA AND THE SURVIVORS OF THE HOLOCAUST

Leonard Dinnerstein. The first to tell the sad story of America's response to the survivors of the Holocaust. Confronts the extent to which American anti-semitism contributed to the shaping of displaced persons policies, putting these events in the scope of our national ethical history at large. 400 pp, $19.95

AMERICAN INTERVENTION IN GREECE, 1943-1949

A STUDY IN COUNTERREVOLUTION

Lawrence S. Wittner. The October '81 sweep of Greek elections by Papandreou's Socialists set the stage for the latest round in a decades-old conflict between the Greek Left and American military, political, and economic intervention. 432 pp, $19.95

COMPUTERS AND POLITICS

HIGH TECHNOLOGY IN AMERICAN LOCAL GOVERNMENTS

James N. Danziger, et al. Based on data collected as part of the Urban Information Systems Project carried out in 1973-1978, this detailed and comprehensive book offers an up-to-date survey of the major technological innovations introduced into the operations of local government across America by computers and electronic data processing. 320 pp, $25.00

LIBERAL DEMOCRACY

A CRITIQUE OF ITS THEORY

Andrew Levine. A critical analysis of the key notions of liberal democratic theory—freedom, interest, rational agency—and a discussion of the historic peculiarity and conceptual weaknesses inherent in the ideas that support and justify Western political institutions. "Levine is one of the most acute and wide-ranging young political philosophers in the United States."—Robert Paul Wolff. 272 pp, $25.00

AMBIGUOUS PARTNERSHIP

BRITAIN AND AMERICA, 1944-1947

Robert M. Hathaway.
A close study of British-American relations in the critical period when the concerns of policy-makers in both nations shifted from how to win the war to how to order the post-war world. 448 pp, $25.00

GOVERNMENT AND SOCIETY IN CENTRAL AMERICA, 1680-1840

Miles L. Wortman. The first intensive study of the critical influence of government over society during the nearly two centuries in which Central America evolved from the baroque period and isolation through the age of enlightenment to independence and twentieth-century economic and political turbulence. 464 pp, $27.50

MARXISM

AN HISTORICAL AND CRITICAL STUDY

George Lichtheim. Offers an authoritative analytic survey of the course of Marxism from its origins to what the author regards as its petrification in the post-World War Two period. "One of the best single volumes, if not the best, on its subject, and a model for anyone writing intellectual history."—*American Historical Review* by Walter Laqueur. *A Morningside Book* 412 pp, $25.00 cl, $10.00 pa

NOW IN PAPER:

THE U.S. CRUSADE IN CHINA, 1938-1945

Michael Schaller. "A powerful and superbly researched narrative detailing what the author terms America's arrogant struggle to 'become the arbiter of change in China.' ... a sordid tale of America's disastrous military, economic, diplomatic, and political ambiguity toward China ... a compelling argument."—Los Angeles Times 352 pp. $20.00 cl, $10.00 pa

THE POLITICAL ECONOMY OF REGULATION

CREATING, DESIGNING, AND REMOVING REGULATORY FORMS

Barry M. Mitnick. An original approach to the problem of assessing the effectiveness of government regulation of business. "A prodigious, encyclopedic effort to bring some order to the vast literature on the politics and economics of regulation."—The American Political Science Review 400 pp. $22.50 cl, $15.00 pa

WATERGATE GAMES

STRATEGIES, CHOICES, OUTCOMES

Douglas Muzzio. The first book-length application of game theory to a historical political event portrays the major "players" of the scandal in a new and unfamiliar light. Innovative and persuasive. ***New York University Press*** 176 pp. $17.95

ETHICS, ECONOMICS, AND THE LAW

NOMOS XXIV

J. Roland Pennock and John W. Chapman, editors. This annual publication is devoted to popular economic approach to the law, the deontological-utilitarian argument, ethical questions on foreign aid policy, and an historical study of 19th-century legal developments. Contrasting views contribute to a dynamic forum. ***New York University Press*** 336 pp. $25.00

UNDERSTANDING CANADA

A MULTIDISCIPLINARY INTRODUCTION TO CANADIAN STUDIES

William Metcalfe, editor. A wide-ranging introduction to the United States' northern neighbor. An array of interdisciplinary essays with a fresh and thorough perspective. ***New York University Press*** 624 pp, $35.00 cl, $17.50 pa

THE GOVERNMENT AND POLITICS OF THE PEOPLE'S REPUBLIC OF CHINA

THIRD EDITION

Derek Waller. A straightforward account of the governmental structures and actual workings of China and current Chinese society. Already established as a classic. ***New York University Press*** 224 pp. $22.50 cl, $9.00 pa

KONOE FUMIMARO

A POLITICAL BIOGRAPHY

Yoshitake Oka. Designated as a war criminal after the defeat in the Pacific, Konoe, prime minister in the '30's and '40's, took his own life. Here is the dramatic story of the man, his times, and his fate. ***University of Tokyo Press*** 210 pp. $14.50

JAPAN'S PRACTICE OF INTERNATIONAL LAW, 1961-70

Shigeru Oda and Hisashi Owada, editors. A look at international law as practiced and interpreted by the Japanese government in the sixties. Records and scrutinizes primary sources. ***University of Tokyo Press*** 550 pp. $45.00

MOBILIZATION, CENTER-PERIPHERY STRUCTURES AND NATION BUILDING

A VOLUME IN COMMEMORATION OF STEIN ROKKAN

Per Torsvik, editor. Comprised of essays by friends, disciples and collaborators in honor of Rokkan, one of the world's leading social scientists, and his work in comparative politics to which he dedicated his life. ***Universitetsforlaget*** 500 pp. $38.00

Send check or money order to Dept. JN at the address below, including $1.80 per book order for postage and handling.

Send for our free Political Science Catalog

136 South Broadway, Irvington, N.Y. 10533

new!

The Rise and Fall of Childhood

by **JOHN SOMMERVILLE**, *Department of History, University of Florida*

"Go to school. Stand before your teacher, recite your assignment. . . . Be humble and show fear before your superiors."

—A Sumerian scribe to his son, c. 1800 B.C.

Since the dawn of history, parental admonitions to children have projected certain unchanging assumptions. Yet while some tenets of child rearing have remained constant over the centuries from Sparta to Spock, Sommerville pinpoints many significant changes in adult perceptions of their offspring. This readable history of children highlights changing cultural attitudes, expectations, and fears adults have harbored about the young. Sommerville describes major transformations in the upbringing, health, education, morals, and work patterns of children and adolescents over the course of Western civilization. Illustrated with vignettes and commentaries from different historical periods, **The Rise and Fall of Childhood** will be a useful guide and text for professionals, scholars, and students interested in social history, families, children, education, social welfare, and related areas.

CONTENTS: Introduction / 1. As Other Times Might See Us / 2. The Dawn of History, and Children Already a Problem / 3. Athens and Jerusalem: A Lifetime of Learning / 4. Rome and the Collapse of the Trustee Family / 5. Christianity and the Reversal of Status / 6. A Dark Age and the Revival of Family Authority / 7. Civilization Begins Again / 8. Renaissance Childhood and Creativity / 9. Childhood Becomes Crucial: The Religious Reformation / 10. The Nation-State Takes Up Child Care / 11. Children and Progress: An Early Social Movement / 12. The Glorification of the Child / 13. The Business of Entertaining Children / 14. Concern for the Child's Survival / 15. The High and Low Point in the History of Childhood / 16. Growing Pains and Revolution / 17. The Standardizing of Childhood / 18. The Demythologizing of Childhood / 19. The Liberation of Children / 20. The Identity Crisis of Our Civilization / Notes

Sage Library of Social Research, Volume 140
1982 (Apr./May) / 256 pages (tent.) / $20.00 (h) / $9.95 (p)

SAGE PUBLICATIONS
The Publishers of Professional Social Science
275 South Beverly Drive Beverly Hills, California 90212

AVAILABLE FOR CLASSROOM USE

SPECIAL ISSUES of SOCIAL PROBLEMS

DEVELOPMENTAL PROCESSES AND PROBLEMS: GENERAL TRENDS AND THE EGYPTIAN CASE, *edited by* Mark C. Kennedy, Volume 28:4 (April, 1981)

SOCIOLOGY OF POLITICAL KNOWLEDGE: THEORETICAL INQUIRIES, CRITIQUES AND EXPLICATIONS, Volume 27:5 (June, 1980)

ETHICAL PROBLEMS OF FIELDWORK *edited by* Joan Cassell and Murray L. Wax, Volume 27:3, February, 1980)

THEORY AND EVIDENCE IN CRIMINOLOGY: CORRELATIONS AND CONTRADICTIONS, Volume 26:4 (April, 1979)

EDUCATION: STRAITJACKET OR OPPORTUNITY? *edited by* James Benét and Arlene Kaplan Daniels, Volume 24:2 (December, 1976)

SSSP AS A SOCIAL MOVEMENT, *edited by* Richard Colvard, Volume 24:1 (October, 1976)

FEMINIST PERSPECTIVES: THE SOCIOLOGICAL CHALLENGE, *edited by* Lillian B. Rubin, Volume 23:4 (April, 1976)

PAPERS ON WOMEN AND WORK: IN HONOR OF CAROLINE B. ROSE, Volume 22:4 (April, 1975)

SOCIAL CONTROL OF SOCIAL RESEARCH, *edited by* Gideon Sjoberg and W. Boyd Littrell, Volume 21:1 (Summer, 1973)

Subscription to SOCIAL PROBLEMS is by membership in the Society for the Study of Social Problems. Non-members may subscribe at the individual rate of $35.00 or the library-institutional rate of $45.00 per annum. (Add $5.00 per year for subscriptions outside the U.S.) Single copies of issues may be purchased at $9.00 each. (Add $2.00 per issue for orders outside the U.S.) (Discount for bulk orders. All orders must be prepaid in U.S. currency.)

For information on these special issues, subscriptions to SOCIAL PROBLEMS and membership in the SSSP, write to: The Society for the Study of Social Problems
State University College at Buffalo
208 Rockwell Hall, 1300 Elmwood Avenue, Buffalo, NY 14222

EARLY CHILDHOOD EDUCATION AND PUBLIC POLICY

Education and Urban Society, Volume 12, Number 2 (February 1980)

edited by WILLIAM M. BRIDGELAND and EDWARD A. DUANE,
both at Michigan State University

This Special Issue addresses major policy concerns posed by the nurturance and development of young children. Topics include the effects of diverse programs on early cognitive development, professional views on early childhood programming, and legislation and policy formation in this changing area.

CONTENTS: Introduction: Early Childhood Education and Public Policy W.M. BRIDGELAND and E.A. DUANE / Child Growth and Development: A Basis for Policy F. ROBERTS / Early Childhood Education: A National Profile of Early Childhood Educator's Views D.B. SPONSELLER and J.S. FINK / Child Care and Parent Education: Reformist Rationales for Governmental Intervention K.H. DUNLOP / A Prekindergarten Program: Policy Implications of the Research M.D. HORAN et al. / Prekindergarten Educational Politics: An Inquiry in Three States W.M. BRIDGELAND and E.A. DUANE / Early Childhood Policy-Making: Inputs, Processes, and Legislative Outputs P.D. FORGIONE, Jr. / Early Childhood Specialists as Policy Makers S. KILMER

$5.50 (Individual) **$11.00** (Institutional)

Orders under $20 must be prepaid. **Order from:**

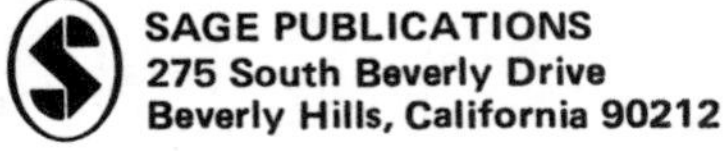